Adventures of a Wonky-eyed Boy *The Short-arse Years*

Jason Byrne is one of Ireland's best-loved comedians. He is consistently the biggest selling act at the Edinburgh Fringe and sells out venues across America, Australia, the Middle East, Europe and Asia. He has many television credits to his name including *Ireland's Got Talent* and *Last One Laughing Ireland*.

Nicky Phelan is an award-winning illustrator. He also works in animation, where he was Oscar-nominated for Brown Bag Films' short film *Granny O'Grimm's Sleeping Beauty* and won an Emmy for directing the BBC hit *Bing*.

ADVENTURES OF A WONKY-EYED BOY

The Short-arse Years

Jason Byrne

GILL BOOKS

Gill Books, Hume Avenue, Park West, Dublin 12 | www.gillbooks.ie

A CIP catalogue record for this book is available from the British Library. | 5 4 3 2 1

Gill Books is an imprint of
M.H. Gill & Co. | © Jason Byrne 2016, 2023
First published in 2016. This paperback edition
published 2023. | 978 07171 79053
Illustrations © Nicky Phelan | Designed by
www.grahamthew.com | Copy-edited by Rachel
Pierce at Verba Editing House | Proofread by
Jane Rogers

Printed and bound in Great
Britain by CPI Group (UK) Ltd, Croydon,
CRO 4YY | *The paper used in this book comes from
the wood pulp of managed forests.* | All rights

MIX
Paper | Supporting
responsible forestry
FSC® C171272

Contents

FAMILY TOP TRUMPS

JASON (ME)

SKILLS:	having a wonky eye, fast runner, professional rat.
HOBBIES:	shitting it, running, seeing double, music (but only the type the lads were into, nothing weird) and shitting it.
SPECIAL POWERS:	hypnotising people with wonky eye, opening sweets inside pockets.
DISABILITIES:	professional rat, sweets, tea and toast, milk, beans, accident-prone, not being able to judge distance, height or depth.

MAM

SKILLS:	washing, cleaning, vacuuming, cooking, ballroom dancing, running to get washing in out of the rain, going to mass, being small and lethal.
HOBBIES:	laughing, smacking, telephone chats for hours, peeking out blinds at neighbours.
SPECIAL POWERS:	slaps, clips round the ear, power of voice in sing-songs, mammy power.
DISABILITIES:	doing too much, not looking after self, pleasing others.

SKILLS:

HOBBIES:

SPECIAL POWERS:

DISABILITIES:

DAD

SKILLS:	having a jar, empty threats, dead-pan wit, paying bills, bringing stuff home from work.
HOBBIES:	having a jar, sitting on the jacks for hours, worrying about bills, not going to mass.
SPECIAL POWERS:	making up facts, daddy sayings ('Don't mind your mother', 'I'll take the arm off ye', 'Ah jaysusss', 'He's only a bollix', 'Pint and a small one').
DISABILITIES:	having a jar, smoking, telling too many people to 'ask me bollix'.

ng to
ng

s

ERIC (OLDER BROTHER)

SKILLS:	being the eldest, art, battering me.
HOBBIES:	being out all the time, coming home earlier than I thought.
SPECIAL POWERS:	calling me a spa, being bigger than me.
DISABILITIES:	girls and motorbikes.

SKILLS:

HOBBIES:

SPECIAL POWERS:

DISABILITIES:

RACHEL (YOUNGER SISTER)

SKILLS:	being nice all the time, crying at sad things (dead birds, squirrels in a sling, etc.).
HOBBIES:	collecting fancy paper, brushing her hair, helping Mam.
SPECIAL POWERS:	taking on the sins of the world, being worried about everyone else.
DISABILITIES:	fancy paper, My Little Pony, helping too many animals.

EITHNE (BABY SISTER)

SKILLS: being cute, having curls, vomiting and then laughing straight afterwards.

HOBBIES: being lifted up or down off something, getting jockey-backs, hanging out in buggies, running fast and landing on face.

SPECIAL POWERS: getting people to lift her up, sitting on your head while you watch TV.

DISABILITIES: falling asleep anywhere, eating stuff off the ground.

KARE

SKILLS:

HOBBIES:

SPECIAL PO

DISABILI

KARL (BEST MATE)

SKILLS:	being best mate, brave, robbing, burning stuff, legging it.
HOBBIES:	burning stuff, robbing, making swings, breaking his limbs, smoking, making me do mad stuff.
SPECIAL POWERS:	being two years older than me (a power I could never have over him).
DISABILITIES:	hanging out with a professional rat like me, hedge porn (see Chapter 10).

CHAPTER 1
OUR HERO ARRIVES

'Mrs Byrne, you've a beautiful, very pale, ginger-haired baby boy with a wonky eye.'

As she was handed me by the midwife, my mother wept for all the wrong reasons. She could have shagged a platypus and I still would have come out better than this. My mother later admitted to trying to tilt newborn me slightly, like one of those hand games we had as kids with the small steel ball ('steelie') you had to get around a maze and into the hole at the end. She basically tried to roll my wonky eye back into the middle, where it should have been, but as soon as she stopped tilting me, the eye wandered back towards the nose area.

People tried to be kind when they looked into the pram. They'd manage to smother the 'sweet suffering Jesus' that bubbled up and instead say things like, 'Isn't he ... a lovely boy? He's the image of, he's the image of, he's the image of ... a baby.'

They brought me to the doctor when I was four years old. The doctor said my eye was lazy and needed to be made work. The correct term is Amblyopia. Sounds fancy, like I had super powers from a nuclear explosion, but the doctor lacked imagination and preferred the more offensive names: lazy eye, or squint.

Squint (strabismus)

'A squint is a condition where the eyes do not look together in the same direction. One eye looks straight ahead, while the other eye turns to point inwards, outwards, upwards or downwards. As the eyes are not straight (aligned), they focus on different things. The result is that the brain ignores the signals from one of the eyes to avoid seeing double,' the doctor said to my mother.

There's no getting away from it: no matter how you try to dress up a squint, it's just hilarious every time. I mean, how could you rattle out that explanation and not fall around laughing?

My mother tried to make me feel better by telling me I had a magic eye, or a special eye as she called it. No one else had a special eye, only me, which meant I was very special. I felt great about that, for a short while.

The bottom line was that I had a wonky, lazy, gunner, cock, turned-in, broken eye. So how did they fix this? At the age of four I already had big glasses that magnified my eye. But the good doctor, summoning all his skills as a surgeon or optometrist or torturer or whatever, decided to add a patch over my good eye. My *good* eye. Now I didn't even have one straight eye to aim at people. I had a turned-in eye, accompanied by a massive patch with bottle-end glasses over it – you couldn't have made it more comical if you'd tried. People were looking at me now, with my wonky eye, the patch over it and just in case people couldn't see it from a distance ... *it was all magnified by thick as shite glasses!* Jesus God, help me.

You can understand why I struggled through my early years. I was forever trying to hide my glasses so I wouldn't have to wear them.

TiPS ON WHERE TO HiDE YOUR GLASSES WHEN YOU'RE FOUR

1. In the toaster.

2. Inside a large sliced pan.

3. In the dog's basket.

4. Behind, under, in or down the couch.

5. Under your pillow.

I know they're crap places to hide things; I was only four.

Despite being an odd-looking chap, I got on well with my brother and sisters. When I was four, I had one older brother, Eric, who was two years older than me. Two sisters, Rachel and Eithne, were to come later.

One day, when I was five or so, I got quite ill and started to vomit a lot. My mother was worried because she couldn't work it out. She asked me if I had eaten anything bad. 'No.' She asked again: was there anything at all I had eaten that she should know about? She was suspicious because I had a reputation as a kid for putting anything into my mouth. The word 'repulsive' didn't exist for me, everything on the planet could be on the food pyramid if you were hungry enough, or gullible enough. My mother was well used to sitting me on the potty and going through my poo to find the one pence piece I had swallowed.

THiNGS I SWALLOWED

1. A penny
2. Flat Lego piece (two-square)
3. Flat Lego piece (one-square)
4. Lego man's head
5. Moth balls

This was different. Whatever I had swallowed this time wasn't going to be coming out so easily into the potty. She walked me around the kitchen to see if I'd point out what had made me ill. I knew exactly what it was, but I didn't want to get my brother into trouble. Eric had said he'd kill me if I ever told on him. My mother kept at me, though, asking over and over again if I'd eaten anything weird. She kept at me because she knew I was lying. She knew I was lying because whenever I told a lie, my wonky eye would turn in. It gave me away all the time.

CAUSES OF EYE TURNING IN

1. **Lying**
2. **Tired**
3. **Angry**
4. **Sneezing**
5. **Coughing**
6. **Excitement**

My mother wouldn't stop with the questions about what I'd eaten and my eye was flying around in my head like mad-eyed Moody from *Harry Potter*. Eventually I cracked and screamed that it was the caramel wall.

'The caramel what?' my mother asked.

I let it all out in floods of tears. 'Eric told me not to touch the caramel that you make on the wall like Willy Wonka's magic walls, but I couldn't help it, the caramel was just too nice, Mammy. I'm sorry for robbing your caramel!'

Mam had no idea what I was talking about. 'Caramel? Where?'

'Behind the cooker.' I pointed to the thick grease that gathered on the wall behind my mother's 1970's death-trap of a cooker.

'The grease on the wall?' she yelled.

I was chased up and down the house by that woman while she slapped me bum with a slipper. I only got some respite when my brother passed me on the stairs and she went after him, for telling me it was caramel. The two of us couldn't sit down for days. I continued to eat off the caramel wall for at least another year. I was hooked on the stuff.

THINGS NOT TO EAT IN THE 1970S, DESPITE YOUR OLDER BROTHER TELLING YOU IT'S OKAY

1. Grease behind the cooker: it is not caramel.
2. Chewing-gum off the ground: it is not kept out there to stay fresh.
3. Dried dog food mixed into your cereal: it is not Coco Pops for dogs.
4. Scented soap: it is not French white chocolate.
5. Licking the back of the cat: it does not give you climbing powers.

(P.S. Do not use white dog poo as chalk for hopscotch either.)

So, a pretty eventful little life I was having, helped along by my special eye and my brother, Eric. If my mother had a womb for a handbag, I'd be still in it. I was with her all the time. The first time I was separated from her for a long period was when I was sent to crèche, or playschool as it was known then. 'Only posh people and Italians go to crèche,' my dad would say. He was a man of few words but when they did come out, they were pretty strange words.

The crèche was at the top of our road – in fact, everything was at the top of our road.

TOP FIVE TOP-OF-THE-ROAD PLACES

1. **Crèche**
2. **School**
3. **Church**
4. **Swimming pool**
5. **Top of the road**

Yes, most importantly, at the top of the road was the top of the road, and that was where most people met. It was like our very own Clery's clock. 'Meet you at the top of the road.' It was always there, and it would be the top of the road forever. It's still there now, at the top of Ludford Drive, but funnily enough it had no bottom because our road curved around at the end, so there was never, technically, a bottom of the road. We had to make do with a top of the road.

So me and Mam went to the top of the road, up to the crèche. It was called 'The Rec', which is short for recreational building. It was a rectangular red-bricked '70s yoke, plonked beside the school like a bad cousin nobody spoke about. They had 21st parties in there, birthdays, all type of recreational activities. It was about a fiver to rent and it smelt of the swimming pool, which was at the back. In fact, we could see them all swimming while we sat in the crèche, smelling of chlorine.

My mother brought me inside and dropped me into the sandpit. There were mothers dropping kids all over the crèche, like the Luftwaffe sheet-bombing Britain – there were kids launched into the building-block area, drop and cry; the plasticine section, drop and cry; the fuzzy felt area, drop and cry. Little bundles of weeping and sniffling kids, with their arms outstretched for their mothers to pick them back up and take them home. Some mothers had to jemmy their children off their legs with umbrellas. The teacher was doing her best to help, but it was chaos.

At one stage I saw a kid holding onto his mother's legs, and the teacher had the feet end of him, and the kid looked like Stretch Armstrong as the mother forced her way out the door, until suddenly the child recoiled into the teacher's arms with a thud, almost knocking her over.

I was the only one not crying. I was sitting in the sandpit with my huge glasses and my special eye beside Kenneth Cook, who was crying so hard his eyes bulged as he pushed out the tears.

My mother was wailing like a banshee as she was guided out by the teacher. I later found out that she was crying because I wasn't crying, and she thought that meant I didn't love her. But truth be told, by then I had learnt not to cry unless totally necessary because it either filled up my patch or fogged up my glasses. By the time the mothers left, the whole place was red-eyed, even the teacher. Although the red-eyed teacher was due to the fact that the crèche was joined onto the swimming pool, separated by a window that wasn't floor to ceiling, so the chlorine would creep over the top and burn the eyes off the poor teacher.

As soon as the last parent left and the door closed shut, all the children stopped crying, turning off the water-works like a tap. Even I was confused.

These children loved the crèche, they were all only three and four years old, but I could see in their eyes that even though they were happy out, this was something they did every day and that they knew what they were doing. They cried just to upset their mums. Evil! It was like looking around a room full of Stewies from *Family Guy*. I liked it, I liked it a lah (silent T, à la Jim Carrey in *Dumb and Dumber*).

So I played in the sandpit with a now non-crying Kenneth Cook. He didn't want to share the sandpit and kept trying to edge me out. I got angry. He stared at me in the eye and said, 'Get out of the sandpit' and gave me a hard push. But the more angry I got, the more my eye turned in, and he watched the eye going from middle to nose from middle to nose as I tried my best to control it. I was seeing two Kenneth Cooks. But just as I was about to push him back, he started to get dozy-looking, his eyelids got heavy and he lay face-down into the sand and fell asleep.

My eye had somehow hypnotised him. I had no idea how this had happened, but I made my way through the whole crèche that morning, putting children into a trance as I stared at them in the face with what I now believed really was a *special eye*. I had everything to myself, whatever toy I wanted, until I came across David O'Connor, the only other human being I'd ever seen with class-A special eyes. *Both* of his eyes turned in and, as only one of mine did, we put each other to sleep as we fought and stared for territory over the toy boats in the basin of water.

I was woken up by the cries of a room full of toddlers as the door to the outside was opened again and the mothers came running back in, full of guilt because their children looked like they'd been crying for the whole two hours of crèche. Little bastards, but clever little bastards, I thought to myself, if I had known that word then, but I thought clever little somethings as I tried to cry as my mother carried me out. As the crèche and David O'Connor disappeared into the distance, I stared at both of them, mentally preparing to fight another day in crèche!

'Happy Birthday, dear Jason, happy birthday to you!' My little sister Rachel, who was now three, leaned in and blew out my candles. Hell was starting for me because I was now the *dreaded middle child*!

It's an awful feeling being in the middle, you're neither here nor there. You're not the youngest or the oldest. Your mother shouts at you when you get in trouble with your little sister because 'you should know better, you're older than her'. 'I'm only five, for God's sake.' On the flip side, 'No, you cannot go to the shops on your own until you're old enough, like your older brother.' *Arghhhhhhh.*

THE CURSE OF THE MIDDLE CHILD

1. Not many photos of you anywhere.
2. Too young to go out.
3. Old enough to stay in and babysit.
4. 'Should know better, she's younger then you.'
5. 'Grow up like your big brother.'
6. 'Make the tea.'
7. 'Change the channel.'
8. 'Answer the door.'
9. 'Close the curtains.'
10. 'Open the curtains.'

Rachel was getting all the attention and Eric was getting all the clothes. So that was that, time to run away – they didn't need me anymore and wouldn't miss me and my special eye, with the stupid patch.

So I packed my Action Man backpack, which wasn't even mine but a hand-me-down from my *older* brother Eric. I put my dad's lighter in there, four Fig Rolls and my Action Man's eagle eyes, as he had a telescope in the back of his head and I would sometimes use that to help me see better, especially when I had the patch over my good eye. That was all I could fit in.

TOP FIVE THINGS TO TAKE WITH YOU WHEN YOU RUN AWAY, IF YOU COULD FIT THEM ALL

1. Action Man's eagle eyes (as above).
2. Ten cooked sausages (to put bloodhounds off the scent).
3. A Stretch Armstrong (as trip-wire).
4. Bed sheet (to make yourself into a ghost to scare away police).
5. Pet dog (for protection and warmth).

And off I went. Goodbye stupid big brother, little sister, mother and father.

★ ★ ★

The hours passed. I looked around with my Action Man eagle eyes to see if anyone was coming. Not a soul. I had done it, I had run away and they'd *never* find me. Suddenly I heard a door slam. Then I heard my dad calling my name. Then my mother said, 'I thought he was with you?'

'No,' said my dad.

I munched down on a Fig Roll as my mam and dad started to shout my name. I didn't answer, I stayed put. I had run away for a reason, and that reason was to never come back. I was five, I had my whole life ahead of me and I would never come back.

More time passed and I have to admit, I was boiling hot in my new home. The Fig Rolls were all gone, but they had made my mouth dry. I could hear my mother crying to a couple of our neighbours. They were saying things like, 'You'll find him, he can't have gone far.' That's told them, ha, now I'm getting notice, I will not come home, but damn I need water.

I heard my dad say, 'I've looked everywhere, me hair is soaked from standing in the rain looking for him, I'm going to get a towel.' I heard his footsteps getting nearer to me, suddenly I could see his shins, he opened the door to my new home, pulled out a towel, all the other towels fell out, with me in them. *THUD!* I hit the ground right at his feet.

'You little bollix yeh! I found him.'

He dragged me out of my hiding place and down the stairs to my mother. My mother and her friends were so happy to see me that my mam took off her slipper and slapped the arse off me.

> MAM: *(weeping)* Thank god *(slipperslap)* we found you *(smile, weep, slipperslap)*. You gave me the fright of me life *(slipperslap)*. I thought I lost you *(slipperslap, hug, kiss, slipperslap, smile, weep, collapse)*.

She was too tired to keep going, so she passed the slipper to one of the neighbours.

> JOAN: You frightened *(slipperslap)* the life out of your mother *(slipperslap)*. Don't do that again *(hug, slipperslap, hug, slipperslap, lights fag)*.
> MAM: Where was he?
> DAD: In the hot press, the dozy little bollix.

My mother cried as she gave me one last slap of the slipper. She was more furious now that I had ruined her weeks of washing and ironing. 'My good hot press, yeh little brat.'

Hot press description for people who do not live in ireland

A hot press is a cupboard used by the Irish mammy to dry or air towels, sheets or clothes. All these things are stuffed into the so-called hot press and jammed in all sides of a boiler that is used to heat the water. This activity is no doubt dangerous, as I'm sure boilers need a bit of space to breathe and operate properly.

There is normally a switch in the hot press, labelled BATH and SINK. Please, for God's sake, always have it on Sink – unless it's a special occasion, then leave it on Bath, but only for a few minutes or else your dad will need to take out a second mortgage on the house to pay the bill, or so he says.

OTHER ITEMS THAT COST A FORTUNE, OR 'AN ARM AND A LEG', TO RUN IN THE '70S/'80S HOUSE, A.K.A. THE I'M NOT MADE OF MONEY! LIST

1. Telephone (had a small padlock on it. In case of emergency, jump out window and forget about calling for help).
   DAD: 'If you stay on the phone any longer, I'll chop your arm off. I'm not made of money.'

2. Kettle (boiled 743 times a day, more when Mam involved in major neighbourhood gossip).
   DAD: 'If you boil that kettle one more time, I'll chop your hand off. I'm not made of money.'

3. Hot blanket (put on most nights, took three hours to heat up, then it was too hot to lie in the bed anyway).
   DAD: 'Don't leave that blanket on or I'll chop the hot legs off yeh. I'm not made of money.'

4. Immersion (i.e. Bath or Sink switch, *always* to be left on Sink).
   DAD: 'Leave that immersion on Sink or I'll chop yeh all up and leave your bits in the bath. I'm not made of money.'

5. **Sockets and lights (unplug every plug, switch off all sockets, even if plug not in socket, whole house to be in darkness at night – unless on holidays, then landing light to be left on, so the robbers think you're home, clever Daddy).**
DAD: 'Unplug the telly, lamps, switch off all the lights or I'll poke your eyes out. I'm not made of money.'

NOTE: my dad threatened us all the time with the above and he wasn't even a butcher. I'm sure he wouldn't even know where to start with the chopping and if he was made of money, he'd be an art installation in Paris somewhere. Which is where my mother wished he'd go.

Anyway, back to the runaway story …

I was sent to bed early that night, my brother grinning as I passed by him, my sister hugging my mother's neck. I'd get them back, I was thinking, I'll get them all back, every one, yes I will. Then vengeful thoughts interrupted as my dad shouted after me, 'Don't have that bedroom light on all night up there, or I'll dig the eyes out of yeh. I'm not made of money.'

Primary school

First day of primary school, September 1977. No barrage of bawling kids, as most of them have been found out at this stage and that 'playacting' gets them nowhere. So we all waited outside the school with our mothers, not a dad in sight. My mother said they had to work.

My dad made Guinness, that's all I knew. His work involved getting to work – 'I haven't all day, where's me breakfast?' – where he made Guinness, then he came home – 'I haven't eaten all day, where's me dinner?' – and then he went to the pub – 'I haven't all day, where's me coat? I need to relax after a day like that' – then he came home again that night, smelling of chips.

My mother was an ex-professional ballroom dancer. She had trained in England and had two crates of winner's cups in the attic. She never took them down to look at them. She should have had them in a display cabinet in the living room, but I think it just reminded her of her show biz, no babies days, and let's be honest, those were great days.

She stayed in a girls' dance college in Soho, London, danced on *Come Dancing* (a BBC dance competition long before anyone had heard of Craig Revel Horwood) and could have been a judge on *Strickly*. But she would go home to Ireland on weekends because she missed her mammy. It was on one of these weekends home that she met my dad. He just said, 'I don't like dancing much', then he asked her to marry him. She gave up dancing because to marry a man who worked in the Guinness brewery was like winning the Lotto.

REASONS YOU SHOULD MARRY A GUINNESS WORKER

1. Free health care
2. Free medicine
3. Free dental
4. Solid pension
5. Free feckin' Guinness. *Free!*

I would have married him.

So, like most of the mammies in those days, my mam didn't work.

A NOT WORKING MOTHER TOP TEN

1. Vacuum whole house.
2. Wash any dishes by hand and dry them, put them away.
3. Wash clothes, iron all clothes too.
4. Hang out washing, use ancient pole to hold up clothes-line, break back while trying to lift line into the air with pole.
5. Make all beds, so a penny could be bounced on them.
6. Feed pets – cat, dog, parrot, fish – clean out cages, if necessary.
7. Go shopping, walk, no car, dad uses car for work, real work.
8. Carry all bags of shopping down the hill while your fingers bleed.
9. Get in, put shopping away, get the dinner on.

10. **Do absolutely nothing for yourself, you only serve your family.**

So yeah, my mam didn't work, only Dad did.

Primary school. First day. We waited for our new teacher to open the door, all of us grabbing at our cardboard collars and itchy willy areas. The people who invented these school uniforms didn't plan to have humans in them. The mammies were all proud of their little ones and would say, 'Look at yeh', just look at yeh, you're only massive'. Other mothers would come up to you and say, 'Look at him, just look at him,' then lean into me and say, 'Look at yeh, just look at yeh, he's massive', as my mother would repay the compliment to their child, 'Look at him, just look at him, now *he's* massive', lean in, 'look at yeh, just look at yeh'.

'Massive' meaning amazing, not the actual size of a thing, but how big it is in amazingness.

EXAMPLES OF 'MASSIVE' FROM MAM

1. **You look only massive.**
2. **Your new hair is massive.**
3. **That is a massive car.**
4. **The dinner was massive.**
5. **Massive is not the word.**

We could go on forever.

All the mammies were at it, they sounded like the seagulls in *Finding Nemo*. But deep down, only their own child mattered, all the other children didn't matter in the slightest. I learned this from all the time I'd spent at home with my mother. A woman would come to visit her, they'd sit and drink tea and laugh and be the best of friends, then as soon as my mother had closed the door behind her she'd say, 'That bloody woman, she's full of it, and as for that runny-nosed little brat, he has an attention problem. He's just a little brat who needs a clip around the ear and a boot up the arse.'

'Will yeh look at all of yehs,' our new teacher yelled as she opened the door. Sister Francis Xavier was her name. We filed into a very big classroom. There were no sandpits, no water basins, no Marla (Irish plasticine). Instead, there were numbers on the wall, and big letters, with animals and other things entwined in the letters. I thought to myself that they looked like a periodic table for infants ... no, I didn't ... I wasn't even sure what letters were up there.

My mother sat me into my seat, pinned my name badge on, fixed my hair, checked my eye-patch, straightened my massive glasses, kissed me on the forehead, then all the mammies left in one group together, weeping quietly to themselves like a North Korean would when their leader dies ... I didn't think that either, they just left weeping and went home to do doing no work.

Teacher said goodbye to them all, locked the door and turned around to us all. 'Right, *Jesus!*' We all jumped. Sister Francis Xavier went to a huge picture of Jesus on the wall, his chest was all open and you could see his heart. It was like Sister Francis

Xavier was possessed, she would bang her ruler against the wall, saying through gritted teeth: 'Jesus will help you all learn, as long as you believe in him. If you don't, you will all become stupid little boys and girls.' She whipped around and faced the class. 'Who believes in Jesus?' We all put up our hands. Then she walked over to me. I knew she was going to walk over to me. I would always, in my later life, attract attention. The mad person at the bus stop would always talk to me. I'd get picked out by the clowns at the circus, no matter where I sat. And it all started here, in Sister Francis Xavier's classroom.

'This little boy … name, boy?'

'Jason.'

'Jason has a handicapped eye, the Lord has done that to him. And if he's a good little boy, his handicapped eye will straighten up.'

The class laughed, and that was me done in.

That day was us doing letters, drawings, numbers. I drew a picture of Jesus on a skateboard. Sister Francis Xavier smacked me for that. That's pretty much my memory of primary school: go in, letters, numbers, draw, get smacked, go home. Until one day, Ms Higgins said we were going to do a school play. My first school play, oh yeah! I always wanted to be an actor, not a comedian. It was the acting end of things that really excited me. My first chance to tread the boards was to be in *Snow White and the Seven Dwarfs*.

Amanda Hayden, the best-looking girl in the class, got the part of Snow White. That wasn't difficult for her as the rest of the girls were, well, let's just say very, very Irish looking – and the boys even more so. Amanda's mam was Russian or something, so the Irish had been bred out of her. So the part of Snow White was gone, what did that leave?

CAST AND CHARACTERS OF SNOW WHITE AND THE SEVEN DWARFS

1. Snow White ... Amanda Hayden.
2. Seven Dwarfs ... two Davids, Alan, two Toms, a Terry and a Ken.
3. Woodsman ... Brian Curtin.
4. Queen ... Debra Jolly.
5. Etc.
6. Etc.
7. Etc.
8. Etc.
9. Etc.
10. Trees in the Woods ... Glen Amber and Jason Byrne.

Opening night. Huge excitement. I looked down from the edge of the stage as all the mammies waved at their children. Amanda Hayden was going down a storm, even mammies that weren't her mammy were waving at her. There wasn't a daddy in sight, they were all just home from WORK! They needed a rest in the pub. 'Take a picture of the play, sure he won't even know if I'm there or not.'

Suddenly, the lights on the stage changed – well, they dimmed them down to 50%. Sister Francis Xavier pressed Play on the tape-recorder, the wind howled from the tape-recorder and into the mic, which then fed back. Snow White was on her own in the deep, dark woods.

Sister Francis Xavier looked at me and Glen and whispered loudly: 'Cue the woods, cue the woods, go boys.' On me and Glen shuffled. We both had cardboard wrapped around us, painted brown, shower caps with leaves stuck to them and in our hands, held down by our sides, we were carrying a couple of branches, and of course one tree also had big glasses, a patch and a special eye.

SNOW WHITE: Oh … no … I … am … lost…in … the … forest.

SISTER FRANCIS XAVIER: Sway boys, sway.

We swayed back and forth, the best forest an audience had ever seen, although I'm not too sure if we were a forest as I don't know the official amount of trees needed to qualify for the word 'forest'.

I saw my mam, I got excited, it wasn't my fault. I started to wave my big branch arm towards my mother. As I did this, I caught Amanda Hayden by the hair, but with the lights in my eyes I had no idea what was happening. I was dragging her backwards and forwards by her long hair, which was now stuck in the branch at the end of my arm.

Cut to: show ending early, Amanda Hayden with heavy bruising to the head, my mother mortified, as the Irish would say, and I know she was because she said it all the way home as I tried to walk down the road still dressed as a tree. My mother didn't even wait for me to get changed, we made a quick exit before she was taken down by the other mammies.

Mam didn't go to mass for two weeks, until things cooled down. I was made say sorry in school, at the front of the class, to Amanda Hayden. She said she didn't mind. But with the bruising and cuts, she now looked like one of us. Ah life, and I had had only had five years of it so far … more to come.

CHAPTER 2
A LICENCE TO SIN

His breath smelled like he'd eaten a dog's bottom for breakfast. I really wish this guy would get out of my face.

'I'd say, by looking at this little boy, he'll be needing the three-wheeler bike, with that wandering eye comes a wandering mind.'

He leaned back out of my face, and now I could see the whole scrapyard as my dad stood beside me like a proud chimney. I say chimney because my dad smoked all the time – not a chain smoker, as chain smokers tend to light one fag off another, my dad magically had a lit fag in his mouth all the time.

'Sure why wouldn't yeh? Yeh could drop dead tomorrow,' was Dad's advice on all things in life.

TOP FIVE 'SURE WHY WOULDN'T YEH? YEH COULD DROP DEAD TOMORROW' THINGS TO DO

1. Smoke your face off.
2. Drink your head off.
3. Eat all fried everything, forever, as much as you can.
4. Relax and do nothing at all, I mean at *all*.
5. Buy something stupid.

Right, I have to remove the fifth item there, in fact, as Dad never made a stupid purchase in his life, was never in debt, owed nobody nothing, ever. We once got a credit card, for four weeks. When the bill came in, there was uproar in the house. Dad was running around as if the Mafia were coming to get him. He couldn't grasp that money had been spent, yet he had never held the money in his hand.

'It's like fresh air money! Jesus Christ, we'll be on the streets at this rate, walking into a shop with fresh air money that you can't see, how are you supposed to feel if your pockets are any lighter?'

He got a scissors and cut the card in half in front of all of us, something he'd seen in an American movie. He then got his coat and went off to the pub, with real money in his pocket, so he could calm down.

When he'd gone, my mother picked up the credit card bill. It had two items on it: 60 Silk Cut purple, and £20 worth of petrol. Total amount on bill: £26. Jesus Christ, thank God he cut that card up, we nearly lost the house.

So you get that my father was not the kind of man to go wild with his money. For my first bike, then, he brought me to a type of scrapyard. Most children would have gone to a bike shop, but my dad said it was my first bike and that you wouldn't buy a Ferrari as your first car.

So there we stood, while the creepy old scrapyard man went off to rummage around his yard for a bike. There were mainly spare car parts, and the whole place looked like a sprawling metal city, with rats as the occupants.

My dad knew Frankie, the scrapyard fella, well. Frankie used to come around our area on a horse and cart, collect bits and pieces from people's houses and give cash for it. So in the '80s when Ireland was in recession and everyone had 25% mortgages, cash from Frankie the scrap man came in handy. People were nearly throwing their kids up there on his cart.

'Here we go, I didn't think I'd find it, but here it is.' Frankie placed a three-wheeled bike in front of me.

It could not have been a more *watch out, here's the special child!* bike. It was impossible to fall off it because it couldn't be cycled more than five miles an hour as the wheels were buckled. And it had a flag on the back, *a flag on the back*, and, get this, it had no tubes in the tyres, just a strip of rubber glued around the tyres. So when you cycled it, your balls, brain, spine, everything rattled. It was designed to make you feel like you were always cycling down a set of steps.

We arrived into the driveway and Dad beeped the 'we're home' beep. *Beep! Beep!* Two quick presses of the horn. My mam came out to see the new bike, along with my brother and my sister Rachel, who was now five.

I jumped out of the car. I may have just gotten a rubbish bike, but I was still excited by all the excitement around me.

'I don't believe it, Paddy, you mean auld shite,' my mam said.

'What?' said my dad, in a tone that suggested he knew exactly what she was upset about.

My brother started to laugh and jumped up on my bike. 'Nice one, Dad,' Eric said. 'You've brought me bike back.'

'What?' said my dad again, in another tone of *jaysus, I'm caught here*.

'Your son's first bike and you get him that, you mean auld shite.' Mam walked back into the house.

Cut to: two years previous, and Frankie the scrapyard man is going around the doors collecting stuff. My dad brings out my brother's first bike, a three-wheeled, no-tubed bike with a flag that I was too young to remember. Dad throws it up on the cart, saying it's a grand bike but way too bashed up for Eric to cycle now. He gets £5 for it off Frankie.

So to sum up, my dad – who is, I'd be fairly sure, the only dad in the world to have done this – went back to a scrap-dealer to find my brother's cheap bike that he had thrown out/sold to Frankie two years before to give to me, two years later, in two years' worse condition.

Still, we had a ball on that old bike. There was a sort of step on the back of it, so I could carry my best friend, Karl, around on the back, and we cycled that bike into the ground. When Frankie came around a year later, my dad sold it to him again. 'Well, that's the last you'll see of that bike, lads,' Dad said, as Frankie slowly pulled away with the bike on top of his pile. Me and my brother just gave a small smile to my sister. No doubt her first bike would be *very* similar.

TOP FiVE WAYS DAD CUT CORNERS iN THE '80S.

1. Took the Club Milk out of the wrapper, ate the bar, made the wrapper back up to look like there was a bar in it so mam wouldn't think they were gone and buy more.
2. Put water into the milk bottle to make it last longer.
3. Took light bulbs out, 'Sure what's the point in having a

light bulb in a room that's never used?' Irony: we never had a room we didn't use.

4. **Fed the cat dog food and fed the dog cat food.**

5. **Went to buy a new car, traded in his old one, drove the new car for a few days to test it before buying it (he knew the bloke in the garage). Brought the new car back, said he didn't like it, and took his old car back, which was now fully serviced with four new tyres on it. They attempted to charge Dad for this but they didn't have a leg to stand on. It was swiftly dealt with – a quick 'Ask me bollix' cleared the bill.**

There was massive excitement around the school when Holy Communion letters were put in our bags. The date was set. 'Jesus Christ, the communion,' my mam screeched as she read the letter while seated at the kitchen table. 'We'll have to get the house ready, it's a mess.'

Holy Communion was a pretty big deal in our house, except for my dad: 'When you're gone, you're gone.' In other words, he didn't believe in life after death or any of the holy promises held out for later on, when you'd kicked the bucket. He only went to mass when someone died, got married or there was a Communion or a Confirmation. My mother did go to mass, but the religious aspect wasn't her focus when it came to the Communion. She wanted new carpets in the house as the neighbours and relatives would be coming in to have a look at me in my suit.

I say neighbours and relatives, but I never was really sure who was my real uncle or my real auntie because everyone who walked into the house was called uncle or auntie. Our house was the party house of the road. It was a long-standing arrangement. What happened was that, back in the 1960s, when we weren't born and my mam and dad had just bought the house (for £4,000, a sum that wouldn't even buy me a second-hand car now – *see below*), the local pub opened up at the top of the road. Well, it was top of the road and around the corner actually.

THiNGS YOU COULD BUY iN THE '60S FOR £4,000

1. **A house**
2. **A speedboat**
3. **A houseboat**
4. **At least four cars**
5. **A garden full of bouncy castles**

Anyway, on the first night the pub opened, my dad went around and knocked on all the neighbours' doors. He told the man of each house that it was the first day the pub was opening and he invited them up for 'a jar'.

A jar

This is what your dad said he was going to have when leaving the house for the pub. He was going for 'A Jar', not a new jar for your mother's homemade jam or, in fact, a method for holding a door open for a small amount of time, but to have a drink. Oddly enough, when entering the pub they would never ask for 'A Jar'. In fact, you told people you were going for 'A Jar', which turned into 'A Pint' when you asked the barman. As far as I know, these men never drank Guinness from a jar in their lives. You might see it nowadays in those craft beer pubs, which my dad wouldn't even be able to talk about without setting himself on fire.

Whoever left their house that day and came up to the pub with my dad was his drinking buddy for life on the road. Whoever didn't come, my dad never spoke to them again. He said he asked a few fellas, but their wives appeared at the door and said, 'No thank you, he's helping me unpack'. Door closed, husbands' balls in their hands *forever*.

'Jesus Christ, you have to able to go for a drink with your mates now and again, it's a God-given right to a man,' Dad would say. He felt sorry for those poor men. 'Well, I tried, there's nothing I can do for them now.' So the men who got out that night and headed to the top of the road for a pint became extended family and would be seen at sing-songs in our house for many years to come.

So on Sunday nights, the day of Our Lord and the day before going back to another week of school, the house would be peaceful and quiet. My little sister was fast asleep in the room we shared, while Eric was asleep in the box room.

The box room

Named for being the shape of a box. It was tiny, the smallest room in the house, and could barely fit a single bed. There are four walls in a box room: one with a door in it; two outer walls, named *outer* because it felt like you were literally sleeping outside because those walls were so cold, no insulation whatsoever; and another wall, because there had to be to hold up the roof, but that wall only had room for posters. Really thin posters, you don't want thick ones that will take up room in the box room.

If you are ever asked, the box room in the '70s and '80s was the room where a child was sent to freeze to death. In fact, it was so cold, and this is no joke, my mother used to put the trifle in the box room to set. I would be just nodding off when I'd see the door push open, and my mum would gently place the trifle down on the small table in my room. She would then poke her finger in the door every hour to see how it was setting. When I woke up in the morning, it was gone.

'I never set a trifle in your room when you were smaller,' my mother would yell at Christmas, around the table, when me and my siblings told stories of our childhood in the house. '*Or ever laid a finger on any of us*,' we'd all sing out, like a weird table choir.

The box room was so cold, I would go to school with mould growing on me. When the teacher asked what it was and I'd say mould, she'd reply, 'Serves you right'. I never knew why it served me right, but apparently it did.

While I slept in the box room as a kid, a low whistling noise would blow through the window. 'This is a *draught*,' I explained to my Australian friends in later life. 'A draught? *In* your house?' 'Yes,' I would say, 'surely you have draughts in your houses?' 'Only if the window is open or the front door. How in the name of God do you have a breeze blowing through your house?' 'It's a draught,' I'd tell them patiently. 'The door is closed and there's a snake (draught excluder) lying along the bottom of the door, there's also tissue in the keyhole to stop any draught getting through there. But it still blows around the house, otherwise the house can't breathe.' (I took that useless quote from my dad, who insulated nothing, ever.)

So for most of my childhood I slept to the sound of a low whistling noise coming through the frame of the window. I think Irish people are the only people in the world who listen to that and immediately wrap their duvet around themselves tighter and say to themselves, 'Oh lovely, I'd hate to be out there, just hate it, it's way nicer in here.'

If the fridge was being defrosted, sometimes the box room was used to keep the food cold. *I slept in there, for God's sake*, but at any moment I could be surrounded by meat and ice cream.

More often than not, though, we were sent into Maura's house, next door. Mam would pack up all our fridge food and we'd be sent next door with it because Maura had a big fridge in her garage. Then on Sunday, we'd be sent in to get the Raspberry Ripple from Maura's big fridge. I'd come back with the Neapolitan, only to be sent back immediately: 'It's far from Neapolitan you were raised, young man, now go get the Raspberry Ripple.'

So even though the box room was – sometimes literally – a fridge, it was a status symbol because normally the eldest child got it and had their very own bedroom. But in our house, the box room history went like this.

BOX ROOM HiSTORY

1. Eric's room.
2. Along comes baby sister, bunk-beds put in.
3. Eric thrown out of box room, put into room with me.
4. Eric gets too old, girls and me all in same room, Eric gets box room back.
5. Eric leaves home, I get box room.
6. I leave home, girls get a room each, with box room for eldest sister.
7. We all leave home.
8. Mammy takes box room because of Dad's roaring snoring.
9. Dad lonely, goes to box room.
10. No room at the inn, Dad evicted.

Right, that's your crash course in the box room. Back to us happily asleep on a Sunday night. The front door opens, it's midnight. 'Horrah, get in there Paddy and get the music on.' Literally, and I do mean literally, the whole road arrived into the house. Woken up by the noise, I stood at the top of the stairs watching man after man, woman after woman, walking into the house.

I went back to bed and lay down and tried to sleep, but all I could here was muffled Perry Como coming out of the record-player, and the whole of downstairs singing along. I couldn't sleep, so I went down, pushing past the people on the stairs, who seemed happy to see me. 'How're yeh little Eric? 'It's Jason.' 'Of course, of course, the little fella with the funny eye, making his Communion this year?' 'Yeah.'

I got to the bottom of the stairs and the place was thick with smoke, all I could see were floating, laughing adult heads. I could hear my mam laughing somewhere, but it was hard to track the laughter as the entire place was warbling 'Maaaaagic moooomentsssss!' It looked like a roomful of smoking and singing Muppets, all swaying from side to side as they all sang. They rubbed me on the head as I travelled by them, searching for Mam.

Finally, I found my mam in the corner. She was beside my auntie Betty, who's not my real auntie of course but my godmother, and on the other side of her was my uncle Paddy. In terms of names, there was a Paddy overload in those days. It's hard to believe now, but 65% of that room was called Paddy.

> BETTY: There he is, Eithne (my mother's name, by the way). Are you making your Communion this year?
> ME: Yes, I am.
> 'Maaaagic mooooomentssss!'
> BETTY: Aren't yeh, love, making your Communion?
> ME: Yes.
> BETTY: Look at him, just look him, making his Communion this year, isn't that what you're doing, making the Communion? You're going to look massive.
> ME: Yes.

'Maaaagic mooooomentssss!'

BETTY: Is he making his Communion, Eithne?

MAM: Yes he is, Betty.

BETTY: Look at the size of him, making his Communion, Eithne.

MAM: I know.

BETTY: He's huge.

MAM: I know.

BETTY: Huge for Communion.

MAM: I know.

BETTY: We'll have to put a brick on his head, won't we? Won't we!

ME: Yes.

'Maaaagic mooooomentssss!'

BETTY: Here's a fiver.

MAM: Not at all, Betty.

BETTY: Ah go on, it's for the Communion.

MAM: You will not.

ME: (*takes fiver*)

MAM: (*takes fiver out of my hand*)

BETTY: (*takes fiver out of Mam's hand, stuffs it into my PJ pocket*)

BETTY: Go on now, go son, and enjoy the Communion.

MAM: You're terrible, Betty.

BETTY: Ah but look at his eye, all turned in. He's happy, Eithne, aren't you happy, son ... ?

I stood for a moment in front of my mam and Betty, rubbing the smoke out of my eyes, and then I cut Betty off saying, 'Mam, I've got school in the morning and I can't sleep with all the noise.'

The record came to a stop, people stopped singing and they all looked around at me, it was like a scene from Roald Dahl's *The Witches* ... pause ... long pause ... and then my mother said 'Ooooooooooooooo, you have to be in school in the morning!' She howled with laughter, along with the rest of the room. Betty and my mam fell back into the couch, kicking their legs in the air, laughing themselves silly.

Suddenly the whole room jumped into 'Tie a Yellow Ribbon Round the Old Oak Tree' and they were all back into Muppet mode. 'Go on up to bed, and give your auntie Betty a kiss before you go.' I had to kiss every auld one (Irish for old lady) while I made my way back to my bed. I now smelled of cigarettes and booze, and I was only seven. They sang on into the early hours of the morning. Perry Como had a lot of songs to get through.

I remember being tired and angry that night/morning, but when I look back now, I was in the middle of Irish history – the neighbours, the booze, the singing, the *craic*, people trying to shove money into your pyjamas, it's what Irish people are made of. It's about fun and forgetting and generosity, and that lot had it in spades.

We don't see it as much anymore, unfortunately, because of our more money, our smoothies and healthy frappacino shite, and exercising at every opportunity.

I'm guilty of it myself. I recently ran the NYC marathon for Temple Street Children's Hospital, and when I told my dad I was doing it he said, 'I know a fella who dropped dead from that. You only get a certain amount of heartbeats in your life, you'll stress the heart out of your chest.'

To this day my dad goes out to his shed out the back garden, has his whiskey and his cigarette, barely moves and lets the world stress around him. He's as fit as a fiddle at seventy-five years of age. That, my friends, is the key to a happy life right there: don't use up your heartbeats too quickly, and let all the other idiots stress for you, relax and sit on your arse, and you'll live forever.

Des Kelly day. Time: around 11.30am

Me, Eric and Rachel were all in Des Kelly's carpet show-rooms with Mam and Dad. Dad was walking around, rubbing carpets with his hands, as Mam talked to Des Kelly. She was telling him all about the Communion and how they had got new curtains downstairs for Eric's Communion, but this time they were going all out and getting downstairs and the stairs done and, if there was a little left over, then a bit of lino in the kitchen as well.

Us three kids loved going to Des Kelly's carpets, the warehouse was huge and, unlike now, there were no safety guidelines in place at all, anywhere. My dad would say it's the yanks' fault you can't move about freely anywhere anymore, because of the yanks suing everybody. He blamed 'the yanks' for a lot of things. Des Kelly's warehouse was a brilliant playground for kids. There were huge rolls of carpet, all piled one on top of the other, with very skinny lanes running through the stacks of piled carpet. Me, Eric and Rachel loved running around in there. My mother would let a roar at us to 'SHUT UP', then she'd go back to her posh accent to talk to Des Kelly about the carpets.

My dad wasn't talking to Des Kelly at all, just rubbing carpets, my Dad never spoke to these people until the deal had to be done. He'd let my mam do all the talking and ordering, then he'd step in with his cash card, see the price and yell, 'Yeh can ask me bollix, do you think I'm made of money? We need a few carpets for the house, not the relaying of Lansdowne Road.' (For those of you wondering, this was a rugby stadium, knocked down, rebuilt and now called the Aviva Stadium, soon to be called the Pizza Express stadium. Of course, my dad said it was the yanks' fault when all this happened.)

We kept running and rolling around the carpets as my dad explained to Des Kelly how much money he didn't have. That was when it happened. My brother told me to squeeze through two carpets, through the small gap between the roll above and the roll below. My sister was too small to manage it, and just kept sliding around on stuff, so I said okay to impress my big brother. I pushed myself into the gap between the two rolls of carpet, pushing and pushing, but then I got wedged. Stuck fast. I cried for help, feeling my brother pulling my legs but knowing I wasn't going to budge.

Then I heard the muffled sound of my mam and dad. Des Kelly, too. I felt a couple of pulls, then that stopped, then talking.

Cut to: the car on the way home. I had carpet burns all over my face, legs and arms. I looked a mess. Des Kelly had to get this massive

Russian man who worked for him to pull me out really quickly –
they were applying the same logic you apply to a plaster on a child's
leg: fast equals less painful. I came out so fast, it was like a match
striking sulphur, I nearly set the place on fire with the friction.

You'd think I'd be in trouble, or that my brother would be for
making me do it. But afterwards, Dad bought us all ice creams,
to cool down the burns, he said. Any normal family would have
gone straight to hospital, to get the child treated for shock or
burns, but not my parents. No, a couple of ice creams should
do the trick. 'Sure if you're half happy, you're on the road to
recovery,' Dad would say.

They had strange ways of curing us in the '80s. We didn't have antibiotics when I was a child, we had FLAT 7UP. You're in bed sick, a fever of 110, lying in sweat-covered blankets, and you turn to Mammy, with the palest face ever …

> ME: Mam, I don't feel well at all.
> MAM: Oh that's no bother, I've taken the fizz out of the 7UP, it's nice and flat for you, so just sip on that and you'll be right as rain.
> ME: Mam, I think I'm blacking out, call a doctor …
> MAM: I don't think you can hear me, son. I said I've taken the fizz, now the FIZZ OUT of the 7UP. It is now flat, therefore ready for sipping – *sipping* mind you, not gulping – all flat and ready to take on any illness.

I don't know how we survived in the '80s. My mam would have been at my funeral saying, 'I don't know how this happened, I gave him flat 7UP for months. I think he died to spite me.'

Dad was happy for a very different reason, though. We later found out that my dad had threatened to sue Des Kelly for damage sustained to his burnt faced child. He stood me in front of Des Kelly and said, 'Look at him, he looks like he's been in a fight with forty ferrets.'

So Des Kelly threw in the lino for the kitchen for free. We were in the money as we drove home that day and while I was feeling a bit burnt and sore, Dad was right: I was half happy with my ice cream, so I didn't really feel the pain.

As he drove us home my dad was talking to my mam, saying, 'Ah we're on the pig's back now, Eithne. The house will be massive for the Communion. Hurray for the yanks!'

'Gobshite,' she answered.

The Communion was getting nearer now, and Sister Francis Xavier was in hyper-drive about the whole thing. She was telling the class about transubstantiation. We were seven years old, for God's sake, and she had this massive word written across the blackboard; our copybooks weren't even wide enough to take the word.

The Catholic religion just doesn't do itself any favours with its massive words, guilt and fear. 'Transubstantiation,' she'd say, then she got the class to repeat it.

> CLASS: Trans ... sat ... or ... tent ... aaaaa ... ttentionnnnnsss.
> SISTER FRANCIS XAVIER: NO! Again, again, again.

We had to have all this stuff right for the Bishop on the day or we wouldn't be able to make our Communion. This was bollix, of course, I mean, what bishop is going to turn away a little seven-year-old from the altar if he can't say transubstantiation?

For the pagans of the world: transubstantiation
Transubstantiation is when Holy God's son – who is Holy God and who is also the Holy Ghost, so he's three people in one –

changes the bread and wine into the Body and Blood of Christ.

'Is Jesus a magician?' I asked Sister Francis Xavier. *WHACK!* Right across the head with the Bible. 'Get outside, *now*.' I had to stand outside the classroom. I was then brought back inside after ten minutes of sniffling and crying outside the door.

So, today was to be our First Confession. The day we all head across the road to the church to tell the priest all the grievous sins we have committed ... as a seven-year-old. As we didn't have any sins, which should have been fairly obvious to anyone, Sister Francis Xavier had to make up sins for us. We were all told to go in and say that we had cursed and hadn't washed the dishes and our mammies were cross at us.

This was a disgrace, I remember thinking, these are not my sins, I didn't do anything bad, this is like admitting to a crime I didn't commit. 'I haven't done any of those sins, Sister!' I shouted up to her. She came down with the Bible in her hand again. 'You were a sinner the day you were born, son.' I remember to this day what I said back to her, and well done to seven-year-old me: 'Is there dirty dishes in your mammy's belly?'

Sister Francis Xavier's face filled with red rage as the Bible was raised up and I was belted with it again and again. 'Little, sinning, disgraceful ... language, boy.' She calmed down, then told me to tell the priest what I had just told her when I went into the confession box.

In the church, we all sat in rows on the hard pews, hands pressed together to make us look extra holy. The church smelled of incense, and there were old people scattered around the place, like a waiting-room for Heaven. The old people would pass us and nod, as if to say, you're all in trouble now, yeh little sinning bastards.

It was all very scary for a child. There was the huge Jesus on a cross right in front of us on the altar, and I was sure he was looking at me, but with my patch and special eye I couldn't really be sure. I looked over at the confession box and it was terrifying looking, too, all dark wood and creepy, which made it look like the entrance into hell. We were all frightened and had no idea what was inside there. God, but this religion really knew how to put the shits up yeh.

There was a red light above the door to the confession box and it lit up when you went inside, then after a while the light went off and out came a child, red-faced.

My theory of the red light was this: as you went in, you told the priest your sins, then he would press a button that basically cooked you in there and cleansed you of your sins. A bit like a holy microwave. You then came out red.

'Next, next!' I looked up, and it was me next. God I was scared, I put my hand on the door and the red light went on above. In I went, full of sin.

I walked into a completely black hole, a pitch-dark room. (I know this is very like Frank O'Connor's first confession, but we've all been going into that box for nearly 2,000 years ... good story, though.) I couldn't see a thing, it was terrifying, I didn't even know which way to face. Then suddenly I heard a slide of wood, and a small shaft of light appeared above my head. A voice came from the shaft of light: 'Bless you, my son, welcome to the confession box', or something like that, I was never going to remember what he said in my future life because the Catholics scared that out of me too.

ME: Hello? Jesus?
PRIEST: No, it's Father Murphy.
ME: In the light?
PRIEST: No, up here son, here.

He tapped the weird little mesh window he was looking through, but I couldn't make him out at all, his face looked like a jigsaw.

ME: Hello?
PRIEST: What do you say?
ME: Hello?
PRIEST: Bless me, Father, for I have sinned, it's my first confession ...
ME: Right.

SILENCE, FOLLOWED BY AN ANGRY BREATH OUT.

PRIEST: (*sigh*) What sins have you to confess?
ME: I didn't do anything.
PREIST: Yes, you must have sinned.
ME: I did the dishes, and I never swear because my mam

would batter me.

PRIEST: You're a sinner, child, you have sinned.

ME: No, I'm all good, thanks.

I looked around to see if the box was about to light up red, like an oven, and cleanse me. I remembered that something similar had happened to Superman when he gave his powers up for Lois Lane, he got into a chamber that cooked him and took away his powers. In the same way, I thought, if I tell this priest any sins, he'll press the button and I'll be fried of my sins. It sounded painful!

Maybe that's what Sister Francis Xavier was talking about when she said, 'Jesus died on the cross so he could fry us of our sins'.

PRIEST: Just tell me what Sister Francis Xavier told you to say.

ME: (*to myself*) How did he know that?

PRIEST: Go on.

Cut to: outside the confession box, and all you could hear from the inside was ...

PRIEST: WHAT?

I was hurtled outside and made say ten 'Our Father's', and not the fast way, where you don't pronounce the words, but the slow way, every word heard.

I'm glad I told the priest that I thought my mammy had dishes in her belly, because it distracted him and didn't give him time to press the red fry button, so I took the ten 'Our Father's' gladly.

TOP TEN THINGS TO DO BEFORE THE COMMUNION TO MAKE YOU EVEN MORE HOLY

1. Mam gave me her mother's rosary beads, which belonged to her mother. I was delighted as a young boy to receive a scary necklace with Jesus hanging out of it.

2. A prayer table was put into my bedroom, with holy water, a bible, a cushion to kneel on, and a crucifix at the end of table leaning against the wall.

3. One moving statue of Mary, so called because we kept moving it around on my mam and she thought it was doing it on its own. At one stage it was sitting at the table in the kitchen and we heard her talking to it like it was real.

4. Got blessed each morning at the door by my mother from her holy water bottle.

5. Had to go to extra mass on Saturday and Sunday; it was like my mother was trying to clock up extra holy points.

6. Made stand at the side of the road for the day and help old people cross the road. My older mates loved this and came to jeer me, and did impressions of the old people behind me as I helped them cross the road. My mother

said I had to do it because Jesus did it. I'm pretty sure Jesus
didn't help anyone cross the road.

7. Speed praying training so you could get through the
   rosary as fast as possible. My mam was a black belt at it.

8. Meet people less fortunate than you. My mother brought
   us to meet Protestants in their local church. She always
   felt sorry for them because they didn't believe in Mary,
   and she just couldn't understand that.

9. Draw endless pictures of Mary, baby Jesus, sins, sinners,
   guilt and hate.

10. Holy homework for the priest. We had to bring it into his
    office in school one at a time and sit way too close to him
    as you read out a holy poem or showed him a drawing of
    some miserable scary bit of the Bible.

Finally, it was the day of the Communion, and Mam was running
around the house getting us all ready. I had my suit on with the
giant rosette on my chest, looking like a horse that had just won a
prize. My hair was brushed down flat to my head so many times
that it looked like Lego hair. I was then put in the hard-backed
chair in the hallway and told not to move until we had to go or
else I'd crease my suit.

My big brother plonked down beside me. He passed on his compli-
ments to me by giving me a dead arm and calling me a 'Spa'.

Spa
Very much a slang word; we had no idea it wasn't PC. In fact, a
'PC' to us in those days was a copper off *The Sweeney*.

My little sister sat up on his lap. My mam then ran around the house, giving her brand new Des Kelly carpets a last run-over with the Hoover. Every room in the house had a different pattern. I remember later in my life, when I showed my mam my new house and it had the same colour carpet all the way through it, she said, 'How are you supposed to know which room is which? I can't tell where your good room is.'

The good room

The good room was the nicest room in the house, kept immaculately clean, but almost never used. It usually had: a dining-room suite that the family only ate at on very special occasions; a massive mahogany unit that held plates that were never to be used; and, in the centre, a drinks shelf, with the posh whiskey and scotch my dad had stolen over the years. Nobody was allowed to go into the good room, because then it would become bad.

Once the carpets were vacuumed and we were deemed good enough to go out in public, we went out and got into the car, my mother up the front, three of us in the back. Mam kept beeping the car horn for my dad to hurry up and come out. Eventually he came out, got into the car and said, 'I was having a shite, for God's sake, woman. Can a man not have a shite now?'

TOP FiVE REASONS YOU HAVE TO WAiT FOR YOUR DAD TO COME OUT OF THE HOUSE AND INTO THE CAR

1. He's having a shite ('Can a man not have a shite now?')

2. Finishing his cup of tea ('Can a man not finish his cup of tea?')

3. Tying his tie ('Can a man not leave the house looking well now?')

4. Looking for his wallet ('Oh so now we don't need money anymore?')

5. Locking doors and closing windows ('Oh right, so you leave all the windows and doors open for the robbers? I thought you had to lock the house up, more fool me. Jaysus, now a man can't even lock up his own house!')

When we arrived at the church, it was mad busy. All the mothers were calling out Hellos and saying, 'Will you look at him, he's only massive' and 'Will you look at her, she's massive. *(whispered)* Not her weight of course, but her dress'. All the fathers stood in a circle, swapping cigarettes, wearing the same suit but in different shades of blue, all saying that they had gotten the suit for 'bollock-all' from a bloke in town, and 'fair play to him'.

The mass began. It looked like a huge multiple wedding. All the boys in suits, all the girls in little white wedding dresses. My mam said we were all getting married to God. Man, this religion was weird.

We all queued up for our first taste of Holy Communion, the round white wafer that the priest would give to us. The line was long, but I just kept repeating in my head what I had to say and do at the top:

PRIEST: The body of Christ.
ME: (*tongue out, wafer on tongue*) Amen (*bless myself*).

I repeated this to myself over and over again as I neared the priest. Just as I reached the top of the line, I spotted my family, and on the end of the pew was my brother. I passed by, trying to ignore him, but just as I stepped forward he said 'Spa', and that threw me.

I heard the girl in front say 'Amen' and already it was my go. The priest looked down at me, wafer (I mean, Body of Christ) at the ready. He said, 'Body of Christ', I stuck my tongue out and put my hands out at the same time. The priest didn't know where to put the wafer, so he put it into my hand and then pushed my hand toward my mouth, and the wafer went onto my tongue. I then looked him right in the eye and said 'Spa', then moved to the side. The priest wasn't sure what he'd heard because I'd said it with my mouth open, tongue out, with the wafer on my tongue. I continued to walk back to my seat with my tongue out and the wafer/Body of Christ melting on my tongue.

I sat back into the pew, and my brother was in tears laughing to himself. 'You're supposed to swallow the bread, yeh mickey.' SMACK OF THE HEAD, for my brother, from Mam. I then did my little prayer, and I prayed that the priest didn't hear me say 'Spa'. The ceremony went on for a while, then finally it was over and the first to leave the church were the dads, followed by evil looks of their red-faced wives, who would be killing them later for being so obvious about it. 'So a man can't go outside for a cigarette now!'

We got home to the house, then came the most embarrassing thing about an Irish Holy Communion: the door-to-door visits. My mother pushed me out the door and said, 'Go and show people how you look'. People reading this outside Ireland or who aren't from Ireland, I swear to you, this is the absolute truth.

We had to call into the houses on our road, to show the neighbours our new outfits, and the whole road was full of kids going

in and out of houses. All you could hear around the estate was *KNOCK, KNOCK* or *DING DONG*, doors opening and then, 'Will you look at you, you look massive!' At that, the whole family would come to the door. Then the mother would go off to find 50p to give you, and while she was gone the bigger brothers or sisters would stand there in the doorway, staring menacingly at you, whisper 'Spa' at you, then the mother would come back and give you money. Money for what? For looking like a little groom, that's for what.

Then back to my own house again, which was now full of pretend uncles and aunties from the road. Everyone was shoving money into my jacket, rubbing my head, then straightening my glasses as they knocked them askew with the rubbing.

The party went on long into the night, and everyone loved my mother's new carpets and the lino in the kitchen. All except auntie Olive, that is, who dropped her cigarette onto the lino and burned a tiny hole in it. She started to cry, saying she was so sorry. My mam, who was holding back the tears, said it didn't matter, she'd get it replaced, all the while knowing full well she'd never get it replaced because we weren't made of money, for God's sake. That cigarette burn stayed in the lino for about fifteen years, before it was finally replaced with a new square of lino.

The cigarette burn in the lino incident didn't stop them all smoking more, drinking more and singing into the early hours of the morning. As they drank, they got more drunk, and more generous. They just kept giving me money, it was like a scene from *Goodfellas*. By the time I went to bed, I must have had about 55 quid, which was the most money I'd ever seen, let alone held, let alone owned. My head hit the pillow and I drifted off to the strains of 'Tie a Yellow Ribbon Round the Old Oak Tree'.

We returned to school on Monday, all feeling really big and holy. We could now go to mass on our own to receive the Body of Christ. It was like getting your 'L' plates taken off your car – we were no longer learner Catholics, we were qualified Catholics, licensed to sin and ask for forgiveness straight after.

Sister Francis Xavier went around the class asking each of us what we had bought with our Holy Communion money.

> ALAN BENNETT: Half back to the church, the rest on a new Bible, Sister.
> CORA MURPHY: A new Holy Mary statue for the hallway in the house, Sister.
> JASON BYRNE: A new swing.
> *WHACK!* over the head with the Bible, eye turned in immediately, made to stand outside class for half an hour to reflect on my greed.

It was good to be a fully qualified Catholic now: guilty, miserable, but cashed up.

CHAPTER 3
BLOBS, BEATINGS AND BABIES

Mam at the pillar of the gate along with all the other mammies at their gate.

ALL MAMMIES: Dinner!

We all headed towards our mother's voices like baby lambs being called for a bottle feed. Then it was in for dinner, around the table, the whole lot of us. It was never a surprise because my dinner was nearly always the same.

JASON'S DINNER MENU FOR AT LEAST TWENTY YEARS IN LUDFORD DRIVE

1. Mashed potatoes, beans and chicken.
2. Mashed potatoes, beans and mince burger.

3. **Mashed potatoes, beans and sausage.**
4. **Mashed potatoes, beans and Granby burger.**
5. **Mashed potatoes, beans and fish fingers.**

Except for this day, when my mum handed me mash potatoes, beans and some sliced meat that I didn't recognise. I had no idea what it was, so she told me it was sliced-up burger. I ate it and I loved it. My mam didn't tell us for years that it was lamb's heart. Puke!

It was only 25p for a lamb's heart in the butcher's, gross I know, but it just shows you, if you don't know what you're eating, then you'll just down it anyway.

My dad was at the table with us and he loved to moan about anything that was handed to him. On this day my mam handed him fish and potatoes. He had to have his dinner when he arrived in the door as he was exhausted from work, real work, not the work that my mother was doing as we discussed earlier. She would hand us all our dinners, we'd start eating, then ten minutes later she'd arrive in with her own dinner. She'd sit down, and my dad would start.

'The skins are on the potatoes, Eithne. I thought you'd peel them.' My mam stared at him like she was going to kill him. 'I can't peel these potatoes myself, Eithne. They're too small and if I have to concentrate on something as small as peeling the skin off these potatoes, then my blood pressure will rise and I could have a heart attack right here at this table.'

He'd be the first man in the history of the world to have a heart attack from peeling baked potatoes. So my mother grabbed the plate from him and, more fool her, peeled his potatoes for him.

Dad was moaning about peeling his potatoes because they were too small, while right beside us, on the coffee table, was his jigsaw puzzle, with its tiny, tiny pieces making up a picture of thousands of people walking in a square somewhere in the world, I think it was Rome, but Dad never finished it so I never got the whole picture. Surely you'd get high blood pressure from trying to find where a stupid jigsaw puzzle piece went, but oh no, potato peeling seemed to be the killer in our house.

'Can I have my ice cream and jelly now, Mam?' 'Finish your dinner,' she'd say. I ate like a bird, I hated dinners because I had such a sweet tooth. I held the road record for fifty blobs in my mouth at one sitting. I know that blobs are now a slang word for condoms in most places, but it wasn't fifty condoms in my mouth. On the southside of Dublin, in Ludford Drive, blobs were from Menan's shop and they were little sections of chewing gum. My gums resembled a hamster's face when I was finished beating the record.

I'd roll my dinner around the plate until my mam gave in, then Yeah!, jelly and ice cream. We were allowed eat this in the sitting room, in front of the telly. My small sister Rachel would make an absolute mess of the jelly and ice cream, Eric had it finished before we sat down, my dad ate his while my mother fetched him a basin of hot water filled with Dettol. She'd put the basin in front of my dad's chair, then he would lower his bare, white, Irish feet, accompanied by long toenails as he couldn't be arsed cutting them – my mam had to do that for him too – into the basin, so the room smelled of feet and Dettol as we tried to eat our ice cream and jelly.

We had to watch the News because there was only one telly, but as soon as it ended Dad wanted the channel changed, and that's the only reason he had us in there, to change the channel for him. In those day's you had to get up from your chair, walk over to the telly and press the button with the name of the channel on it.

CHANNEL BUTTONS

1. **RTÉ 1**
2. **RTÉ 2**
3. **BBC 1**
4. **BBC 2**
5. **HTV**
6. **BLANK (later became Channel 4)**

Your dad's chair was very important in the '80s. One day my mother had the priest in for tea. He often called into whatever house he wanted to, for food, but what he was really after was the whiskey.

My mam and all the other mothers treated him like royalty. He was just a priest, for God's sake, but they never understood this.

So on this day, my dad came home from work and he must have been in a bad mood. He walked into the house and the priest was in the living room having sandwiches and whiskey, while seated in my dad's chair. My dad walked into the living room, looked at the priest in *his* chair, looked at my mother and said, 'Who's he?' 'You *know* that's Father Murtagh, Paddy,' my mam squeaked out with a very, very red face. My dad said, 'I don't give a bollix who he is, he's in my chair, get him out.'

The priest had to go into the kitchen with my mother as my dad sat into his chair. My mam didn't speak to my dad for about a week, which he didn't even notice, so my mam gave up trying to ignore him.

I have children now and if I say they're sitting in my chair, they just laugh at me. A man doesn't have a man's place in a house anymore. Today's houses are all about the family, a unit, no higher status or lower status, parents together as one, and the children to be disciplined together as one. There's no more beat it into them, now it's all about talk it into them, and that's why they're not afraid of us anymore. They can sue us if we do anything wrong to them. (Blame 'the yanks' for that, too.) Imagine if I'd threatened my dad with Childline when I was a kid? He would have shoved the phone up me hoop.

Well I say that, but he never went near us, never once hit us. His hands were like hammers; if he'd ever hit us, he'd have sent us into next week. No, no, it was that little 5 ft 3 in. ninja mad woman who battered us.

You could be in the kitchen with your brother and sister, and a plate would drop and smash, and if your mam was upstairs, you'd hear her drop whatever she was doing and then come hurtling down the stairs like something from a horror movie.

A spiral staircase we had, by the way, one of the most lethal things to have in a house. My dad got it in because he said there'd be more room in the hallway. He was right, but we fell up and down that stairs for years. My mother slid down it with dirty washing in her arms, my baby sister, bog rolls, you name it, my mam slipped down that stairs with it, but because she was a black-belt mammy, she always landed on her feet.

WALLOP! Right across the bum went the slipper. My special eye didn't know what to do, it was turning into my nose, back to the centre, back to the nose. I didn't even drop the plate, but my sister and brother had split out of the kitchen.

I just ran into the path of my mam, then around the kitchen table as she chased me with one slipper in her hand, limping as she ran. I was nervous. When I'm nervous or in trouble, my eye goes in, but even worse, and what riled my mother even more, was that I'd start laughing. So there we were, her with the slipper and her mad anger, me laughing and running.

She chased me into the hall, caught me and whacked my bum even more. I tried to block the smacks with my hands, but ended up with red hands.

Super Nanny would not have lasted a second in the '80s. Can you imagine her walking into my mam's house while my mam was belting the arse off me with a slipper?

> SUPER NANNY: Mrs Byrne, Mrs Byrne, why are you hitting that child?
> MAM: You know something, these little brats have me so angry I can't even remember why I'm hitting them.
> SUPER NANNY: Maybe you're depressed?
> MAM: Depressed? Depressed? I'd love to be depressed, I haven't got time to be depressed.
> SUPER NANNY: Look, Mrs Byrne, you just need to put him on the naughty step, and if he gets up and runs away, go get

him and put him back gently. If he runs away again, go get him
and put him back gently again. Keep doing this till he learns.

MAM: Oh if I put him on that step, he won't move.

SUPER NANNY: How's that, Mrs Byrne?

MAM: Because I'll nail the brat's knees to the steps with his
father's hammer!

So in the '80s we had no choice but to take the slaps on the arse.

FAVOURITE MAMMY BEATING ITEMS

1. **The slipper (bum area).**
2. **The other slipper (bum area).**
3. **Back of the hand (head area).**
4. **Front of the hand (used on bum area).**
5. **Anything loose she could grab as she ran (normally
   thrown at you, so pot luck on the area of strike).**

After all that, I went out to finish off a football game. We played
until it was dark, then we all sat down in the field. My mother
was first to appear at the pillar and shouted down into the field,
'Jason!' Before I could answer my mate Ciaran shouted, 'Yeah?'

MAM: Get in here, it's dark.

CIARIAN: Ask me bollix, Maaa.

I was battered to sleep that night, you could read the make and
size of her slipper on my arse.

A few weeks later we were all having dinner at the table. Eric had finished first, my sister was making a mess, I was playing with my burger, my dad was lifting up his fish and saying, 'This could have done with longer on the pan'. My mam looked up at us all.

MAM: (*deep breath*) I'm going to have a baby.
RACHEL: Yeahh!, a little baby.
ERIC: (*doesn't care*) Right.
ME: But you're too old, Mam.
MAM: No I'm not, it will be great.
DAD: Another baby! I'm not made of money, you know.

As if my mother had gone out and gotten herself pregnant with a sponge and a stick. My dad was in a pretty bad mood for a while, as he now had four mouths to feed, but that was just the way it was going to be.

My mam's belly got big quick, that baby in there was growing fast. My mam would let me talk to the bump, and I'd tell it jokes and do silly vibration stuff on it.

Then the day came. We were watching *Scooby Doo*, well, me and Rachel were watching it, Eric was out playing in the field and Dad was at work. My mother leapt from the armchair with pain. I asked if she was alright. She said, 'I'm fine. Go get Joan next-door.' So I called into Joan next-door and told her my mam was having a baby.

JOAN: Jaysus!

Joan came rushing in. My mother was very red-faced and breathing hard and trying not to scream with pain. How were they going to get to hospital? There wasn't a car on the road as all the dads had the cars and they were all at work.

'Hello? Hellooooooo.' In walked Bernard the breadman, in his brown coat. 'The door was open and … jaysus,' as he caught sight of my mother.

JOAN: We need a lift to the hospital, now.
BERNARD: Call an ambulance.
JOAN: We won't make it, you'll have to bring her.
BERNARD: But it's just a bleedin' bread van.

Cut to: me in the front of the bread van, with Rachel beside me on the seat, Bernard driving as fast as he can and my mam in the

back of the van with Joan and a load of sliced pans flying all over the gaff (place). My mother was doing her short breaths and Joan was helping her … while munching down on an éclair.

> BERNARD (*looking in the rear-view mirror*) They're going on your bill, Joan.
>
> JOAN: Ah shut your mouth, it's an emergency here, yeh dope.

We drove for what seemed like forever, got to the door of the hospital, Bernard jumped out and they all ran in as my mother waddled toward the midwife.

Sitting in the waiting-room, Rachel asleep on my lap, Joan reading a magazine and Bernard still sitting in his brown coat. Doctor comes out, walks up to Bernard.

> DOCTOR: Are you the father?
>
> BERNARD: No, the breadman.
>
> DAD: I'm the father, not that bleedin' eejit, no offence, Bernard.
>
> BERNARD: None taken.

Dad had just arrived in with Eric.

> DOCTOR: It's a baby girl, smells of doughnuts, but a baby girl all the same. You can go in and see her now.

Myself, Eric, Rachel, Dad, Joan and Bernard the breadman all headed in to see my mam. The midwife stopped us all at the door. 'Only immediate family, please.'

'I'm the dad, these are my children, Joan is our neighbour and that's our bloody breadman. For God's sake, if it wasn't for him, we wouldn't have a large slice pan on the table each day, and that bun there that was in the oven would've popped out on my living-room floor.' So we marched in.

'Eithne, her name is Eithne,' Mam said. She was tiny, and oh my god! 'Look, she has a wonky eye.' 'No son, all babies have wonky eyes, there's only a few that hang onto them like you,' said my mam. 'Spa,' said Eric.

TOP FIVE ADVANTAGES OF A NEW BABY IN THE HOUSE

1. Eric would bring the baby outside so the girls would swarm around him.
2. The baby would keep Mam busy and away from us.
3. I now had a new pet to play with.
4. We all smelt of baby, as mam dried us with talcum powder to save on towels. She would cover us with it.
5. I could watch younger cartoons again and just blame my little sister if anyone walked in.

TOP FIVE DISADVANTAGES OF A NEW BABY IN THE HOUSE

1. Never too sure which stains were chocolate and which were poo on the couch, floor, wall, etc.
2. Eric would forget to bring her back and lose her now and again.
3. Mam was too busy so Dad had to make our dinner sometimes (puke).
4. We all smelt of baby, as mam dried us with talcum powder to save on towels. She would cover us with it.
5. She wasn't a pet so she never landed on all fours when she ... AHEM ... fell off the couch, chair, counter, etc.

Myself, Eric and Rachel stood in a line like three orphans in front of my dad in the living room. My mam wasn't coming home for a few days and Dad had to mind us. This was going to be similar to letting a monkey fly a jet airplane.

He had no idea what we ate, how we dressed, what time our schools started at, how to iron, wash, basically he had no idea who we were. That's how it was in those days, your dad was this fella who hung out in the house like an extra big child and your mam looked after him the same way she looked after her children.

Dad stared at us with wonder. 'Right ... everyone into the car. Chipper.' Yes, yes, yes!

★ ★ ★

As a kid, and even now, when you hear the word 'chipper' it's like a shot of adrenalin, we always associated the chipper with excitement. We loved it when we were in the house and Dad would ring from the pub and tell my mam to heat the plates under the grill, that he was bringing home chips. Mam would put on the grill, heat the plates, then Dad would wander in about 11.30pm and we'd all sit around eating chips. I've no idea why my mam heated the plates, as the chips were boiling anyway. So we all sat around, cooling our chips before putting them into our mouths, '*Hoo, hoooo, hoooooo*', we sounded like a family of owls in a circle.

MOST POPULAR THINGS YOU'D FIND IN A CHIPPER

1. Fresh cod and chips.
2. 20 Silk Cut purple.
3. Drunks.
4. Very, very busy mammies (*red-faced and embarrassed*): 'Jesus, I didn't have time to put a dinner on'.
5. Young fellas up to no good.

MOST BATTERED ITEMS IN A CHIPPER

1. Battered burger
2. Battered fish
3. Battered onion

4. **Battered sausage**
5. **Battered young fella**

So we were very much in my dad's way of living, we even stopped at the pub on the way home from everything. This time we had to stop off on the way home from the hospital, with the chips and burgers. It's as if he didn't want to upset the barman. We sat around the table, all digging into our burgers and chips. The barman came over and gave us our fizzy drinks.

> BARMAN: They're not allowed eat chips in here, Paddy.
> DAD: Ah shut your mouth, their mother is in hospital, where else are they going to have their chips and burgers?
> BARMAN: In the house, Paddy.
> DAD: And how in the name of jaysus am I supposed to have me pint if I'm stuck in the house with that lot?
> BARMAN: Fair point, Paddy.

Oh, the love of a father.

We loved being in the pub, it was so different from the way it is now. People nowadays don't like it when you bring children into bars, but we spent most of our childhood there, along with the rest of the road.

There were only two places you'd find out news in the area when I was a kid. The news on telly and the papers? Wrong, it was either: 12.30 mass on a Sunday, as people hung around to get gossip off each other and there was no mass coming in after so you could linger; or in the pub.

Mind you, info from the pub about someone else could be sketchy, because drink was in the mix.

> MIKE: Did you hear Tony McCarthy dropped dead last night of a heart attack?
> DAD: You're joking, I was only talking to him yesterday.
> MIKE: Yep, dead as a doornail.

Next minute, in comes Tony McCarthy through the pub doors.

> MIKE: Tony? I thought you were dead?
> TONY: What? I'm not dead.

(Love the way the Irish say stuff like this as if it's totally normal, telling people around him that a walking, talking man is not dead.)

> MIKE: (*angry that Tony is not dead*) Well somebody's dead, that's for sure.
> DAD: Bleedin' gobshite, Mike.

On a Saturday afternoon the pub was amazing. The system was as follows: all the dads drove the mam and the kids up to the supermarket. Mammies all headed into supermarket. Dads brought the children into the lounge, a bright part of the pub, bought them a packet of crisps and a 'lemo', which was my dad's word for a 'lemonade' but we always ordered Cokes. Another lovely word my dad would use was for a whiskey, which he called 'A Henry': 'I'll have a pint and a Henry,' he'd say to the barman and the barman knew what he meant.

All the dads would then leave all the younger kids to be minded by the older kids, and off they would go into the bar. The bar was a much darker place, with no women or children. It wasn't that women weren't allowed in there, it was just that the ladies left the misery of the bar to their moany husbands so they could talk shite to each other. Oh, and the pint was 10p cheaper in the bar. I think this was due to lack of light, the bar must have made up the money on not using too many lightbulbs.

So all us kids would play together in the pub, running around the lounge, off our heads on lemo and crisps. The dads would knock back the pints and talk shite. The mammies pushed the trolleys around the supermarket, squeezing bread and smelling fruit. The dads had it in their heads that …

> DAD: Sure, the women love shopping, that's where they're happiest.
> MIKE: You're dead right, Paddy.

Wrong shops, lads! Ladies shopping for *themselves* is what they like, not pushing a heavy weekly shop up and down aisles and around corners in the supermarket, with a small child on board, usually in a trolley that has a mind of its own.

SCiENCE OF A SHOPPiNG TROLLEY

1. Push forward (turns left).
2. Push forward (turns right).

3. **Pull towards (bashes left or right into shelves).**
4. **Try to turn left (goes forward).**
5. **Try to turn right (goes forward).**

Note: trolley is also magnetised, so as soon as it gets to the car park, it manages to steer itself towards every car in the car park.

DAD: Me car!

Eventually, Mam would come into lounge looking for us, trolley parked outside in the pub porch. She'd round us up, then we'd all go in and get Dad. Dad drives us home. Mam doesn't even get a packet of crisps as she needs to get dinner on.

'Baby Eithne is coming home,' squealed my little sister. Thank God, the three days were up. We were sick of burgers and chips, none of us had got to school on time and we ended up wearing random variations of our school uniforms. We had a note, though, which explained: 'THEIR MOTHER IS IN HOSPITAL, FOR GOD'S SAKE, signed Paddy Byrne.'

'I've a surprise for you all to celebrate the coming home of your new sister,' said Dad. 'A video-recorder.'

My God! I had seen one of these before alright, but *Wow!*, now we had one.

'The rules of having this video-recorder is that you can't tell anyone we have one or the house will be broken into and the recorder stolen. It cost a fortune,' Dad said.

And it did, in those days. These massive rectangular boxes cost around 800 quid, I think my dad had got a loan or something to pay for it. To be honest, a burglar wouldn't have had the strength to rob this thing, they weighed a tonne. They were cool, though, ours had a top-loader mechanism and, again, no remote control, just massive buttons to press to make it do what you wanted. And when you put the 'size of a house' video-tape in, the video-recorder made a noise as if it was chewing up the tape and trying to spit it out, but the the noise settled down and it eventually played the film.

So now we had one, and that's why we ended up in the video shop before my dad had to collect my new sister and Mam.

Years after this, we used to have a fella in a van who would pull up outside the house, you'd give him a fiver and he'd hand you a pirate copy of a movie that would be in the cinema. *E.T.*, we got one time.

That was, without a doubt, one of the worst copies of a movie ever. I think it was recorded in a cinema in America on a tape-re-corder, then the sound was played beside a video-recorder that got its power from mouse droppings. You had to watch it with squinty eyeballs, then the sound went in and out like a station on LW (long wave) – why did I bother writing LW if I was going to put long wave in brackets? And now I've wasted even more time typing this sentence.

You were better off going to the cinema, less stress and a pound dearer, but where's the fun in that?

The video shop was full of my mates and their dads all walking around the shop, all pretending to each other that none of us had video-recorders in our houses. No, we were all just having a look around to see what all the fuss was about. I had to keep people talking at one end of the shop as my dad, looking shifty, joined the video shop queue at the other end. The man then gave him a video.

Eric, Rachel and me were sitting on the couch. From outside we heard my dad beeping the *beep beep, we're home with good news* beep, and we all ran outside. My mam got out of the car with this tiny bundle in her hands, with tiny little fingers waving out at us. We all tried to see inside the bundle, while Mam tried to get into the house.

My mam sat on the couch while my new little sister gurgled in her arms. We all had a go at holding little Eithne. Then my dad walked in with a cup of tea for my mam. My mam stared at him in slight horror.

MAM: Is that for me?
DAD: Course it is, cup of tea for my lovely lady, and, and ...

My dad uncovered the video-recorder, which was under a tea towel.

DAD: ... a video-recorder, so you can watch a movie whenever you want.
MAM: Jesus, how much was that thing?
DAD: Ah not to worry, sure you can't put a towbar on a hearse.

Dad then leaned down, put the video in and it made its alarming churning noises.

DAD: (*to me*) The curtains, Jason, get the curtains.

I closed the curtains, and we all sat and started to watch our first ever VHS video-recorder movie.

The movie started. It was about these college boys getting up to no good, first came the drinking of the cans at the back of the school, then, then ... the sneaking into the showers to see naked ladies. Oh my god! The movie just got worse and worse, boobs, men's bits, ladies' bits everywhere, we were all red-faced watching it.

RACHEL: (*pointing at the screen*) Willies!

My dad and mam didn't move, it was like they were in shock, like if they moved, they might bring more attention to what was happening on the screen. The tape then started to make a really weird noise, the picture left the screen, thank God. The machine had chewed up the tape as if we were all willing it to. Then, blank screen.

Silence swamped the room, the only thing we could hear was my new sister, gurgling.

MAM: Tea anyone, tea?

Everyone in the room said yes, at the same time, then we all ran to different parts of the house to try and understand what had happened – except for my sister Eithne, she had no idea what had happened.

Apparently, my dad had hired *Porky's*, which was basically a soft porn movie. When my dad was all shifty in the video shop earlier and he'd asked the owner, 'Have you got anything good? I don't want the rest of them to know,' the owner thought he meant anything racy because my dad looked so shifty.

So my dad greets my new baby sister into our house with *Porky's*. 'Welcome home, sis.'

CHAPTER 4
DEATH-
DEFYING!

FLASH! BANG! 'It's okay, girls, I've got you,' I said.

My two younger sisters and I, all in a bunk-bed in the box room. One of the nastiest storms Ireland had ever seen howled outside the window, and given that we were all huddled into a bed in the box room with its freezing walls, we may as well have been outside in the thick of it.

Mam and Dad were up in the pub, I was babysitting, and big brother Eric was, well, wherever he went at night, no one knew. It was quite common to babysit at a young age in the '80s. If anything went wrong, you just called into one of your pretend auntie's or uncle's houses to ask for help.

FLASH! BANG! went the thunder and lightning again. The girls were crying, but I was telling them it was alright, not to worry, that it was just thunder and lightning, but every time the thunder banged, my eye turned into my nose with fright. I had never heard thunder like this before.

HUGE FLASH OF LIGHT AND THEN … *BANG!*

ME: One, two, three, four, five, six, sev …

FLASH! BANG!

I told the girls that the storm was moving, now it was nearly seven miles away. When you see the flash, start counting, every second you count before you hear thunder again is a mile away. That was our homespun science on the matter anyway.

There was silence for a bit, then the window lit up as if the sun had exploded, followed by the loudest noise in the history of noises.

BAAANNNG!

All the lights went out in the house, street, everywhere. It was pitch-black, and my eye was frightened, it was flying around in my head. The girls were really scared now. 'It's just a blackout,' I said, 'the storm has knocked out all the electricity.' We waited in the bed for a while, not sure how long, then I heard the doorbell.

'It must be Mam and Dad. You stay here.' I walked down through the dark house. I say this like it was a mansion, but the walk from the bedroom to the landing and down the spiral staircase, which was tricky enough to tackle in the daylight, took forever in total darkness.

As I came down the stairs, there was banging at the front door and the doorbell was going as well. This was not my mam and dad. All I could see was the silhouette of a huge head, almost like an alien's head, through the glass door. In fact, a bit like Michael J. Fox's uniform as he steps out of the DeLorean time-machine car in *Back to the Future*, when he crashes into a barn and the farmer thinks he's an alien and … No? No? Nothing? ... Ah, Google it.

More banging on the glass door, the lightning lighting up the figure outside from behind. It was like a horror film.

MONSTER: Hello, hello, anyone in there?
ME: Yes.
MONSTER: Open the door.
ME: No.
MONSTER: Open the door, it's the fire brigade.

I opened the door, and the monster came into focus. He *was* a fireman, his helmet was the thing that had scared me. He stepped inside and more firemen rushed past him.

'Where's the rest of your family?' 'Upstairs,' I said. The firemen ran up the stairs, while another took me out into the driveway.

There were four fire engines outside, all with flashing lights. Every neighbour was in our driveway, along with most of my mates. I was wrapped in a blanket and held by our neighbour Joan. Seconds later, my sisters were taken out, then my brother arrived into the driveway.

ERIC: What have you done now, yeh spa yeh?
ME: Nothing.
ERIC: You're dead when Mam and Dad get back.

Then, in the middle of it all, my parents came down in their blue Ford Cortina from the pub. The whole road watched as they drove up to the house. My dad jumped out in his usual calm manner.

DAD: Holy shit, who the???, what's happening???, what are all these people doing in me garden, the fire brigade!!!!!!!!!!?

He continued to run in and out of the house and around in circles in the front garden in a complete panic. He had no idea what was happening as the house wasn't even on fire, he just couldn't work it out.

HOW MY DAD DEALS WiTH A PANiC-TYPE SiTUATiON

1. Panic.

2. Panic.

3. Panic.

4. Panic.

5. Panic

My mother held us all in our blankets as the neighbours looked down their noses at her. Bad Mammy, bad Mammy, she'd dropped the ball. She was always there in case of a crisis, then this happens. Poor Mammy.

The next day I was in the garden, along with the rest of the road. Our house was famous and the newspaper was here to take a photo of us all, well, all except for my dad because he was up in the pub calming down after the ordeal that he never went through. The lightning had hit our chimney, which exploded into a million pieces, then all the bricks rolled down the back of the house, smashed all the slates, fell into the boiler house and smashed that as well. The lightning had also raced down any electrical cables it could find and blew up appliances along the way.

> DAD: I told yous to plug things out at night, now look what's happened.

Yes, Dad, of course, you're right this time, but what's the odds of a house being hit by lightning, and right on top of a chimney? I think we were the only house in Dublin it ever happened to.

> MAM: That bloody man wished that lightning here, now he's quietly delighted it blew up the chimney. We'll be plugging out our knickers at night now because of him.

My best mate, Karl, who lived across the road, was looking out watching the storm that night, with his finger on the blind, and he is the only person who saw it all happen. Apparently, the lightning hit our chimney and when it did, it gave Karl a shock in his finger, across and up the road, at least ten houses away.

Karl then roared to my auntie Betty/his mother that 'Jason's house has just been blown up', but auntie Betty was in the pub with Uncle Paddy/his dad, where they were having a drink with Uncle Paddy Byrne and Auntie Eithne Byrne. So my best friend, still to this day he is, rang the fire brigade himself, 14 years of age, ringing the fire brigade to help his mate.

I was so grateful to him, but as always my best mate's answer was, 'Shut up you, I only did it to see all the fire brigade come, who gives a shite about you,' followed by a headlock, a wrestle to the ground, grass shoved in my mouth. Sign of best mates.

We were all in the local paper. I think they got nearly the whole road into that photo, well, all the mammies and the kids anyway, the men were all away, *ahem*, working, oh and worrying.

I was very close to my best friend, Karl. His mam and dad were my godmother and godfather. Karl and his sister, Orla, ended up being my sister's godmother and godfather. It was like the gypsies on our road, except we didn't live in caravans.

Karl was way braver than me, he wasn't even afraid of the old man who whistled. We called him The Whistler, he was this really old man in our area who would take out a comb and pretend to play it by whistling the tune. I was so afraid of him. He was really old and bent, but he once trapped me against a wall when I was walking home from the shops, shoved his face near to mine, then whistled a whole song at me, after which I ran home, screaming and crying. The old man was harmless, but I had him made out to be a horror character. So I ran whenever I saw him, leaving Karl to deal with The Whistler on his own, which normally meant Karl walking around him. Very brave, Karl.

We did everything together, me and Karl, we got into a lot of trouble together. But with Karl's bravery came accidents.

One year in the '80s, it became very fashionable to wear roller-skates, or boot skates as they were known. We would head up to the school at the weekend and skate around on the tarmac in the yard.

There was a very steep hill at the back of the school, and Karl decided to roll down it on his skates. I didn't. Karl hit a tiny stone, went straight to ground, and smacked his front teeth off the hill. I went to help him and he said not to tell his mam what had happened, that she'd kill him, so instead we'd tell her that the wheel broke on the skate and that made Karl fall.

When I got into my house, my mother confronted me. 'I've just been off the phone to Betty, she said Karl's after falling and he broke his two good front teeth, is that true?' My mother watched my eye closely; it started to turn in. 'Don't you lie to me, Jason Byrne, your eye is turning in, it always turns in when you lie.' I couldn't help it, I was the worst liar in the world because of that bloody eye.

It came flooding out of me. Through tears I said to her, 'Karl was skating on the hill where we're not supposed to and he busted his teeth.'

Some best friend I was, but I couldn't help it.

★ ★ ★

Another time, Karl was climbing a tree, and while I would go only halfway, he always went to the top. Of course, he fell out of the tree and smacked his chin off the ground. I helped him up again, and again he said, 'Don't tell my mam I was climbing trees, she'll kill me.'

Cut to: my house, my mother standing over me, phone just put down to Betty, and some major eye watching going on. Through tears I said to her, 'Karl was climbing a tree that he wasn't supposed to and he fell out and smacked his chin!'

What a little rat. Why was I wired like this? I was the worst mate ever.

Then came the big one, the move of the year. Karl and me were walking down along Dundrum Road, when a girl we knew and her sister came cycling by and got off their bikes to say hello. Karl, messing, pretended to steal one of the girl's bikes. As he wasn't used to her bike, he was wobbly on it, so he wobbled out onto the road, then a car hit him, sending him flying.

And what did his best mate do? RAN AWAY. I ran all the way home, sobbing wildly. I thought Karl was dead. I was going to go to prison for robbing a bike with my mate and then killing him. I got into the house and ran upstairs, there was no one home. Then, after about an hour of me hiding under the covers – big eejit that I was –I heard my mother come in the front door. Karl was definitely dead by now. This was it, I was going to jail for sure.

'JASON! JASON! Karl has been knocked down and is in hospital. JASON?!' My mother found me in the bedroom, she didn't even have to ask. Through tears I said, 'Karl robbed a girl's bike and cycled out onto the road, I think he's dead. Am I going to jail?'

Turned out Karl didn't die. The man who knocked him down drove him home and delivered him to his sister, Orla, at the door. This was all happening as I ran home through the back fields. The man didn't even bring Karl to a hospital, just dropped him off at his house and then drove away. Karl's mam drove him to the hospital, and we never found out who the man was. It was a hit-and-collect-and-deliver-and-run, for the first time in history.

We ended up hanging out in Karl's back garden for weeks because he had broken his leg, in full plaster. Plus, thanks to me, he was grounded for weeks too, not allowed even out the front garden. I was also grounded, but mainly to Karl's back garden.

TOP KARL ACCIDENTS

1. **Knocked down.**
2. **Fell out of tree.**
3. **Roller-skated on Danger Hill.**
4. **Slid on cardboard downhill and into metal fence.**
5. **Set eyebrows and hair on fire while lighting a bush on fire.**

The shops, same year: my go for an accident

I loved going to the shops for my mam. It was a short walk up the road to the shops. It was a small shop, where we got sweets, milk, bread. You would never do your main shop in there, that was saved for Superquinn on a Saturday, so we could go to the pub. No, no, this was the small shop.

This day, I had to get a pint of milk for Mam. The milkman hadn't left milk that morning. So I got the milk, then I was walking home. I was in a world of my own and, as we've discussed earlier, my special eye had a habit of wandering, so sometimes I wouldn't see very well.

I crossed the road, and I still remember to this day where it happened. Something hit me in the hip, I flew up in the air, landed on something, slid, then landed on my feet, still holding the milk, then I walked on.

I heard footsteps running up behind me. It was one of the neighbours, and she was rubbing my head and checking my legs and arms.

> NEIGHBOUR: Jesus Christ, son, are you alright?
> ME: Alright? Why?
> NEIGHBOUR: You've just been knocked down, son.
> ME: What?

Apparently I had crossed the road, thought I'd looked both ways, but because of my eye, both ways could have been me looking on one side, if you know what I mean. I walked out in front of a car, it hit me in the hip, I spun up in the air, hit the bonnet, and rolled off onto my feet. The shock of it must have helped me to keep walking.

Then a man I didn't know ran up to me.

MAN: Is he alright, I didn't even see him, are you alright, son?

I was so confused that my answer was:

ME: I'm not allowed talk to strangers.

The neighbour brought me into her driveway and gave me water. I seemed fine, so the driver left. I gathered up my milk and walked home. But my God, if that happened now, you would not let a kid walk on home on their own, but the '80s was tough and we were tough kids, had to be.

I walked into the house, terrified to tell my mother, but I was as white as a ghost.

MAM: What happened? Are you alright?
ME: Yes.

Oh my God I did it, I lied and got away with it.

MAM: Really?

Damn, the 'Really?' trap.

ME: I was knocked down by a car because I was or wasn't, I'm not sure, looking where I was crossing. I didn't spill the milk and I think I'm alright now.

MAM: Paddy!

I'm not sure how we survived life as kids back then, because we were always trying to kill ourselves.

Here are a few of the things we tried to do but managed to survive.

The valley of death

One year in the '80s up to 4 ft of snow fell. Schools were closed, and it was the best winter ever. We loved when it snowed – even if there was only 1 in. of snow the school closed as they couldn't get the heating on due to frozen pipes. So we built snow forts in the field and had full-on snowball fights. On that occasion we were proper snowed in. I remember going down to the dairy on a small sheet of plastic, being dragged along by my brother, because the milkman wasn't able to get his electric milk cart through the snow. It felt like war-torn Russia, but this was the southside of Dublin and we were walking to get milk as we would die without milk, never mind food. Milk was the number one item needed to survive in the '80s

THINGS THAT MILK WENT INTO OR ON

1. Tea.
2. Coffee (if you were just home from a foreign country or you were foreign).

3. **All cereals.**
4. **Glass (as in, glass of).**
5. **Dog's eyes, when sore.**

So me and Eric were despatched to the dairy, got the milk, home again, milk all safe in the fridge, then knock at the door, it was Karl, Brian Roche and Ken Newman.

> KARL: Everyone is heading to the golf course for a massive slide-down.

1980S' FRIENDS

1. Karl
2. Ken
3. Brian
4. Tally

I don't have enough room for the other 120,000 kids on the road.

I grabbed my coat, ran out, pretending to be excited, because of course I was crapping myself. The massive slide only happened when it snowed, and it didn't snow that often. I had heard from my bigger brother about the massive snow slide and it sounded awful.

> ME: Great, can't wait, boys!

I could have pooed right there and then.

★ ★ ★

We arrived up at the golf course, and there was already a couple of kids up there.

KARL: There's the rest of the lads. Lads!

We went over, there was about twenty lads from the road there, all different ages and sizes, standing at the top of a very steep and long hill. It was at the par 5 hole on the golf course and when you played it, you basically shot down into a valley. That was where you went on the plastic sheet.

I say *you*, I really mean *us*. Ordinary children would have had a small sledge each, or a bit of cardboard to slide down on, but oh no, not us! We were in the business of killing ourselves, and you had no choice but to do this because there was no other way down than to slide.

One of the lads took out a massive, and I mean *massive*, sheet of plastic. We all helped him roll it out, and when flattened out it made a kind of square about the size of a small garden.

KARL: Right, listen up everyone. The only way this works is that we stay off the sheet, rest it here on the edge of the hill, then we all run at the same time, jump into the middle and off we go.

I was crapping it, I wanted to go home, my heart was beating like mad in my chest, but this time I had no choice. I had to run with the lads.

KARL: Three, two, one ... leg it!

We all ran at the sheet and, like a suburban Olympics team, we all leapt in the air at the same time, landed on the plastic at the same time, fell on our arses at the same time.

LAUNCH!

The sheet pushed over the edge as we landed on it, it started to move and *Holy Jesus!* it picked up some unbelievable speed. We were all moving around on the sheet, cry-laughing with fear, we had no idea this thing was going to get up to this speed. We would have passed out a toboggan.

We were all battling to get to the back of the sheet because no one wanted to be at the front when it got to the maddest bit at the end of the hill. I was climbing on top of Ken Newman, Brian Roche was on top of me. Karl, of course, was trying to stand up.

Karl: (screaming and pointing) THE JUMP!

We hit the end of the hill in what felt like two seconds. There was a lip at the end of the hill, like a ramp. We hit the lip of the ramp. Every single one of those twenty children went high up in the air, the sheet kept going without us, then we all landed in a huge snow-drift. No one dead, but my God, I think I laughed five years of laughter in that second we landed.

We then went home ...
we did in our arses, we did it all day long, till
some owner spotted us wrecking his golf course.

> ARSEHOLE: Get off the course, you're wrecking
> it, you idiots.
> KARL: How are we wrecking it? It's covered in snow.

Kids are experts in smart answers. As adults we can't do it, but
for some reason as kids we can do this for days. Then how do the
adults reward us for our smart answers?

> ARSEHOLE: Don't be smart, son.

We all left, trying not to be smart.

I got to bed that night, covered in bruises, every time I turned
in the bed I felt a bruise, but I just giggled myself to sleep. I was
so proud that I had joined in a near-death experience, around
forty-three times.

The tunnel

This was another mad idea that somehow didn't end in death for all concerned. All the lads on the road had climbed a tree in the tunnel in order to build a swing.

Our housing estate not only had a road with a top and a curvy bottom, lined with thousands of semi-detached houses, we also had a field beside us, and alongside the field there was what we called The Tunnel. This was a dried out riverbed and we used it for kissing, tasting beer, swings, catching rats, lighting fires, hide-and-seek; what you did there depended on your age. At twelve, I was still in the hide-and-seek age.

Quite often I'd go hide, only to find one of the big brothers from the road snogging his girlfriend in the hidey-hole – as in, that boy was in the place where I wanted to hide, not that he was in snogging her hidey-hole. I really didn't mean to type this, but it just made me laugh out loud, so from now on I will call that bit 'the hidey-hole', and my wife will be delighted.

TOP STUFF NEEDED TO MAKE A GOOD SWING IN THE '80S

1. A tree with good branches.
2. Rope, stolen from someone's dad's car boot.
3. A good thick stick for the seat.
4. A nice launch-pad area, normally high in another tree.
5. Dangerous area to swing over.

Karl got on it first, of course. He climbed up into the tree, then we handed the stick up to him. The idea was you put the stick between your legs, but only *after* you had jumped. So you would take your body weight on the rope, then using your legs you would manoeuvre the stick so you could sit down on it, and you had roughly two seconds to get this right or you would be hanging on for dear life, by just your hands, as you swung over the 'death bush' (not in a hidey-hole sense, I mean shrubbery).

It's hard to explain how dangerous this was, but you were at least 15 ft in the air at the start point, then rising as you swung over the empty riverbed, which meant that at the midway point you would be at least 30 ft off the ground. The laws of physics then brought you to even higher heights, so you were at least 38 ft above the death bush, and under no circumstances could you fall in there.

People swung on that swing all day, all week, for months, before I even thought of going near it. I was terrified of what I saw, but I had to get up there eventually. I'd done the snow slide, so I had to do this. I was the only kid among us not to have done it yet, and things were getting bad for me in the gang. I was in goal for all the football matches at this stage.

So I left my house on this one Saturday and headed to the tunnel. The lads were already over there on the swing. The girls watched on: they would never go on the swing as they had sense. 'You're bleedin' dopes for getting on that swing, dopes.'

I announced to the lads that I wanted to have a go. 'Deadly, man. Fair play to yeh, you'll love it, Jay,' they all said.

I was so nervous climbing into that tree. They say when you're about to do something dangerous, like sky-dive, bungee-jump, rock-climb, surf, you need to be relaxed or you could cause yourself an injury with the nerves.

Well. I was the most nervous little boy you have ever seen. I hugged that tree as I climbed up its massive trunk. My face rubbed along it as the ground moved further away, my huge glasses not helping at all as they dug into my nose. I can still smell that tree to this day.

I reached the launch area. Karl, my best mate, who I ratted out constantly, had climbed up with me. 'Throw up the rope, Brian.' The rope was swung up to Karl, and he held it for me and stood on that branch with no fear. 'Here you go, Jay, you'll be alright, I have yeh. Just swing out, legs around the stick, sit down gently. It's deadly fun, man.' My hands were shaking as I took the rope, the rest of the lads looked like little men at the bottom of the tree. The girls just shook their heads as if they knew what was going to happen.

I held the rope, stood on the branch for longer than I can remember, with all the lads shouting at me to jump, and Karl telling them to 'Shut up down there.' Then all I remember was jumping out, my heart pumping. I managed to get my legs around the stick, I sat down and YESSSSSSSSS!

I was swinging! It was the best feeling I have ever had in my life. I swung backwards and forwards. The lads all cheered. Karl whistled as he held onto nothing while standing on a branch. This was it, I was one of the lads. I was the man. I was swinging, boys, swinging!

SNAP!

Before I knew it, I couldn't feel the weight of the rope holding onto the tree. The thick, dangerous death bush got bigger as I hurtled towards it.

Within seconds, I was in the thick bushes. The swing rope had snapped. Months of lads swinging on it and nothing happened, then I get on it for the first time and it snaps.

'Someone get his maaa!' I heard someone shout. If you hurt yourself it was normally, 'Someone get his maaa!', except in Karl's case, because he didn't want his ma to know.

I was upside-down, with rope coiled all over me, but the lads couldn't get to me because I was lying in the middle of the death bush, head first, legs flailing. If it was a diving competition, I would have got a clear 10. 'Help me!' 'Someone is getting your ma, Jay.' I was upside-down in that bush for about half an hour. Then I saw a ladder appear over my head, then my dad's head. All he could see was a red-headed child, with massive, now broken, glasses and a special eye that by now had a life of its own.

DAD: You bleedin' gobshite, yeh.

My dad reached into the bush and with his massive bull hands – my dad really did have the biggest hands ever – picked me up by my legs. I hung upside-down in one of his arms, looking like a chicken about to be beheaded. He then threw me over both of his shoulders and we climbed down the ladder. The lads all cheered. I walked away with no injuries.

We got home just as my mother got in from shopping.

MAM: All alright?
DAD: Oh yeah.
MAM: Nothing strange?
DAD: No, no.

My dad winked at me. He never ratted us out to Mam, he was a deadly dad like that. But I wasn't very popular on the road for a while as now making swings was banned. I'm not sure how the parents found out I fell off that swing. The lads said nothing, and my dad said nothing.

Bath night.

MAM: Why have you a cut on your back there?
ME: (*through tears*) Because I was on a swing that I wasn't supposed to be on, it snapped, I fell into the bush and dad had to save me with a ladder. Sorry.
MAM: *Paddy!*

CHAPTER 5
BOOO.
HOLiDAYS...

I looked out along the tips of the blades of grass. I used to imagine what it would be like to be an ant walking through the huge blades of grass. I'd lie on my side in the field beside our house, with one good eye in line with the tips of the grass, then I'd pretend I was an ant looking out along this amazing assault course that was the blades of grass.

I was just lying around, hanging out, it was the summer now, Communion had been made, and Sister Francis Xavier was a distant memory.

We got a good deal with the summer holidays in Ireland. I have tried to explain the school summer holidays many times to my foreign friends, so here it is again for those of you who are not from Ireland.

Irish school holidays

If you are in primary school, you get July and August off school as your summer break. I know, two whole months. If you are a first, second or fourth year student in secondary school, you get June, July and August off. What? I know. There are exams for third years and sixth years in June, so if you aren't sitting those exams, you get that extra month off. Boom.

PS. The final school exam, which you sit in sixth year, is the Leaving Certificate. It's called 'The Leaving' because after you finish it, you leave school foreverrrrrr.

'Are you playing or not?' A huge game of football was about to start in the field.

We were a very sporty lot on my road, and the football games were legendary. I was eight when I started playing in these games; the top age could run to 13 or 14. The skills needed were massive. We all loved being in that field, there could be up to 150 kids there at any time playing games.

The norm was that the game was up to a score of 100, or when we lost daylight. We had loads of different types of football games. World Cup, for example, where you'd pick a country to be and if you scored, you stood to the side. The last player to score was out. This was played until it was down to two players. A favourite of mine was Bum And In, which was where you could only volley the ball off your arse to score. We never stopped laughing at this.

We'd play after school, maybe get to a score of about 48-52, then all our mothers appeared at the gates, with their cardigans around their shoulders. They'd stand at the pillar of the drive and roar for their child, like prison guards at lock-up time. We'd stop playing, head to the house and just as we did this, the dads would start to roll around the bend at the curve of the road in their cars, coming home from work. They'd have to slow down as the whole road was full of kids, all walking back to their houses, and we often used the road as a path.

Then into the house, and out would come the Dettol and the basin for Dad's feet, I'd eat me dinner like a pigeon, have a large

bowl of jelly and ice cream, then back outside to finish the game until it got dark.

We loved being out there until around 10.00pm. The game would end, then we'd sit in a circle talking about all sorts of stuff.

Now, the only bad thing about being off for the summer holiday was the fact that you had to go on holidays with your parents. The last thing you wanted to do as a child was to be dragged away from your mates, who were having the *craic* in the field without any parents watching.

My mam and dad liked to go to Spain ... without us. They said it was too hot and we wouldn't like it, we'd boil to death, so they thought we were better off left at home with a mad auntie or random neighbour.

So the only holidays we went on as children were cold ones. The two favourite cold places were Mosney Holiday Camp, in County Meath, and the Isle of Man.

Mosney was near a town called Drogheda. It was the Butlin's of Ireland, basically, but with extra misery. All I remember as entertainment was 12 ft x 6 ft snooker tables with faded balls. The sunlight had done that to the balls. Or you could go to a really stinking pond where you tried to row a boat around an island while rougher kids treated it as bumpers and came at you with maniacal grins wide across their faces.

But my favourite was the dining room. The dining room?, I hear you say. Yes, the dining room. The dining room had a window that looked into the bottom of the indoor swimming pool, so naturally, it being Ireland, as you ate your food all you could see was young fellas flashing their willys and arses at you. I howled with laughter as my mam made us all change seats so we'd have our back to the window.

I mean, who was the bright spark who decided to put a window there? It can't have been an Irishman. If an Irishman had suggested putting that window there in the company of other Irishmen, the other Irishmen would have said, 'You can't put a window in the dining room, kids will be flashing their mickeys at the diners.' No. It had to have been a German or a Swede who came up with it. In those countries they'd have a bit of respect for the diners and swim normally at the bottom, but oh no, Irish people are born messers. So when the pool first opened, I'm sure there were a bunch of Irish people at the edge of the pool looking down into it saying:

'You know there's a window down there facing into the dining room.'

'Is there?'

'Yeah, let's jump down and flash our mickeys at the diners.'

And so the flashing pool window was born. It was a skill to dive down, get your pants down and flash, all in one breath.

I remember seeing a bloke jump in, get his boxers down, spin around and stick his arse onto the window like one of those sucker fish that cleans your fish tank. Now he had technique. I looked around at the diners and was surprised not to see them holding up score cards.

The other top bit of entertainment in Mosney was the slot-machine area. One day me and Eric popped in there, and Eric being the cool dude he was, he had gathered up a few mates around the camp for a bit of mischief. He was now going to show me the best way to get money from the pushing slots. I don't know what the machine is actually called, but it's the one where you put your money in the top, your coin slides down a shaft, lands and hopefully pushes money down onto another level, which in turn will push teetering-on-the-edge money out into the collection cup.

The things was, my brother needed a few of us to do this, but the slot-machine manager was a right miserable shit, who kept saying we weren't allowed in there without our parents.

But this was perfect for Eric's plan. The plan was this: when the manager went down the other end of the slots area, away from the pushing slot-machine, we would run at the machine, as quick and as fast as possible, hit it full force, the money would fall out into the cups, then we'd grab the money and run.

We waited and watched. The manager walked to the other end of the slots area.

'RUN!'

We all legged it in the door, like a pack of wild horses. BANG! We nearly sent the slot-machine over on its side, but it came up off the ground, leaned back, then came towards us and landed again with a THUD!

Money started to fall into the cups, but as this happened, the alarm on the machine squealed for attention.

ERIC: Quick, grab the coins.

We grabbed as many coins as we could, then we all ran out towards the boat lake. This bit was genius: we hopped in a boat and hid the money out on the island in the middle of the pond. It felt like we were pirates! We stashed the money under a tree on the island, saying we'd come back and get it each day, bit by bit so as not to arouse suspicion.

We then got back into the little boat and rowed back to dry land. No one was going to catch us now. We had committed the perfect crime.

YEAH, *IN FAIRYLAND*!

In reality, we were caught immediately. The manager knew us from trying to get into the slots, people had seen us robbing the money, and in Mosney on a given busy holiday weekend, there were probably about twenty-eight families staying, so no need for Inspector Morse on this one.

A man called to the door of our chalet, asking questions. My mother and father swore blind that their children would *never* rob.

MAM: I didn't raise my children to rob.

TOP THiNGS YOUR MOTHER DiDN'T RAiSE YOU FOR

1. To rob money.
2. To be like that.
3. To give back cheek.
4. To talk with your mouth full.
5. To not clean your face, hands, etc.
6. To be too near the telly.
7. To pick your nose.
8. To be at yourself.
9. To leave your shoes there.
10. To rub whatever that is in the couch.

Man sent away, door slammed shut, then they battered us with shoes, slippers and handbags, as they knew well we had taken those coins.

Our other nightmare holiday destination was the Isle of Man. Now that was a different trip from Mosney, which was really only my mam and dad, me and my brother and sisters all wedged into a tiny chalet, surviving each other for a weekend.

No, we would head to the Isle of Man with all my real aunties and uncles, grandparents and cousins.

First, we would board what was known as the Isle of Man Bucket, well at least that's what my dad called it. It docked on the northside of the quays down at Dublin Docklands.

We'd all board, normally in rough weather; I actually do not remember ever getting on that boat in calm seas. The adults spent the whole crossing in the bar. My mam has a picture in her photo album at home that shows my granddad, my dad and uncles, all with their feet hooked under the bar that ran along the bottom of the bar counter, so they wouldn't fall over as the boat swayed front left to right, or port to stern, or from starboard to star track.

While the adults drank, the kids were allowed play around on the ship. I'll just repeat that: kids of all ages, unaccompanied, running around on a very rocky ship in rough seas, where the chances of falling in were very high.

It was dangerous out on deck as the spray came up over the side. Here's the best way to get the image of it in your head: go watch an episode of *Deadliest Catch*, one where they're in the high seas and trying to trap crab with waves washing over them. Well, that was the Isle of Man Bucket, except we had it way worse. It was slippy and with, this is no lie (hold in your dinner), layers of vomit all over the deck from people being sea sick. Grosssssssssss!

Meanwhile, we went into the bar to visit our parents so we could get some Coke and crisps off them for the forty-ninth time.

The trick to this was to ask your mam and dad when they were sitting beside your auntie and uncle. Your mam and dad would say, 'No, you've had enough', then your auntie and uncle would step in and say, 'Ah let the little fella have a Coke and a crisp', then your auntie and uncle would buy it, just seconds after they had said no to their own children, and just seconds after your mam and dad had bought your cousins another Coke and a crisp: 'Ah let the little mites have a Coke and crisps, it's the holidays, for God's sake.' Simple.

TOP iTEMS YOUR PARENTS SAiD THAT YOU OR THEY HAD HAD ENOUGH OF

1. Coke
2. Crisps
3. Lip
4. Cheek
5. Enough is enough

We arrived at the Isle of Man, but it took a while to get off the boat as the high seas would push the walkway about a foot up off the dock. As the walkway slammed back to the ground the sailors would shout, 'Go, go, go', and one family at a time, cases and all, would leg it before the waves sent the ramp into the air again.

Finally, we all got off the boat.

SHIP'S LOG FOR THE BYRNE FAMILY: Paddy, Eithne, Eric, Jason, Rachel, Eithne, Cora, Michael, Neville, Simon, Cliona, Winnie, Harry, Glen, Laura, Linda, Pauline, John, Stephen, Helen, Colin, Hilary, Marie, Nana, Granddad.

Hotel lobby was packed. Now these weren't really hotels along the front of the Isle of Man, but more B&Bs with little bars, a bit like you'd see in Del Boy's front room in *Only Fools and Horses*. The front of the Isle of Man was layered with them: from a distance, a nice English seaside town; up close, shacks with doorbells.

The owners hated children, it was like being in an episode of *Fawlty Towers*. The guy we used to go to was tall and skinny and had a moustache – I think he was actually modelling himself on Basil Fawlty.

We'd all get to our rooms. The kids would share beds as it was cheaper than renting extra rooms, while the parents took the nice cosy beds that looked out onto the seafront. Even if it was grey, wet and miserable.

Then the parents, Nana and Granddad would head down to the bar to get a Del Boy pint, and all the kids would make it their mission to annoy the owner.

TOP THINGS THAT ANNOYED THE OWNER

1.   All of us sliding down the stairs on our bums.
2.   Making him reach for sweets on top shelf in the shop.
3.   Playing chasing in the dining room between tables.
4.   Climbing all over his good porch.
5.   Speaking too fast in an Irish accent when he asked you something.

After pints and annoying the owner, it was down to the beach. The beach that had no sand, just rocks. Normally just the kids and the aunties went onto the beach, but the dads went on for a very short time, just long enough to help the mams set up the windbreakers.

Combovers blew wildly in the breeze as the dads tried to hammer the windbreakers into the ground, but it was hard to find ground because there wasn't any, so your dad spent ages trying to hammer windbreakers and those giant umbrellas into rocks and stones.

Then it was off to the pub for the dads, and we were left on the freezing cold beach in our swimming togs, covered by angry clouds and breeze.

I remember being so cold, trying to play at the edge of the water with my cousins, as my mam and my mad aunties shouted at us to 'Get in, get in, you're on your holidays, for God's sake.' We got in.

The minute the water hit your testicles and willy, they all tried to retreat up inside you for cover, my God it was like cruel punishment. You tried to stay in for longer than a minute, but it was impossible, then you couldn't get out because your feet kept slipping on the rocky bottom, nothing to grip onto, until you were eventually washed to shore along with your cousins, like little lost pebbles. But that wasn't enough, because then your mam threw you a ball.

MAM: Play football with your cousins.
ME: But there's no sand.

MAM: Ah don't be moaning, it's the holidays, for God's sake.

ME: But me feet are cut to bits.

MAM: How could they be? Sure sand is tiny stones, this is just big unfinished sand.

When were we allowed to get off this beach? Oh yeah, when the dads returned because they were hungry for their dinner. Then it was even worse, trying to pack everything back into the bags. The windbreakers and giant umbrellas never fit back into the plastic bags they came in, it was like they'd grown while they stood in the sand, well, rocks.

So it always felt like we were all carrying twice as much stuff back to the hotel, across the road, still wearing our wet togs, our mothers telling us they'd change us in the hotel.

The hotel owner then freaked out at all of us as we brought half the beach, well, stones and sea, in with us. My dad used to calm him down with a fiver into the hand; that man was so mean, he'd do anything for money.

We'd all eat dinner together then, all the kids at one table like an Italian wedding, the parents at another, laughing and smoking themselves to death. And in the middle of it all, Basil Fawlty running around, hating every minute of his job and wishing he worked in the Dorchester.

The highlight of the trip was Summerland. But before we went there, the parents would have a pint in the Del Boy Bar. My dad loved ordering the Guinness in the bar and then, as he lifted it up to the light, saying, 'Piss, utter piss this stuff is, bleedin' Brits haven't a clue how to pour a pint.' He drank it anyway.

Summerland

'Ta-daaaaaaa,' the magician ended. He told jokes as he pulled live rabbits out of his trousers. The MC came back on and announced it was time for the raffle, as the magician walked off to four claps that echoed around the room.

The atmosphere heightened as people reached for their beige, salmon, yellow and blue tickets. Summerland had never seen such excitement.

Summerland was an old hall where the dregs of entertainment did shows for half-pissed Irish paddies while their kids played chasing. The raffle, however, was a thing talked about even on the streets in Ireland.

'Oh you have to go to the Isle of Man, there's a massive raffle, stuff from floor to ceiling.'

STUFF YOU COULD WIN IN THE SUMMERLAND RAFFLE

1. **Ceramic cheetahs.**
2. **Ceramic clowns.**
3. **Ceramic elephants.**

4. **Huge teddy bears.**
5. **Remote-control cars (with wire attached to remote).**
6. **Action Men.**
7. **Dolls.**
8. **Big spoons with *Isle of Man* written on them.**
9. **Everything with *Isle of Man* written on it.**
10. **Boxes of wine.**

This is one of the most traumatic events in my young life. We were all sitting at the table, the band played a little intro music, then the raffle began. The Byrnes had tickets laid out all over the table because we had to win. We ran up and down the table, checking the tickets as the numbers were called out, but the prizes were leaving the stage as fast as the Irish leaving Ireland after the Famine. We got more and more worried.

Then the moment came. 'A salmon-coloured ticket, number 345, that's salmon-coloured 345.' The family scanned the table, we had loads of salmon tickets. My dad looked at a sheet he had in his hand, it ended at 344, which meant there was a ticket missing from the bottom. My dad looked at me, then my mam looked at me, my eye immediately turned in.

'Jason!' said my mam. I held out my hand and opened it to show the ticket I'd robbed off the table, the ticket that was being called out. My dad looked at the ticket in my hand, then he screamed ...

DAD: BINGO!
MAM: It's not Bingo, yeh big gobshite.

DAD: Who gives a bollix, he won, our Jason has the winning ticket, here, here, BINGO, BINGO, BINGO!

My family lost the plot, cheering and jumping up and down. They pushed me towards the stage. I walked up these massive steps, light shone in my eyes as the MC in his pale blue suit, breath smelling of whiskey and hair tight with hairspray – if he was any taller, the lights would have set him on fire – guided me towards the prizes.

It was an Aladdin's Den.

MC: And what prize would you like, little boy?

He said this as his cheesy grin spread across his face, like The Joker from *Batman*.

I headed towards the massive section of Action Men. Who to choose? Action Eagle Eyes? Action Soldier? Action Captain? Action Sailor? Action Mechanic? So many to choose from …

But as I walked towards the Action Men, I started to hear shouting coming from my family's table. My dad, mam, aunties, uncles, Nana and Granddad were all standing, shouting at me, and gesturing madly to another part of the stage.

'The wine, get the wine, son, pick the wine' … they kept pointing to the box of wine. The MC watched in horror as I walked away from the Action Men and towards the wine, then back towards the Action Men.

FAMILY: No! The wine, get the wine!

I pointed to the box of wine in confusion.

FAMILY: Yes, yes, the wine!

I bent into the MC's microphone.

ME: (*eight years of age into the mic*) The wine, please.

The MC was stunned, but he blurted out the words anyway.

MC: The little boy ... chooses ... the wine ...

The room was in silence; the only table cheering was my family's. The band slapped together a *well done you got your prize* tune even though they, too, were in shock.

The MC handed me a box of wine, I nearly fell over lifting it, but it was whipped from my hands as my dad greeted me at the bottom of the steps.

My whole family then spent the night drinking the wine at the table, celebrating my win. It's the only thing I've ever won in my life and I could have had that Action Man, but instead they gave me the corks out of the bottles and said if I glued them together, I could make a cork Action Man. They howled laughing at this of course.

★★★

'Just put your hand in and take them.'

The glass door to the ice-cream stall was open, and someone had left a four-inch gap between the glass door and the frame. It was the small window the man leans out of in the day, so you can get an ice cream without having to go inside the shop.

'Go on, put your hand in and grab them.'

My cousin Glen was egging me on to take a box of chocolate flakes, they were just there at the window, tantalising.

It was night-time, and we were allowed to walk up and down the prom on our own, all the cousins on the mess, well, those of us who could walk, the younger ones were in bed. The older cousins went in the opposite direction, so it was just me, Glen, Neville and Colin.

'No way, man,' I said. 'But you've the smallest hands,' Glen replied. I was shitting it, my heart raced, the blood was doing a legger all over my body and my eye was turning in like a mad thing.

But I had to do it. I pushed my small hand between the gap, got a hold of the box and pulled. As I pulled the box, it tore and the flakes fell all over the ground, like a slot-machine (one-arm bandit) paying out.

'Yeaahhhhhh!' the lads cheered and started to gather up what looked like a thousand flakes. We stuffed the flakes up our jumpers, then we all legged it back towards the hotel, laughing as we ran, well, they laughed, I was still shitting it.

SCENE 14. NIGHT. OUTSIDE ON THE PORCH OF THE HOTEL. GLEN, COLIN, NEVILLE AND JASON ALL TUCK INTO CHOCOLATE FLAKES.

GLEN: Now, we don't tell a soul about this or we're all dead, got it?

ALL: Got it.

GLEN: Got it, Jason?

ME: Got it.

NEW VOICE: Hello boys, what's all this then?

My brother Eric had arrived back with the older cousins. They were drinking cans of lager with ladies on the side of the can.

GLEN: Nothing.

ERIC: Where did you get all those flakes?

GLEN: Found them on the beach.

ERIC: Ask me arse! Where did you get them or I'll tell?

GLEN: If you tell on us, then we'll tell on you for drinking.

Just then Paddy Byrne (my dad) arrives out for a bit of fresh air and a smoke. I never understood how you could join up fresh air with smoking.

He looked down at a couple of chocolate-mouthed kids, obviously trying to hide something, then he looked down at a couple of pale older kids, most likely inches from getting sick, also trying to hide something.

My dad took a drag on his fag. We all watched in silence as he exhaled.

DAD: Right, who's going to tell me what's going on?

Everybody stayed tight-lipped. My dad then headed towards me. He bent down and stared at me right in my chocolate-ringed face. All the cousins sighed, as they knew it was game over: Jay the rat was about to spill.

DAD: Jason?

CHAPTER 6
THE OFFICIAL LUDFORD DRIVE ROAD OLYMPICS

'Jesus, it's good to be back in our own house. I'll put the kettle on so we can have a proper cup of tea, then finally we'll get to sleep in our own beds tonight, but not before I put a wash on and get our clothes all smelling Irish again.'

Why do they bother going away at all if they miss their homes so much? Every Irish family to this day says the same rubbish when they get home from holidays. My mother was delighted to be back in her kitchen, with all her bits and bobs in their place.

TOP TEN THINGS IRISH PEOPLE MISS WHILE ON HOLIDAYS, IN NO PARTICULAR ORDER

1. Milk ('The milk is always funny here, the cows eat different grass').

2. Guinness ('They don't know what they're doing with it').

3. Sausages, bacon, etc. ('The pigs are fed different stuff').

4. Cereals ('They've all got the names wrong, Ricicles?').

5. Weather ('Now it's just toooooo hot!').

6. Language ('I don't know what your man is saying, it's all yik-yak').

7. Hospitals ('Don't end up in there, you'll be dead in a week').

8. Newspapers (pre-Internet: 'I don't know what's happening at home').

9. Toilet paper ('It's like sandpaper on your arse').

10. The right side of the road ('They're all on the wrong side of the road').

The Isle of Man was now behind us. 'Jesus Christ, I'll need a holiday after that holiday,' my mother groaned as she hauled the full suitcases up the stairs. My dad hadn't made it all the way home yet.

Every time we came back from holiday and landed at the ferry port in Dublin, we'd hop in the taxi and go straight up to the pub so my Dad could finally have a decent pint of Guinness. We'd have the lemo and crisps, then Mam would bring us on home to get the house ready. She'd say, 'I'd rather head home meself with the kids so their father isn't under me feet while I get the house back in order.'

We were then kicked outside. Eric headed to the field, I headed to my part of the field, Rachel had to take Eithne to her part of the field, so now we were all finally happy again. The family all in their rightful places. Kids: field. Dad: pub. Mam: house.

As soon as we left the house, my mam strapped herself in not for a day of housework but for a day of 'catch up'. She picked up the phone and rang everyone to tell them how much of a great time she'd had, how the weather was great, the food cheap and the kids had a ball. In return, her friends would tell her (because the Irish are begrudging arses) that she'd picked a bad two weeks to head off because the weather in Ireland was the best it had been in seventy-three years, the man on the telly said so, and they wouldn't see the like of it again, and you should have seen this and you should have seen that, Mary from down the road died and rose again, her husband had an accident with the fright, but they're both alright now, but the dog's dead …

The field was buzzing with kids. We now had roughly a month left before we headed back to school. The Road Olympics were announced. This was an event organised by the bigger kids, but we all joined in and we loved it. There wasn't a parent in sight and they had no idea what we were doing. It just looked like a load of kids playing, but playing at a very intense level.

EVENTS iN THE ANNUAL LUDFORD DRiVE ROAD OLYMPiCS

1. Cycling

2. Hurdles

3. Tennis

4. Squares

5. Curbs (or Curby if you're from a rough area)

6. Football World Cup

7. Rounders

8. BMX

9. Knick knacks or knick knocks, depending where you're from

10. Tip the Can (or Kick the Can if you're from a rough area)

These events would vary each year. The head of the Road Olympics was Derek Priestly. He was my next-door neighbour and he and my brother Eric were in charge. Derek was in the FCA (the Army Reserve or something like that, anyway it was the army for teenagers: if you were a good boy scout, you got into the FCA).

This is the way Road Olympics worked: you got maximum points if you won an event; if it was a team event, the points were split down between that team; at the end of all the events, the person with the most points won.

Cycling

The bike section was always won by Damien Farrell, as he had a real racing bike, shaved legs and all, and we would chase him around on our various bikes but never catch him.

The bike I cycled around on was my dad's bike, which he used to cycle to work. Well, I say *cycle to work*. He got it in order to get fit, cycled it once or twice to work, but then announced that …

> DAD: If the cars don't kill yeh, the buses will kill yeh, and if they don't get yeh, your heart will. Bollix to that.

So I had to race on a bike that was too big for me. You often would see kids on bikes way too big for them, you could tell by how they cycled. On a too-big bike you had to cycle from side to side, leaning over and hanging your whole body to one side when the pedal went down, then do the same on the other side when the other pedal went down. I never won that event, needless to say, but I did end up with a lot of chafing and sore balls.

The lid of a bin was banged on the ground – and we weren't even in Belfast – to announce three laps around the estate. All shapes, sizes and ages headed off in a bunch. Damo Farrell was gone into the distance with his shaved legs. The little kids just banged into each other, cried and fell over. The middle pack, which I was often in, tried our best. We must have been so fit to even get those bikes 100 metres down the road, never mind the three laps straight after. But we pressed on. Damo Farrell came past us twice and had the race won before we'd even finished the first lap.

It was all over and Damo was the winner, maximum points for him, the rest of us were given our points. I came eighteenth or something, I say that, but I'm totally making that up, as to remember your placement in a race 30-odd years ago is just a damn lie, but it was around that.

The hurdles

Now, this was the '80s at its best. The hurdles event was always conducted out my back garden. My dad used to work in plastics for a bit. We never actually understood what 'plastics' was, but he made 'plastics'. 'What?' 'Plastics, I said, I make plastics.'

This was during a break in his career from working in Guinness. My dad was a cooper (made wooden barrels with his bare hands, these men were super human), but metal barrels were brought in and the lads all lost their jobs (as sung in 'The Rare Auld Times' by The Dubliners or Luke Kelly, depending on your age: 'By trade I was a cooper, lost out to redundancy'). My dad got a job somewhere in plastics, where he made plastics, and then returned to Guinness to make Guinness. He didn't make Guinness with hammers and nails, mind you, but by drinking the stuff you would think he did.

Whatever it was he did, my dad had got a load of giant plastic Lego-type bricks, so we would line them down the garden and use them as hurdles. We made them all different heights and then timed each other around the garden. We had the most accurate timer ever; Leonardo da Vinci would have been proud of us. One of the lads would shout 'Go', and the group of us would chant.

TIMER: 'One Mississippi, two Mississippi, three Mississippi …'

Genius. Here, what has four eyes but can't see? The Mississippi river. You can have that for free.

Karl went first at the hurdles because he was always good at this event. The fact that he was two years older than me always helped. I was never taller than him (not until later in our teens anyway), but he always made me feel good about it. He'd say to me, 'You don't want to be taller than a girl. You need to be the same height as her girl willy, or you won't be able to do it. I'm taller than most girls, so I'll probably end up single.' We didn't have the Internet then, so I had to guess what that was all about.

Karl sailed over the hurdles and clocked a great time. My go now. Lovely white shorts on me, with a long slit in the side for extra leg spread as I leaped into the air like a gazelle. White,

tight T-shirt for aerodynamics, which we had never even heard of then, and, of course, my big framed glasses and patch, to take in every aspect of the obstacle course.

'GO!' I left the line like a cheetah. I jumped at the first hurdle, didn't really leave the ground, ran straight through the plastic bricks. I kept this up around the whole course. Every time I went to jump, I just didn't seem to leave the ground, instead going face-first into every hurdle, demolishing the course as I ran. The lads stopped counting halfway through. I crossed the finish line.

ME: Yes!

No cheers, no claps, just my brother booting me in the hole. 'Yeh spa, you just wrecked the course.' No points for me on that day either.

The sport played on the road was normally brought on by an event on the telly. The telly ruled our lives, whatever the telly told us to do, we did it.

World Cup, and everyone was out to the field after the matches on the telly with screams of, 'I'm Maradona', 'I'm Pelé!' If Wimbledon was on, the road was covered in children playing up to twenty matches all the way down the road, using the tar on the road as markers for the courts, until Brian Roche started to rip all the tar up out of the road. I don't know why he did it, but Brian just couldn't stop pulling the tar up out of the centre of the road. You could do this on hot days when the tar got hot and soft and pliable. When the road started to crack as a result of his addiction, he got into loads of trouble.

The difference between where I lived in Ballinteer and another place in Dublin was that, if you lived in a rough area, then you got in bad with the cops, or were even sent to prison. In Ballinteer, you just got into loads of trouble, with your mam. Which was probably worse, really – those mammies were badasses.

Knick knocks

A very scary Ballinteer stunt was the knick knock, which was also one of the events of the Road Olympics. While other kids in Dublin were breaking into houses and cars and robbing shops, the Ballinteer possy or 'the Luds', as we were known (only amongst ourselves, mind you, as no one feared the Luds and we didn't tell other roads our name was the Luds in case that sparked a fight and we were all shite at fighting). But the Luds, my friend, the Luds knocked on doors and then ran away. BOOM! Fearless.

This is how you did a knick knock: we would all gather outside a house, normally picking on the house where you would get the best chase. Many a house we knocked on and ran away and they never answered, so we let them be.

But my next-door neighbours, their dad, Bert, would never learn. Every time we knocked on his door, he would chase us out the drive and down the road, and we cried with laughter as he ran after us.

I've no idea what age Bert was then, maybe in his late thirties? But he looked old because all men in their thirties in the '80s looked old because they all had beer bellies and smoked like chimneys. If you look at a late thirty-something men now, they look like they're in their twenties, as they jog back from their marathon or bike ride with half a ton of Lycra shoved up their holes.

You'd get points for how brave you were with the knick knocks, so the longer you waited at the door, the more points you got. I remember my dad catching the older lads doing knick knocks on our road.

The doorbell went and I jumped up, but my dad, being so street-wise, said, 'Don't answer it'. He then switched the hall light off, crept towards the front door and waited. We had no idea what he was doing. He waited in silence at the door, then, out of nowhere, the door bell went again and before the chime could even stop, my dad had opened the door and grabbed a kid by his coat, holding him up as he wriggled like a fish out of water.

DAD: Got yeh, yeh little bollix.

The kid just kept on saying, 'I'm sorry, Mr Byrne, I'm sorry.'

DAD: Don't knock on this door again, or I'll chop the knuckles of yeh.

The kid was terrified. I didn't even know him, he was from a rougher estate. My dad then put him back outside the door and let him go, like he was releasing him back into the ocean.

From that day on, my dad was the coolest dad on the road, the lads said, and out of respect to my dad, no one was allowed to do knick knocks on the Byrnes' door. Out of respect, me bollix! They were all terrified of my dad. Which was cooooooooollllllllllll!

So, knick knocks was another challenging Road Olympics game. After we'd played it, my brother and Derek Priestly checked the points. I wasn't even on the board. Damo Farrell doing really well, Ronan Garvey was doing well, Karl was doing well, but me, Ken Newman and Brian Roche were just doing okay.

We were just about to start the football section of the Road Olympics when the most amazing sight came walking up the road, not the path, never the path, but the road, they looked amazing and smelled great ...

The Spanish students!

We were all wide-mouthed as the most beautiful males and females walked up the road, all speaking Yik-yak, as my dad called it. Lovely brown skin, legs on the girls like you've never seen, some of the blokes even had beards and they were our age!

A few of my mates had Spanish students in their houses, but we never got them. I thought it was because we were too poor, I literally thought for years that you paid them to stay in your house. I loved them so much, I just thought you'd have to pay for the privilege of having such a fine-smelling, good-looking beast around the house.

I remember asking my dad and mam could we have one, like a kitten or something, still thinking we had to pay for one.

> DAD: Ah yeah, and how am I supposed to sit around in me jocks watching telly when there's some sprog talking Yik-yak to me while I'm trying to watch *Countdown*, for feck's sake?

We never argued with our dad, there was no point as he never really made sense, but he stuck hard and fast to whatever he said.

TOP TEN DAD COMMENTS THAT YOU DON'T UNDERSTAND

1. If you look like you don't want it, you'll get it.
2. Best way to get rid of hiccups is to ignore them.
3. I'm telling you because I'm telling you.
4. You had a haircut last week, that's quite sufficient.
5. The only way they'll stop that war is if they stop fighting.
6. I can't hear a thing without my glasses.
7. What's the point in cutting the grass? It will only grow again.
8. We're not getting a cat, we only bought a new table.
9. You'll sleep better in bed if you try to stay awake.
10. Skiing? Sure it's all snow.

The Spanish students would spend the summer sitting in our field. All the girls who normally hung out with us went over to the Spanish boys, they barely spoke English, but they looked like young matadors. The girls loved them. The Spanish girls, on the other hand, didn't really like us, we were pasty, blue-skinned almost, and incredibly shy around these amazing women.

It was like the Grand Prix of blokes had arrived into town, and we were the go-karts, electric ones, not even petrol ones, but shitty little shy, safe electric cars. These Spanish boys just had to click their fingers and they got a snog off an Irish girl. I remember talking to a Spanish girl once in the field, and she just kept looking at me as if she was trying to talk to a bowl of sick.

I have no idea why the Spanish were sent to Ireland to learn English, I can only imagine that it was the low rent the Irish must have charged. One family on the road used to make their kids sleep on couches and on the ground to make room for the Spanish students. Now that's greed at its height.

But I often thought of the Spanish student heading home to Madrid after being in Ireland for a summer.

MAMMY SPAIN: (*in Spanish*) Myyyyy beautiful boyyyy, welcome home to Spain.

SPANISH BOY STUDENT: (*in Spanish Irish*) Shuuuut yer box hole maaaaaaa, and throw a few rashers 'n' saussies on for us, I'm bleedin' famished, knackered from the flight, and I'm dyin' for a huuuuuge dump.

MAMMY SPAIN: *Que?*

The main thing with the Spanish was the football. We played them in a match nearly every day, we were good and they couldn't believe it. They thought we were just a pack of paddies who knew nothing about football, but that's all we did all year, play football, even I was good at it, running around like a human stick with glasses, nutmegging the Spanish boys and burying the ball in the back of the net, which was actually just a pair of jumpers.

We won all the time, and the Spanish went mental. They would scream at each other in Spanish, which we thought was cool. We thought we were especially cool when we all went into our houses for our dinner smelling of Spanish aftershave because the Spanish had been rubbing off us on the pitch.

I'd sit down to dinner, and my mam would sit down, look at my dad, sniff the air and say, 'Are you going out tonight, Paddy?' And Dad would say, 'Now how am I supposed to go out tonight? Me tie is brand new, woman.'

More logic from my dad:

> DAD: It's this fella here, been rubbing off the Spanish again have you, son?
> MAM: *Paddy!*
> DAD: Well he has, don't mind her, son, when I was your age, we'd be rubbing off the French. Oh you'd smell nice after rubbing of a French fella, or the Italians, you'd smell of Ferraris when you headed into the house.
> MAM: At least he doesn't smell of smoke or rats.

Normally, I'd come in smelling of smoke. I used to love setting stuff on fire around the edges of the field, especially in the summer when there were big tufts of grass everywhere. I'd steal my dad's matches and burn everything.

Once, me and Karl lit up a bush, which sparked to another bush, and we started a small blaze. We were shitting it; a parent had to call the fire brigade.

I ran into the house with a black face, smelling of smoke. Karl told me to say nothing. I agreed, as we were dead if we were found out.

My mum smelled my clothes, looked at me, didn't even have to open her mouth.

> ME: *(eye turned in)* Karl and me robbed matches off our dads, then we set all the grass on fire, we didn't mean to do it. *(Followed by crying, followed by my mam ringing Karl's mam, Betty. Karl was grounded for two weeks. Nothing happened to me, little shit, as I was two years younger and Karl should have known better. Poor Karl.)*

He was, and is, a great friend. In that summer we also cut people's grass to make a bit of money. We would get Karl's dad's lawn-mower, wheel it to the petrol station, fill it with loads of petrol and fill a spare can. We weren't supposed to fill stuff up with petrol then, but mad Larry in the garage always let us, he even sold us cigarettes for 10p each.

Then we'd go knock on the doors and ask if they wanted their gardens done. We'd make about a fiver a garden, we were minted.

Except this one time, we got an old lady's house. Karl always said to avoid the old ladies' houses because those gardens would take forever, but we were sure a young family was living in that house. It wasn't our estate, though, which is how we made the mistake. Old lady answers the door. Karl looks at her. 'Bollix.' Old lady sees the lawn-mower, 'You can cut the front and back, lads.'

The front, to be honest, didn't look too bad and it was a small garden, but when she let us out the back, the garden was massive and overgrown to shite. It took us all day and when we were finished, covered in cuts and bruises, she came out to us with a tray.

'Drinks, lads?' she said. I grabbed what I thought was a pint of 7-UP, but it was cheap sparkling water. I nearly puked, as did Karl. We gave her back the glasses, told her we were finished and could we get paid?

She headed to get her purse, this was always the best bit. She then handed me 50p and Karl 50p, then closed the door in our faces. Well, we were disgusted. But then we burst out laughing.

We headed back to our estate, knackered, sat in the field and waited for the ice cream van. It came, as it always did, just before dinner, to annoy the parents. The man who drove the van was called Dracula because he literally looked like Dracula. His jet-black hair was always greased back onto his head and he

hated kids, we drove him mad. But on this day, a day I will never forget, I was leaning against the van, waiting to place my order at the window. Dracula was serving another child, and he poured red sauce all over this kid's ice cream, but some of the red sauce fell onto the ground.

I looked at him and said, 'Lick it up, Dracula.' Now that was cheeky, but before I knew it I was about 3 inches off the ground, dangling in the air. Dracula had reached out, grabbed my hair, hauled me up, then he began to shake me from side to side. I was screaming, and Karl and the other kids were throwing their ice creams at him, and he eventually let me go. I was in tears, it had hurt like hell. Still, to this day, if you pull my hair at all, it sets my temper off.

I ran into the house crying, told my mam. She said, 'Right, don't tell your father', but he walked in at that moment, so we had to tell him.

Holy Jaysus! The next day the ice cream van's tinkly music sounded, my dad picked up a shears and headed out the door, with my mum shouting after him, 'Paddy! Paddy! Don't.'

We all ran out after my dad, the whole road was out now, gathered around the van as my dad waved his shears at Dracula.

Dracula then, mad brave bollix, said to my dad, 'Right, you want some? I'll give you some.' He got out of his van and came around to my dad.

We had never, ever seen him outside of his van, but the man came up to about my dad's belly-button.

My dad threw down the shears, grabbed Dracula by the waist, picked him up and fecked him back into his van through the serving window, which was open.

> DAD: Now take your ice creams, your van, turn into a bat and fly out of here, before I melt ye meself!!!!

(Anger never made sense when my dad spoke it.)

Dracula drove away, and we didn't see him on our road again for maybe a year. But whenever we heard his stupid ice cream bell, my baby sister Eithne used to say, 'Oh, pull hair, pull hair is coming.'

The games had been played, and Damo Farrell was declared the winner of the Road Olympics. The summer was heading towards its end. My scalp was sore from the ice cream van assault, but I had a bit of cash in my pockets from grass-cutting. The Spanish students were all leaving, and the normal smell of the road was reinstated. Holidays with parents all done, now we all faced into a new year in school, which I can't say I was looking forward to.

But … there was time for one more summer stunt before we had to get back to the boring school routine. Around this time, we had seen the microwave oven for the first time. My mother and all the mammies were so excited, it was like the invention of the fridge all over again.

An aside on fridges: my dad once told me that he had no fridge when he was a kid, which meant lateral thinking was required. The Christmas goose lived out in the back garden for a month until it was needed. Jaysus my granny was tough, come Christmas Eve, she'd head out into the garden, chop the goose's head off, skin it, gut it, and have it on the table for Christmas Day dinner. Now Jamie Oliver, yeh big pansy, how's that for a bit of Bish Bash Bosh dinner in fifteen minutes? More like, whack, chop, batter, murder, dinner in fifteen minutes from the hardest bitch ever.

So … the microwave came into the Irish house and my God, what a miracle! Mammies could now make dinners whenever they wanted, relax and get stuff done. The first day my mam used the microwave, my dad arrived in, and he knew something was different in the house but couldn't put his finger on it.

Bing! That's it, Mammy is not up to her ankles in pots and pans trying to time everyone's dinner to perfection.

She set the table for my dad, we had already eaten, and he then sat at the table looking confused. All we could hear from the kitchen was *BEEP BEEP BEEP*, then my mother walks in with a steaming hot plate, the widest smile on her face ever, and puts it down in front of my dad. He too is impressed, he digs in, takes a big spoonful of meat and veg, puts it in his mouth and ... burns the bleedin' mouth off himself.

It took a few weeks of practice and many visits to the Burns Unit before my mam got used to microwaving. But it was her pride and joy, her new best friend, as it was with every mammy.

One day, Karl's mam was out shopping and we were in his house. Karl took a pint bottle of milk out of the fridge, looked at me, smiled and said, 'I wonder what would happen if I put this in the microwave?' As we all know, many a great thing has stemmed from the words *I wonder what would happen if* … Karl popped the milk into the microwave and switched it on. I was shitting myself. The bottle turned around in there for a bit, then *BOOM!* An explosion of milk inside the microwave, it went everywhere. We had to clean it up quickly as his mam was on her way back from the shops.

We had just managed to clean it all up before his mam arrived home. She said hello, then started to unpack the shopping. As she did this, she noticed a full box of milk-soaked tissues. We had failed to notice that it had hit the tissue box as well. Betty looked around at me and Karl. She looked at me, my eyes stared to well up, I took a deep breath in and ...

Karl jumped in front of me. 'It's cool, Jay.' Then *to his mam*: 'Me and Jay blew up a bottle of milk in the microwave and we're sorry. I'll now head to my room for two weeks. Jay, you're free to go.'

Karl grounded himself for two weeks and I went home scot-free, little shit. Poor Karl.

CHAPTER 7
THE CROSS-BEARER

Ohhhhhhhh, the smell of new school books and pencils! We've a new teacher because I'm in fifth class. Just one more year of primary after this and then we're going into the big school.

Sadly, my best mate Karl, who was of course two years older than me, was now gone from primary school. I was so sad. I had plenty of mates, but I always met Karl in the boys' area. Yes, I know, in Catholic Ireland we actual had a boys' and a girls' area, and a mixed area.

Me and Karl used to run down into the girls' area, screaming and chasing the girls with dog poo on the end of a stick. 'POO ON A STICK, POO ON A STICK,' we'd roar as we ran them into every corner of the playground.

Mr Murphy was our teacher. He was cool, he played a guitar and would play it in the morning as we walked in, which seemed to calm us all. At that time, teachers were still allowed to smack us with rulers or with their hand. Many a time I would be chatting to a friend beside me in class and I'd get an unexpected belt across the head. 'But it never did us any harm,' I hear you cry. Well, I went on to be an insane comic, four lads ended up in prison, another murdered someone ... BUT IT NEVER DID US ANY HARM!

A FEW THINGS THAT 'NEVER DID US ANY HARM!' OR WERE, IN FACT, GOOD FOR US

1. A clip around the ear.
2. A smack on the arse.
3. The belt with a belt.
4. A good talking-to (I'd rather a belt).
5. Locked in your room (had no actual lock).
6. Sent to bed with no dinner.
7. Hospitalised by a slipper.
8. Getting the smile wiped off your face.
9. Back of the hand.
10. Being sent to the priest.

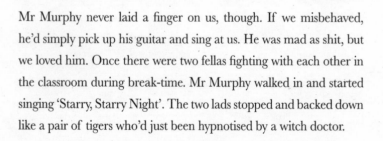

Mr Murphy never laid a finger on us, though. If we misbehaved, he'd simply pick up his guitar and sing at us. He was mad as shit, but we loved him. Once there were two fellas fighting with each other in the classroom during break-time. Mr Murphy walked in and started singing 'Starry, Starry Night'. The two lads stopped and backed down like a pair of tigers who'd just been hypnotised by a witch doctor.

Mr Murphy encouraged us to be active, sports, music or whatever, just as long as we were doing something. One day he came into the class and announced that the priest was looking for volunteers to join the altar boys. If we wanted to do it, we were to go to the priest after school in the church.

Ten of us turned up that afternoon, all boys, of course, as girls were not allowed to serve at an altar, because that would be a holy jaysus sin and absolutely no vagina was allowed near the altar. The only ones allowed up there were those belonging to the old women who gave out the wafers and they were dormant vaginas anyway.

We had a good priest in our school/parish, thankfully he wasn't a fiddly priest at all. We all liked him and he was a decent enough soul, in fact, if anything, he was more interested in the ladies of the parish than in the young boys, and I thought this was healthy.

He said a good fast mass, too. You always looked for a priest who said a fast mass, and that's the one you'd go to.

My dad only ever went to mass if it was a Holy Communion, a Confirmation, weddings, christenings or deaths, otherwise no sign of Dad, he didn't like the Church.

In fact, I can remember the day I stopped going to mass. I was around fifteen, and one Sunday I just stayed in my pyjamas with my big brother Eric. We sat on the floor watching *Hong Kong Phooey*, and my dad sat with us. My mum arrived in looking for us to go to mass, she had my baby sister by the hand.

MAM: Are yeh ready? We'll be late.
ME: We're not going, Mam.

Holy shit, it was like a bomb was about to go off, and my dad didn't help much by saying:

DAD: Sure leave them, they can make up their own minds.

MAM: Right. I'll just head to mass and pray for all you little bastards then. (*Those were her exact words.*)

She left with my sister in hand, embarrassed not to have her family by her side at the church.

TOP TEN TIMES MY DAD HAS EMBARRASSED MY MAM

1. Telling priest to piss off.
2. Telling all taxi men they're robbing bastards.
3. Telling a copper to get his eyes tested, that it was a green light.
4. Telling the desk sergeant to piss off.
5. Telling the whole station to piss off.
6. Oh and if there were any further questions, to 'ask me bollix'.
7. Spitting out food in a Chinese restaurant while screaming, 'This tastes like bleedin' peanuts' (satay).
8. At a graveside, 'Ah well, when you're dead, you're dead.' Then to Mam: 'What?'
9. In someone else's house, 'I'd give that fish a bit more time on the pan', handing his plate back to the host, then looking at my mother, 'What?'
10. 'Sure, I have to iron my own shirts,' said in front of other wives.

The church was cold on the day we applied to become altar boys. The priest ran through what we'd have to do during mass, and told us we'd get paid for weddings and funerals, and get Easter eggs at Easter. We sat up straighter, we *loved* this idea.

The first day I had to serve mass was so exciting. We would meet in a tiny cloakroom-type place, get changed into our white robes, the room was full of wine and wafers, and one of the lads would have a swig of the wine. I didn't because I hated the stuff, so I'd just stuff myself with holy wafers.

So on my debut as an altar boy, we headed out of the room and straight into the path of the priest. He asked me was I all set, but I couldn't answer him because my mouth was so dry from stuffing the wafers in my mouth. He looked at me, and I thought I was caught. But then he rubbed my head and said, 'It must be the nerves, they have your throat dried out'. We headed out to the audience, as I called them, and I had a great gig. I continued having great gigs and rose through the altar-boy ranks. I went from holding the candle at the back of the six altar boys to being the front candle-holder, and then to the best position ever: the cross-bearer.

The cross-bearer

The cross-bearer was the black belt of altar boys. I carried a six-foot stick laden down by a big metal Jesus. I did weddings, funerals, baby head-wetting ceremonies, and we'd get a tenner a service. I was a celebrity on my road. I was the only altar boy who was allowed to carry the cross. When I was sick I had an understudy, Glen Dickson, but then I heard through people that he messed up and got his timings wrong, and when would I be back?

I'm in so many people's weddings photos. If you're from Ballinteer or got married there, I'd get out the photo album now, check if you can see a big glasses-wearing altar boy, as in *big glasses*, not big in frame. In fact, I look like a pole holding a pole with a cross on top, except one of the poles is wearing big framed glasses and an eye patch. I was inches from signing wedding cards for the wedding parties. Proper celeb. I would check in the newspaper or ask my mum if anyone was sick or dying and BOOM!, dropping like flies, old people everywhere, which meant more tenners for Jay the cross-bearer.

But like all fame and fortune, it must come to an end sometime. And oh God did I come crashing to the ground, never to serve mass again.

It was 9.30am mass, and up to this point I hadn't served a 9.30am mass and for good reason. On the morning, I thought nothing of it and headed into the cloakroom to get changed. My minions waited for me with their candles. I then emerged with the very big pole with the cross on top. I checked to see that the priest was behind me, gave the nod to the organist and he started up on his organ (oooh matron! What? Doesn't matter). Business as usual.

We all moved in a perfect formation towards the altar. We looked like a white Red Arrows display, if the red arrows were white and not red, and were altar boys and a priest and not airplanes.

People stood as we walked up the church aisle, and there must have been at least a thousand of them. 'Yeah, that's right, stand, stand for the cross-bearer.' They weren't, they were standing for the priest, but I was gone mad with power. I just thought, since I'm carrying Holy Jesus God on the top of this pole, then I'm the one you want to be standing for, because right there and then, *I* had the direct contact to Holy Jesus God, or God, or Jesus, Holy ghost, apparently all the same fella …

Anyway, my minions placed their candles in the relevant areas under my watchful gaze. I then slotted the very, very important cross into its wooden stand. I could feel Jesus around me, and even he thought I was cool. I then sat in my own head altar boy seat. The priest went behind the altar, opened his arms to the congregation and said …

PRIEST: *Dia daoibh.*
ME: Bollix.

The mass was in Irish, as in the Irish language. Many people reading this book will know that in Ireland, we learn Irish in school for a good thirteen/fourteen years. We can read it, we can write it, but fecked if we can understand it when it's spoken!

The fact was that the 9.30am mass was always *in Irish*. I'd never been at or served a 9.30 yet. And this was the reason.

I was screwed. My minions looked at me and could see the look of horror on my face, and they knew I wouldn't know what the hell the priest was saying for the next forty-five minutes. Glen Dickson was a candle-holder that day, but he had his eye on the cross, and I could tell by the look on his face that he thought it would soon be his. I tried my best. I thought I could follow the mass by watching what the priest was doing. No one would ever know.

I jumped up when I thought he was going for the communion wafers. I brought over the bowl of water as the whole congregation watched me, although in fairness, none of them knew what was going on either. The priest whispered to me, 'Not yet'. I went back to my seat, red-faced. I was up and down to the priest about seven wrong times, which meant I was now the entertainment in the room. I didn't have a single clue what was going on. The priest continued with the mass in his Gaelic language, but suddenly he pointed to me to head to the steps.

ME: Oh bollix, the bell.

I had to head to the steps to ring the bell. The bell in the church had amazing power, it made people stand, sit or kneel. Normally the older women would sit in the front row and, like dancers at a rave on top of the speakers, they would lead the merry dance of standing, sitting or kneeling at the appropriate times.

The old people relied on me to get the bell right. The people at the back relied on the old people to get the standing, sitting, kneeling bit right. Jaysus, what a disaster.

I went to the steps, knelt down like I was about to be beheaded, while the altar boys watched on, sniggering. I lifted the bell in my already sweaty hands, could feel the old people's eyes boring into the back of my head, and off we went.

PRIEST: Ta tu me ag speaking Irish now.
ME: (*not a clue*) DING A LING A LING ...

Congregation stands up at the wrong part, priest stares at me, red-faced with annoyance.

ME: (*in a panic*) DING A LING A LING ...

Congregation sits down, confused. Old people furious.

PRIEST: Ta tu me ag speaking Irish again.
ME: DING A LING A LING ...

Congregation stands up.

ME: DING A LING A LING ...

Congregation sits down.

ME: DING A LING A LING ...

They all kneel.

ME: DING A LING A LING ...
They all stand.

It went on like a Monty Python sketch for several minutes, everyone half sitting, kneeling, standing, no one knew where they were. Eventually, I felt the bell being grabbed out of my hand. It was the other priest. I went and sat down as the other priest rang the bell in the correct spots. People were now kneeling, sitting, standing all in the right places. Order was restored. I sat back in my head altar boy seat, absolutely mortified.

I waited until the end of the mass. Then I grabbed my pole with the Holy Jesus Holy God on top, and stood in the middle of the aisle, waiting for the priest and the other altar boys to join me.

Except they didn't. I stood there for several minutes, until I realised this was my final embarrassing moment. The mass wasn't over, and I was standing at the top of the church with everyone wondering what I was doing there. I don't know to this day why I did this, but I just turned on my heels and walked down the aisle all on my own, holding that massive cross, as the priests, altar boys and the whole congregation watched me.

I got to the end of the church, opened the doors, left the cross leaning at the entrance of the church, threw off my cassock, and walked straight home, leaving my new-found fame behind for Glen Dickson to pick up. People always said I was a great cross-bearer and that it was never the same with Glen Dickson doing it. I also heard that later on in his career, the priest caught him robbing from the baskets and he lost his position.

So that was my altar boy life. It was nice while it lasted, the taste of housing estate fame was good, but just a little too good.

★ ★ ★

The year moved on, it was now October, time for Karl's birthday. I always loved his birthday because his dad, Paddy, would take us out for a treat. I know, I know, a lot of men were called Paddy back then.

LiST OF PADDiES ON LUDFORD DRIVE

1. **Paddy Byrne**
2. **Paddy McBreen**
3. **Paddy Wright**
4. **Paddy McDermot**
5. **Paddy Reid**
6. **Paddy Murphy**
7. **Paddy O'Sullivan**
8. **Paddy Ryan**
9. **Paddy Curtin**
10. **Paddy O'Leary**

Paddy would bring me and Karl to the cinema, just me and Karl and him, popcorn, lemos, the works. It was Karl's birthday so we were going to see *Indiana Jones and the Temple of Doom*, and myself and Karl had bought some magic dust for the occasion. Not heroin, no, actual magic dust, it was a top sweet purchase as a kid in the '80s. You put it on your tongue, held your mouth open and it fizzed and popped on your tongue like tiny mini fireworks. Popping candy, I think it's called now.

POPULAR CANDY / ICE CREAMS IN THE '80S

1. **Magic dust**
2. **Blobs (chewing gum)**
3. **Fizzle Sticks**
4. **Milk teeth**
5. **Cola cubes**
6. **Mr Freeze (good for Mickey Dribblers – if you're in the dark on this one, see Chapter 13)**
7. **Loop the Loop**
8. **Wibbly Wobbly Wonder**
9. **Brunch**
10. **White mice/Fat Frog**

We were headed for the cinema on the Quays (which later went on to become a comedy club, as it happens). So me, Karl and Paddy went into the foyer of the cinema, got popcorn, cokes, etc. Then went to get the tickets, and the little fella behind the desk announces to us that *Indiana Jones* has already started, an hour ago, that the newspapers had misprinted the starting time. Funny that we had to rely on newspapers so heavily then, now our phone beeps when it's ready to head to the movies, not the phone, you, when you're ready.

Couldn't believe it! We stood there with our popcorn, with nowhere to go. Paddy asks the man if there is another movie on now.

MAN: *Jesus of Nazareth*. It's a bit heavy, but it will be good for them.

We headed into *Jesus of* bleedin' *Nazarath*. It was fairly full, but the film went on for *ages*. Karl had brought a farting machine with him that he'd got from an uncle of his in America. It was in a little bag and when you switched it on, it went through a repertoire of various fart noises.

Oh my God, I can say to this day that I have never laughed as much, without actually laughing out loud. Karl switched on the machine in the middle of Jaysus of Naz, then slid the little bag down about four rows in front of us, under people's seats.

It started to go off, little parps at the start, then big woofers, then to a small one again, follow by a kind of *rip rip rip*. I thought I was going to die of barely suppressed laughter, which would look good on your death cert, you'd have to admit. People in that area were shifting in their seats uncomfortably as the machine went off. They didn't know who or what was doing this. Karl had a bit of string on the bag so he could pull it back to him.

The movie was hours long, every time Jaysus would say something important on screen, Karl would set off the machine. Eventually, someone who had seen us laughing got up and left, and arrived back in with the manager, who threw me, Karl and his dad out. In fairness to Paddy, he was crying with laughter too. Just like my own dad, he didn't really give a bollix about Holy God. The manager was disgusted with Paddy, though, and we were all barred.

That was the funniest night of my life. I urge people who are reading this to do the same in your local cinema. You can now get remote-control fart machines, and they are even better. I guarantee you will never laugh as hard and as quietly, although you may poo or wee yourself slightly with the amount of pressure built up by trying to hold in.

Christmas preparations

I had asked Santa for a space shuttle. Or 'Santy', as the Irish call him, like he's some sort of South American dictator. 'Yay, Santy for president.' BANG BANG!

Santy was still very much alive in our house at this age. I had asked for a space rocket and I was so excited, they kept showing the ad for it on the telly.

'SPACE SHUTTLE ROCKET, HEAD INTO SPACE AND EXPLORE THE WORLD ABOVE US, WITH THIS AMAZING SPACE SHUTTLE!' the telly screamed.

I began to build a base for my new shuttle. I mean, I'm not even that old, but I'm going to say it anyway: kids today are spoiled. If they want a base for their rocket, they just ask for it. I had to build mine. It was a load of cereal boxes chopped up and stuck together, with toilet rolls stuck onto the cardboard base, then the whole lot covered in tinfoil. Hey presto! The moon.

Christmas in our house was a mad time. My dad would get up into the attic and drag down all the decorations, including the fake tree. The decorations were years old, but my mam never replaced them. I used to love that, it was great to see the same stuff coming down and out of the boxes.

My mam had a Babycham deer as the star on top of the tree. We never knew what it was meant to symbolise. It was only later we learned that it was to symbolise not the coming of the baby Jesus, but the taking of a lot of booze.

There were Santys that hung on the wall, you would fan out their belly area, and then they became big fat Santys on the wall. Then the room would be finished off with tinsel everywhere, which seemed to get skinnier each year. They started out as thick, shiny, coloured snakes, but ended up as faded bits of strings hung around the lights. But they were still my mam's favourite, and she would wrap her ornaments with tinsel to give them the Christmas look, too.

Then there was the issue of the fairy lights for the tree. Every year they would be pulled off the tree and thrown into the box. They were never carefully put away because if you did this, you might have a stress-free Christmas next year, imagine.

Oh no, first my dad had the lights plugged into the light socket in the ceiling in the hallway. Dangerous? Bleedin' right it was. Then my dad would start with a huge ball of string and lights hanging, and he would have to try and pull it all out, straight down through the hallway. It was a no-go zone for the whole day. My dad on his knees, screaming at us to get out of the way and not to step on the lights.

As he had put the lights back so badly the previous year, he would blow bulbs as he went. So when he finally stretched out the lights, he would gather us all in the hall, switch them on and ...

DAD: Bollix.

Nothing happened. And so would begin the hours on his knees again, this time trying to twist and untwist each bulb to find the loose one or blown one in the chain. He'd have a fag in his mouth as he did it, and the whole time he would be blaming everyone else for what was happening.

DAD: Who in the name of God put these lights back in the box last year?
MAM: You did.
DAD: I did in me hoop. I'd never leave them in such a state.

Bleedin' right he did. He just couldn't remember as he would have had too many Babychams while slinging them back in the box.

BLINK ... BUZZ ... ON ... OFF ... BUZZ ... SPARK ... ONNNNNNN.

DAD: Yes, they're working, now, nobody touch them.
MAM: ... and what use are they all down the hallway? They have to go on the tree.
DAD: I know that, woman, calm down, they're working, aren't they?

My dad would then carefully pick them up and, my God, the swearing flew as the lights went on, then off, as he moved them towards and around the tree.

> DAD: (*on*) Lovely, (*off*) bollix, (*on*) that's it, (*off*) arse, (*on*) steady, (*off*) shite.

He eventually got them all around the tree, but they were going on and off. My dad had had enough.

> DAD: Bollix to them, it will have to do. I can't work out the way they're shorting on and off like, like …
> MAM: Flashing.
> DAD: What?
> MAM: They're on flashing mode, yeh big dope.

Mam would then switch the little box to 'on'. The lights stayed on.

> DAD: I knew that, woman. Do you think I'm thick? I'm off for a pint after that, I'm knackered.

As we all know, pints give you energy. Off he went, the Christmas lighting engineer.

Christmas Eve

My brother was babysitting. My sisters were asleep in bed. It was now time for me to go to bed. My mam and dad were up in the pub, having a pint to settle their nerves, because they too were excited about the day ahead tomorrow.

This Christmas Eve is one I'll never forget. About 11 pm I heard my parents come in the door downstairs. Then I heard them rummaging around downstairs. They started to come up the stairs, and now all I could hear was my mam *shushing* my dad as they came up. They came into my room, and I lay back in the bed, pretending to be asleep.

I looked down the bed sheets at them. They were now both kneeling at the bottom of my bed, and my mother was whispering to my dad.

MAM: (*whisper*) Don't wake him, Paddy.

My dad then did a weird kind of whispering that only my mam could understand. He was whispering so low, it was just insane mumbles, but again my mam knew what he was saying.

DAD: I'm not going to wake him, you're going to wake him, with your shushing and hissing, so if I was you, I'd stop saying I'm going to wake him, cause if anyone is going to wake him, it will be you. Now, hand me the Walkman.

They then proceeded to pick up a Walkman in a box and try to stuff it into a sock. This is an impossible task, as all us '80s kids know.

Walkman

Your Walkman, or portable stereo, was the size of a small house brick. It clipped onto the side of your belt, then dragged your trousers to the ground. It was more a Dragman than a Walkman.

It then used up its batteries after about three songs, so you would end up listening to 'Shout' from Tears for Fears, singing as if they were in slow motion. If you wanted to listen to a song again, you would take out the tape, flip it around, press FF or fast forward. This was canny because it used up less batteries pushing the tape forward instead of rewinding. Rewinding fecked your battery much quicker.

If the battery slowed, the tape would get stuck, then the actual tape of the cassette would unravel as you took it out of the Walkman. You would then spend all day on a chair with the cassette above your head, with a pencil stuck inside one wheel of the cassette, turning it until you had wound all the tape back into the cassette. First world problems … well, working-class problems.

My brother once got the Ferrari of the Walkman family: the tape-recorder.

The tape-recorder

This was a machine that could record your voice, or any noise around it. My brother and I would normally get the tape-recorder, hold it against the radio and wait for the song we wanted to be played by the DJ, and my brother would have his fingers ready on the Play button and the Record button, because you had to press them together. The Record button was red, red for danger, DO NOT PRESS THIS UNLESS YOU TOTALLY WANT TO RECORD, OR YOU WILL RECORD SOMETHING BY MISTAKE!

We waited till the DJ shut up, the song would then play, I'd hold the radio firm, my brother would nod at me and me at him, down went the Play AND Record buttons and BANG!

The bedroom door would burst open.

> DAD: Your dinner is ready, stop messing about and get downstairs.
> ERIC: Dad! You've ruined the recording!
> DAD: I'll ruin your head in a minute, get downstairs.

How many people in the world have a tape with their dad bursting into their bedrooms as they're about to record their favourite song? Millions, I'd say.

Right, back to Christmas Eve and my mam and dad at the bottom of the bed. They just can't get this Walkman into the sock, they're shushing each other and my dad is doing his weird whispers thing. Then I look down the sheet at the both of them. They spot me. They both make eye contact. Then they both just hit the deck. It was the funniest thing I'd ever seen. Two grown adults on their bellies at the base of my bed, arguing.

> MAM: (*whisper*) Well, you've ruined Christmas now.
> DAD: (*still in weird whisper mode*) I've ruined it? I think you'll find with all your bollixing around, you've ruined it.

There was silence for a bit, then I saw one hand go onto the bed and place the Walkman there, then another hairy hand placed the sock on the Walkman box.

MAM: What now?
(Dead silence)
DAD: Roll.

They both rolled and tumbled out of my bedroom and out the door. Best parents ever. Oh and I got my rocket the next morning because Santy made less noise and was in and out downstairs like a real pro as he left the presents under the tree. Even if I thought I had heard ...

SANTY: Bollix!

... as he tripped over the tree.

CHAPTER 8
LiAR, LiAR, PANTS ON FIRE

'L, m, z, q, w, e, s, t, g, y, w, v ...'

'Right, now let's try the chart you didn't learn off by heart while I was talking to your mother, Jason.'

Goddamn it, she's too smart for me. Mrs Large was my eye doctor, as they called her. I went to visit her every few months so she could keep an eye on my special eye.

Crumlin Children's Hospital was the place where she worked. I was always frightened of going because in those days, you had to queue up with loads of other special-eyed kids, all with an array of patches on their faces. It wasn't that I was afraid of the poor, patchy, turned-in-eye kids, it was getting the eye drops. Many people reading this will know what I'm on about if you had these in the '80s.

You see, now you go into an optician's, they look into your eye with a nice light, then they might blow a bit of air on your eyeball, but all pleasant enough. In Crumlin, the door to the nurses' room would swing open and out would come a child holding their knuckles up to their eyes, screaming with pain, as floods of tears poured through the cracks between their fingers.

Then it was your go. In you'd go, into a weird, dimly lit room, sit on chair, light shone in your face, then what can only be described as acid poured directly onto your eyes. It was used to dilate your pupils but because it was so strong, it kept them wide open for hours. All the kids queuing up to see the doctors would be shielding the light coming through the windows into the waiting hall like they were all little vampires. I used to hate that.

While my mam spoke to Mrs Large at her desk, I would sneak up to the eye chart and try to learn the letters on the chart off by heart. But Mrs Large caught me every time.

MRS LARGE: Well Mrs Byrne, I think he's ready.

For what? I thought.

MAM: Oh really, that would be great, wouldn't it, Jason?
ME: What?
MRS LARGE: You're the right age and maturity now for corrective eye surgery.
ME: What?

MAM: Your wonky eye, Jason, they're going to straighten it ... Oh Mrs Large that would be great, we've Confirmation this year and to get that eye back to the middle would look great in the photos.

MRS LARGE: We'll do our best. I'll be on to you about the date; meanwhile, keep that patch on him.

We left the hospital. Mam was delighted, I was confused. What would they have to do to get my eye straight again?

The patch that was over my eye was flesh-coloured. On the bus back home, my mam took off my glasses and took out her mascara pencil, and started to use it on my eye-patch area. She then looked at me like an artist, tilting her head from side to side while admiring her handiwork.

MAM: Now.

Irish people use the word 'Now' all the time, without even knowing it. It's mainly for the beginning or end of things.

TOP TEN TIMES 'NOW' IS USED IN IRELAND

1. (Breath in) sit down (breath out): 'NOW'.
2. (Breath out) slap your knees, stand up (breath in) 'NOW'.
3. Finished the washing up: 'NOW'.
4. Do hair in mirror, all done and: 'NOW'.

5. **Cinema (movie starting): 'NOW'.**

6. **Cinema (movie over): 'NOW'.**

7. **Sex (starting): 'NOW'.**

8. **Sex (over): 'NOW'.**

9. **When your mother thinks you're ready for school (pat on the head): 'NOW'.**

10. **Mother spits on tissue, wipes your face: 'NOW'.**

We stood up to get off the bus, and people were smiling at me as we passed them in their seats. As we stepped down off the bus, the driver was laughing to himself, but my mother was just ignoring all of this.

Got into the house, I went to the loo, washed my hands, then looked in the mirror. OMG!, as they would say in the future. My mother had drawn a cartoon eye onto the flesh-coloured patch. I couldn't believe it, and I couldn't wipe it off. When I went down to my mad mother and asked her for a new patch, she said she didn't have any, and to leave it. I asked her why she did it and she said she didn't want anyone looking at my patch, so she drew another eye so people would think I didn't have a patch on.

Yeah, that would be great if my mother worked in special effects at Pixar, but this eye looked like a four-year-old had drawn it.

My dad burst into the kitchen with a load of daffodil heads clutched in his hand.

> DAD: They're at it again.
> MAM: Who?
> DAD: The daffodil killers.
> ME: (*to myself*) They're back.

The daffodil killers were a group that went around the housing estate chopping the heads off all the daffodils. They did this every spring, but no one knew who they were, or maybe they did but they weren't going to tell me, at this stage of the book we all know why we don't tell Jason stuff.

My dad sat me down, looked me in the eye-patch and said ...

> DAD: Do you ... (*to my mother*) what's wrong with his eye?
> MUM: Eye-patch, yeh fool.
> DAD: Did you draw an eye on his eye-patch?
> MUM: Yeah, good, isn't it?
> DAD: I'll sort that out for yeh, son, in a minute. Now, do you know who's knocking the heads off these flowers?

I just sat still and silent. My parents paused for the usual outburst and turning in of eye. But there was nothing, I actually knew nothing.

> DAD: Right, he knows bollix all, but I'll find the arses.
> MUM: We also got good news, Paddy. Tell him, Jason.

ME: I'm getting me eye pushed back to the middle.

DAD: What?

MAM: Mrs Large says he's old enough to get his special eye centred, so he'll have a proper eye for the Confirmation.

DAD: Well this is all fine, but how much will this cost? I'm not on a wage where I can just pay for any old surgery ...

MAM: It's on the health board, they'll cover it, he's young enough, yeh mean man.

DAD: (*lifting me up*) Great news then, son, no more staring at your nose, and yes, it'll be all ready for the Confirmation. In fact, I'll start on the bathroom at the weekend too, we'll have the place looking smashing for the Confo [Confirmation], but first, to celebrate your surgery, a drink!

Me and my mam cheered. My dad grabbed his coat and left the house, on his own, to head up to the pub to celebrate my surgery, on his own. It was just a given, no questions asked: Dad left the house when he wanted and came home when he wanted.

I once heard him stand up and say the house was too noisy with all the kids running around and that he was heading to the pub for a bit of peace and quiet. He got his coat and left.

Imagine if I tried that now, stood up in a 2016 house and said:

ME: Ehhhhh, I'm just heading out to the pub to calm down.

WIFE: I beg your pardon, what did you just say?

ME: Just heading to the pub for a bit of calmness.

WIFE: (*with gritted teeth*) Isn't that a great idea?

ME: (*fool*) Yes, I think it is.

WIFE: I'll get your coat, just hang on there a minute.

ME: (*fool*) Oh thank you.

Wife helps me on with coat and guides me to the front door.

WIFE: (*even more gritted teeth*) Now off you go (*door opened for me*).

ME: (*fool*) Oh really? Thank you.

WIFE: (*heavily gritted*) Yes, off you go and we'll see if it was worth it in the morning.

I then gently close the door, hang my coat back up, sit back down in the living room and dream what it would have been like to have been a dad in the '70s and '80s.

MY DAD'S LIFE IN THE 1980'S COMPARED TO MINE NOW

1. **No mobile phone.**

   Dad: What do you want one of them for?

   Me: So people can get me.

   Dad: Exactly, why would you want that?

2. **Not at birth of children.**

   Dad: What were you doing there, son?

   Me: To give support?

   Dad: No place for a man, a man shouldn't be seeing that area down there under stress.

3. **No training.**

   Dad: Why are you running around everywhere like a nut?

   Me: To stay fit?

   Dad: Your heart only has a certain amount of beats, you'll drop dead in a park.

4. **Drinking and loving it.**

   Dad: What do you mean you're off the drink?

   Me: To stay healthy.

   Dad: Ah jaysus, you have to have a pint, son, you're a Byrne, it's in your blood.

   Me: Okay, I'll have a wine.

   Dad: Not near me you won't.

5. **School plays.**

   Dad: So you go to the whole thing?

   Me: Yeah, I love it.

   Dad: Too much waving and shite at them.

My dad's secret of life: *Let everyone else worry.*

My dad was, and is, the main man in the pub. When you go into an Irish pub and you see a group of men in a huddle with one of them dishing out 'Great Advice', my dad is the fella with the knowledge, hilarious knowledge, but knowledge all the same.

I went to the pub once with him to sit with him and his mates, and they are the most entertaining people in the world, just so funny. We were all on pints of Guinness, and the lads were talking about the *Titanic* and how it sank, whether it was the iceberg or the bad rivets that sank it.

Well ... I did something that I regret to this day. I told them all to calm down, I'd find out on my phone. My dad grabbed the phone off me, dropped it into a pint of Guinness.

I'll stop there, my eye is turning in as I speak. My dad didn't drop my phone into a pint of Guinness, he would never disrespect a pint like that, he just grabbed it off me, explaining that in this pub they have conversations, conversations that last for hours, and they leave the pub late that night not knowing if anyone was right or wrong, that is what conversations and arguments are all about, not popping out your phone after one minute and what could have been hours of chat, laughter and roaring ends up in a really annoying accent (Siri) telling you what it thinks is the right answer.

What my dad was about to say next proved to me that we should never bring out a phone to check a fact in a conversation or argument, because these drunken chats/arguments end up being gold.

I told my dad and his mates that when I was travelling home from Dubai on a plane one time, a very drunk Arab was causing a lot of trouble. He was sitting in other people's seats when they went to the loo and swearing at the air hostess, shouting at her to 'Get me another drink, woman!' He was a bollix.

My dad took a deep breath in, and all the lads leaned in as they knew Paddy Byrne was about to release some of his very expert knowledge. He held his pint in his hand and pointed with his index finger, he loved to hold his pint whenever he did this, in fact he'd never do this without a pint in his hand, I think he was literally talking through the drink.

> DAD (Paddy Byrne): You see, son, that Arab is a Muslim, and the reason he's drinking on a plane is because their religion prevents them from drinking on the ground, so as soon as a Muslim gets in the air, it's drinks trolleys are us (*doing plane motion with other hand*). You see, he's up in the air drinking and so, technically, he's not anywhere, so no rules if you're not anywhere, soon as you land … Bang! Muslim again.
>
> ALL THE REST OF THE MEN: Oh yeah Paddy, you're dead right there, totally right, very unusual people.
>
> DAD: I am right. Just the way we're not allowed eat meat on Friday, unless we're heading to Lanzarote, then it's burgers for all up there.

I reached for my phone automatically, but then thought, Bollix, I never want to know the real reason for that Arab drinking in the air. If my dad's not right, it's still brilliant.

DIY dad

When my dad approached a task or a day out, he would do it very slowly. Many a time we'd be in the car waiting for him, he'd get to the hall door, pause, then go back in for a poo. We'd be in the car for about half an hour before he'd come back out again.

So when he approached a DIY job, he would take it all very slowly. He said if he went too quickly at something, he'd have a heart attack. So, doctor's orders were to take his time, but they were actually his orders because he never went to the doctor. Now, he was to put in a new sink in for the Confirmation. The reason for this was because my mam wanted people to go upstairs, use the loo, then when they returned say, 'I'm loving the new sink, Eithne, very nice'. My mam: 'Oh that old thing, Paddy just plumbed it in for the Confirmation.'

My dad had done a lot of DIY around the house over the years. I would always try to help him, but he'd forget how weak and skinny I was. We had a back 'good room' and the front living room, with a wall separating the two. My dad knocked down that wall and rebuilt it so many times.

DiFFERENT PHASES OF LiViNG-ROOM WALL

1. Knocked down completely, all made open-plan.
2. Part of it put back in. Reason? It was a supporting wall.
3. All put back in, house too cold with wall down.
4. Middle taken out and French doors put in (neighbours came to see this very, very foreign idea, French doors then started to appear all over the estate).
5. French doors taken out, gap left. Reason? 'If I bang me tea tray off those poxy doors one more time, I'll rip them off the wall' (he did and he did). Wall put back in, still there to this day.

I watched my dad take that wall down the first time. I stood there with my huge glasses as he chipped away at the wall on his own with a mallet. The man was strong. He drank a bottle of Guinness as he belted the wall.

DAD: Bollix, shite, bastard wall, bollix, shite, bastard wall.

That's what he'd chant as he knocked it down.

He handed me a hammer and I chipped away at it too. I didn't need goggles as my dad said my glasses would stop the stone. We had a small rest and my dad gave me a taste of Guinness. Muck, it tasted like muck ... I wasn't to start drink properly until I was about 18, mainly because of that moment. Well done, Dad, method in your madness.

So my mam gathered us all into the kitchen, sat myself, brother and sisters down at the table.

MAM: Right, we better all stay here.
ME: Why?
MAM: Your father is putting in a new sink upstairs, best stay out of his way.

We then listened in silence to the hammering and banging upstairs.

BANG, BANG, BANG ...

DAD: (*from upstairs*) Ah for jaysus' sake!

BANG, BANG, WHOOSH ...

DAD: For jaysus' sake, there's a pipe behind this wall. Why didn't anyone warn me there was a pipe behind this wall!

The DIY went on for a few days, and we had to use the sink downstairs. Finally, after two weeks, the new sink was ready. My dad brought us all upstairs into the finished bathroom. There were a few holes covered up with plaster, but my dad said it just needed a lick of paint, he pointed at most of the bathroom and said, 'Lick of paint'.

But the huge surprise in there was the massive bathroom mirror, which covered a whole wall in the bathroom. My mother was very happy, she cried and hugged my Dad. Dad said he put a mirror on the wall so it made the bathroom twice as big.

NOTE: DO NOT PAY FOR AN EXTENSION ON HOUSE ... USE MIRRORS.

MAM: Jesus Christ, you're right, Paddy, the bathroom is huge. I love it, and the sink is only massive.

So she set up a show-off night. She invited her mates to the house for a drink on Saturday, then spent the whole time urging them to use the bathroom.

We sat on the couches, looking all neat, like this was the opening of a new store, shop or school.

> OLIVE: So you're making the Confirmation?
> ME: Yes I am.
> OLIVE: Your mam tells me you're getting a new eye for the Confirmation.
> MONICA: Ah that'll be nice, a new eye for the Confirmation. Kenneth got a new tooth for his.
> MAM: They'll all look beautiful on the day.
> MAM: Are you needing the loo, Olive?
> OLIVE: No I'm fine, Eithne.
> MAM: I'd say you've had a lot to drink there, Olive, I'd use the loo if I were you.
> OLIVE: No, I'm okay.
> MAM: Bernie? No? Betty? No? Monica? No? Will somebody just use the feckin' loo!

They all sat in silence for a few seconds.

> OLIVE: I ... eh ... I ... think I need to use the loo, Eithne, is that okay?
> MAM: (*in her posh voice*) It's at the top of the stairs, turn right and it's at the end of the hall, Olive.
> OLIVE: I know where your bathroom is, Eithne, I've been using it for ten years.

All the women cackled like witches. I love the way my mam also said 'end of the hall'. When you got to the top of our stairs, you only needed to turn right and take two steps and you'd be at the end of the hall. Gotta love that house. Olive went up, but she knew what my mam was after.

We all waited in silence. My mam listened as Olive walked up the stairs, she got to the top, took two steps to the right, the bathroom door opened anddddddddddddddddddddddd ...

> OLIVE: (*from the bathroom*) Holy Mary, Jesus and Joseph, is that a new mirror and sink in here, Eithne?
> MAM: (*from the kitchen, posh voice*) Oh that old thing, I nearly forgot, we had it installed for the Confirmation.

Installed? I love it. More like Dad spent ages swearing at the wall and sink and then it went in.

The other women then lost the plot, running out of the kitchen and up the stairs.

> BERNIE: Oh give us a look, Eithne.
> BETTY: I can't miss this.
> MONICA: I'd say it's massive.

I stayed downstairs. All we could hear from upstairs, was:

> BERNIE: Its massive, look at the mirror, it's massive and the sink is only massive too.
> BETTY: It will look great for the Confirmation.
> MONICA: I wouldn't leave this bathroom, it's so massive.

My mam was in MASSIVE heaven.

Eye op

Crumlin Children's Hospital was a scary place when you went in for an operation. It smelled weird, the floor was cold, the walls were horrible, but the nurses were nice. My mam took my clothes out of my bag and put them into my bedside locker. She got out my wash bag and left that there, too.

She was a bit teary-eyed as she was putting all the stuff away.

FRANK: I'll look after him.

The voice belonged to a young boy about my age, on crutches, wearing a bandana.

FRANK: How're yeh? I'm Frank.

I shook his hand and so did my mam. Frank then sat into his bed beside mine.

FRANK: Nothing to worry about in this place. I came in for an appendix op and they chopped me leg off.

He pulled his up PJs and he did have only one leg. I hadn't noticed.

I gasped.

FRANK: Only messin'.

My mam laughed nervously, kissed me and said she'd see me in the morning.

Frank was an amazing boy. He'd told me that he lost his leg through cancer and his hair had all fallen out from chemo, he said he didn't mind and that he just pretended to be a pirate.

He had a parrot, but his mum wouldn't let him have it on his shoulder, it was stuffed though.

I loved Frank. I wished I could have taken him home with me. We laughed the whole time I was there, we could have been great mates.

That night, my first night, we talked non-stop. The nurses kept coming in to tell us to stay quiet, then we'd pretend to be asleep, then we'd make stupid animal noises so the night nurse would rush back in to see what the fuss was all about, but we'd pretend to be asleep again, all the while giggling into our pillows.

The next morning I was to start a 24-hour fast, no water or food, so Frank kept sneaking out and getting me biscuits and water. The nurses let him go anywhere he wanted, he had been there for a long time. Finally we got caught, and we were locked into our room.

Then this little old woman with a bucket and mop came into our room, she was ancient. She unlocked our door and told us to get up onto our beds and not move while she mopped the floor. She looked like Yoda mopping the floor, she was so old and bent.

She looked at me.

> OLD LADY: What are you in for?
>
> ME: I'm getting my eye straightened.
>
> OLD LADY: I've seen that go wrong a few times, son, careful they don't pop your eye out and it flies across the room, hits the window and slides to the floor.

Bloody woman was nuts! I think she just worked there so she could hear all the nasty details and then scare people.

She looked up at Frank.

> OLD LADY: Well I can tell why you're here, the bald head gives it away, lose your leg to cancer, son?
>
> FRANK: (*in a pirate voice*) Arghhhhhhhh.
>
> OLD LADY: Well you're lucky, son. I work up on the really bad cancer floors, and I've seen boys up there with bags for stomachs, the cancer has eaten away at their stomachs and they've had to get Hoover-type bags put in instead.

She then mopped her way backwards out of the room. Me and Frank looked at each other and howled with laughter.

> FRANK: Hoover bags for stomachs, mad bitch.

We got up on our beds and pulled faces at the mad old cow as she walked away. She just kept on mopping into another room, dying to tell those poor kids something awful too.

★ ★ ★

DOCTOR: ... and counting to ten ...
ME: One, two, three ...

Darkness.

I woke up in my hospital bed, then immediately puked because Frank had been sneaking me water and food pre-op.

FRANK: Jaysus, here, I do the puking around here. How you feeling, man?
ME: Poxy.
FRANK: Well you look great, Jay, you look like you're just back from World War One.

Frank then started up one of his role-playing sketches.

FRANK: (*as a female nurse*) Oh my poor boy, let me rub your head with my boobies till you feel better, that's a bad war you were in there.

'Ahem!' The doctor appeared behind us, with my mam and dad close behind.

DOCTOR: Thank you, nurse Frank, that's enough of that.

Frank jumped up into his bed.

DAD (*To Frank*): How're yeh, son, just the one leg? (*pointing at his leg*)

MAM: (*belt*) Paddy!

DAD: What? He has one leg, just saying.

MAM: He knows he has one leg, yeh feckin eejit.

FRANK: Ah it's alright, I don't mind, Mrs B.

DAD: There you go, he doesn't mind. Cancer was it, son?

MAM: (*belt*) Paddy! He's a boy, not a man at a bus stop. His name is Frank.

FRANK: Well no, it's Eileen.

DAD: Eileen? Jaysus, each to their own.

Frank then stood up on his crutches.

FRANK: No, I lean ... (*Frank then leaned to one side*).

ME: Nice one, Frank, yeh dope, Dad.

DAD: Funny fecker, too. Fair play to yeh, son.

My mum then popped out some sandwiches, ham and cheese, yes!

She gave some to Frank, too. He was from the country and his mam and dad could only see him once a week because they had to work and look after their other children.

The doctor opened the dressing on my eye. It was an amazing op, one that would change my life, I think it was called strabismus surgery. Google it. GROSS!

DOCTOR: I'd say Jason here will be okay to go home tomorrow.

My mam and dad were delighted. I looked at Frank, his face had dropped and so had mine.

FRANK: One last sleepover then.

The adults and the doctor left, leaving me and Frank to our last night. We laughed all night as usual, upset everyone, even had one last visit from the miserable old mopping bitch, who told us the exact same stories again. So we teased her even more.

Frank took his full leg out of his PJs, sat on it, and screamed at the old woman to get a doctor that he had lost his other leg. She ran out to find at doctor, only to come back in with a doctor to find two young boys crying with laughter on a bed.

OLD LADY: You should have more respect for old people.

'You should have more respect for cancer patients, you old bat,' I screamed as the door closed and they couldn't hear us.

Packed the bags. Mam put everything into my suitcase. I had taken down Frank's home address. With no phones, it was the only way. He didn't even have a phone where he was from, Sligo it was.

Big hugs and then I left my one-legged pirate friend behind. He was the bravest kid I ever knew. Never moaned, never let people know he was scared, always made people laugh. I waved to him as he hobbled down the hall, stopping to talk to nurses, roaring at me to go.

I said I'd visit him, but in the '80s it was hard for a kid to visit his mate in hospital miles away from his house. I wrote to him, but never got a reply. To this day, I don't know what happened to him. Being a kid, I just thought he would get out of there, get rid of the cancer and become a full-time pirate.

But as a poxy adult, I'd say he was a very sick boy. But that's as far as I'll take it, and hope to see my pirate Frank friend some day, hobbling up to me for a hug and a pint.

I was in the house a few days later when the doorbell went. It was the lads coming in to see me, Brian Roche, Karl, Ken Newman and Tally. They had a present for me they said, then handed me a bunch of green stakes, stems from daffodils. I was totally confused.

> KARL: How's the eye? Good to see there's a patch over it, so it doesn't rat on us.
> ME: I never rat on yous.

The lads all laughed. They left after a while, and I looked at the empty stalks in the vases on the table. Then the penny dropped: the lads were the daffodil killers all along! But they were never going to tell me, especially with my eye wandering for all to see, but now, with the ratting eye covered, they knew it was safe to kind of tell me.

> DAD: (*holding up the stems*) What are these?

He walked close up to me.

ME: Don't know, Mam must have put them in there.

Oh my God, my eye did not go mental turning in, and I was actually lying. Had the doctor also cured me from being *unable to lie*?

God, Frank would have found that hilarious too.

CHAPTER 9
BITTEN
BY LOVE

My mam was in the kitchen, doing the dishes. Our sink faced the back garden, and at the end of the garden was a wall, and over that wall was THE FIELD. Not a field, but THE FIELD.

As my mam looked up from the dishes, she saw my brother Eric float up into the air on a bike, then disappear down behind the wall again.

MAM: (*to Dad in living room*) Paddy!

DAD: (*from living room*) What?

MAM: Eric is cycling in the air in the back field. He's just gone higher than the back wall!

DAD: Eric! Don't be cycling your bike in the air (*said from behind a newspaper, half listening to Mam*).

MUM: No, yeh eejit, he can't hear you, yeh … oh forget it.

Eric wasn't cycling his bike in the air. What was really happening was that my brother was being a hero, the hero of the road, he was RAMP JUMPING!

The bigger boys, as in Eric and his mates, had made a ramp out the back field, and this ramp was *huge*. It was made from lengths of plywood and a door. Yes, a door. My brother and his mate, Mick Dolan, had gone down to Mick's house and taken the wooden door that opened into the garage from the house. They'd actually unscrewed it off its hinges while Mick's dad was at work.

My brother cycled away from the ramp and circled round for a second jump. This time me and ten lads all lay down on the ground, to see if Eric could clear us. 'Eric Knievel', the road was calling him.

There must have been at least thirty people there watching. No one else would dare do this jump. I was so proud of my brother. We lay on the ground. Eric pelted towards the ramp at high speed, he hit it, and as I lay on the ground, I watched as he soared over the lot of us, like a bird.

BANG!

He hit the ground and rolled on, easily clearing all of us. The kids were all chanting his name, the girls were walking over to him with their new boobs almost on a plate.

I stood up from the ground, turned and bumped into Dirty Deirdre. She was some woman. She was at least two years older than me, so about Karl's age, but in ladies' age she was about 18.

DIRTY DEIRDRE: Your brother is amazing, and you're not so bad either.

Dirty Deirdre walked off, Karl came rushing over to me.

KARL: You should so try and get into her knickers, man, she is up for it.
ME: Yeah, I should.

Dirty Deirdre waved as she headed off. I had no idea how you got into a girl's knickers. I mean, it wasn't something I thought was ever going to happen.

Until this day. Karl brought his girlfriend down to *The Tunnel*. Now if you can remember, The Tunnel was the dried-out riverbed where you smoked, drank, lit fires and snogged girls. And who was with Karl's girlfriend, Gobnait? Only Dirty Deirdre! Oh my God, my heart was racing.

We said Hi, then Karl went further down into the tunnel with Gobnait, so I was left on my own with Dirty Deirdre. She stared at me, took the chewing gum out of her mouth, stuck it to the tree behind my head, said nothing and ...

Jesus, if getting your face raped is a term, then that's what happened to me. I was pushed back against the tree and before I knew it, a boa constrictor of a tongue was inside my mouth.

I had never French-kissed a girl before. It was the most exciting thing that had ever happened to me. Her tongue was twisting and lashing and poking, my trouser area was going mental, it hadn't even fully formed yet so it was like a tortoise's tail flapping about down there.

Every time she kissed me, she pressed herself against me, and that was even better. Man, was this getting into a girl's knickers? I wasn't sure, but I was loving it, my glasses all sideways and steamed up as Dirty Deirdre kept lashing and grinding away at me. I did nothing, she ground, kissed, moved arms up and down and, as far as I can remember, I stood still with my arms down by my side while she worked away. I loved it.

Karl arrived back looking all kissed out, young lady lipstick all over him. Dirty Deirdre leaned away from me, put her boa tongue back in its box, took the chewing gum off the tree, popped it in her mouth, rubbed my head, then said, 'See ya'. The two girls walked off. Karl looked at me and couldn't stop laughing.

KARL: Come on, loverboy.

ME: I sooooo want to do that again. I mean, I can still smell her, she smells like the summer, Karl.

KARL: Jaysus, you're some spa, man, come on.

Over the next few weeks I couldn't wait to get home. I was like a dog in heat. I ate my dinner real fast, no dessert, went out, played football until the girls arrived, then me and Karl went into the tunnel with our ladies. Snog for hours, ladies leave, but it was always only kissing and grinding. I don't know how I didn't set her on fire in the lap area, with friction.

Then one night Dirty Deirdre looked at me and said, 'Do you want to be my proper boyfriend?' I said yes, as I was two years younger than her and this was great. She then put her head into my neck for what I thought was an affectionate hug, but instead I felt pain as she bit my neck, then began to suck it like a vampire. She lifted her head.

DIRTY DEIRDRE: There (*looking at my neck*), you're mine now.

ME: What have you done?

KARL: Oh jaysus, man, look at the size of that love-bite.

ME: Love-bite? What's a love-bite?

KARL: That is.

Dirty Deirdre laughed as she headed off with Gobnait. On the way home, Karl brought me over to the wing mirror of one of the cars parked on the road.

KARL: Check your neck out, man.

Oh. My. God. It looked like Rocky had been practising his punches on my neck, it was so badly bruised. How was I going to hide this from my mam? She'd kill me. We went over to Karl's house and he gave me a lend of a polo-neck jumper. It was too big for me, but better than nothing. Karl's supper was ready, which meant so was mine.

Supper

This was a weird meal where I lived. This is normally how meals went in Dublin:

1. **Breakfast.**
2. **Small break in school.**
3. **Go home for ham-and-cheese toastie at lunchtime (or go to Karl's house, put on *Indiana Jones* and say the words of the movie as the actors spoke; Karl was able to do the German bits, too).**
4. **Dinner that evening.**
5. **Afters, or dessert.**
6. **Supper around 10.00pm (which was normally an auld sambo).**

I headed into the house with the polo-neck all rolled right up. I sat at the table beside my mam, brother and two sisters, dad at the top of the table, and we started to tuck into our sambos.

MAM: Where did you get that polo-neck?
ME: It's mine.
MAM: No it isn't.
ME: Yes it is.

My mum then leaned over to me to check the inside of the polo-neck, to see the make. When she did this, she saw my *love-bite*.

MAM: What ... is ... that ... !

ERIC: It's a love-bite.

MAM: I know 'what' it is, but what is it?

DAD: What?

ERIC: What?

MAM: Little brat, have you been rubbing your mickey off youngones!

ME: Mam!

MAM: Little bastard here, Paddy, and the Confirmation coming up and he's been rubbing his mickey off youngones. You've only got your eye fixed, if you break that eye before the Confirmation because you've been rubbing your mickey off some youngone, I'll brain yeh.

ME: I haven't.

MAM: I know you haven't, you're too young to be rubbing your mickey off youngones, but you've been trying to rub your mickey off something. Paddy, tell him.

DAD: (*face stuck in dinner*) Stop rubbing your mickey off youngones, son.

MAM: Oh that's great, well done, Paddy, if someone doesn't stop him now trying to rub his mickey off youngones, you and me will be grandparents soon.

DAD: Jesus, relax woman, for God's sake.

MAM: Relax? Relax? The boy is making his Confirmation and, by the way, son, Holy God can see you trying to rub your mickey off strange things.

ME: Mam!

MAM: Don't *mam* me, we're going to the priest in the morning after mass, to tell him what you've been up to.

DAD: Sure, what use is that?

MAM: What use is what?

DAD: Why bring him to the priest? He doesn't even use his mickey.

Then Dad just stood up from the table, laughing his head off, and I joined in with the laughter as did my brother, then my mum belted both of us across the head.

The next morning, we sat in the priests' room just at the back of the altar, waiting for him to finish up his gig. We heard the 'Go in peace', then the crowd saying 'Thanks be to God', or how a lot of Irish would have said it, 'Thanks be to Jaysus' (as in, thank God that's over).

The priest then entered the room and my mam stood up, as if the pope himself had just walked in. She held her hand out and did a weird bow.

MAM: Father.

PRIEST: Hello Eithne and Jason, good to see you, now sit down and tell me all about it.

MAM: Well, it's a very delicate situation, Father.

Oh my god, I was so embarrassed. I couldn't believe I was sitting here with this old fart and Mam was about to tell him about my Dirty Deirdre antics.

PRIEST: Yes.

MAM: Well, he's been messing about with girls, and when I say messing, Father, he has a mark of Satan on his neck.

Mum pulled my polo-neck down and showed him the love-bite.

PRIEST: That's quite a whopper there, Jason, now what have you been doing?

ME: (*red-faced, eye trying not to come out of my head*) Kissing.

MAM: And the rest. He's wore a hole in his zipper area, God forgive me for saying it in a church, Father, but the Confirmation is soon and God won't accept this, I know he won't.

Mam always believed she had a direct connection to God. She would always pray for us because she said God didn't listen to our half-arsed prayers, but her black-belt praying, now God always listened to that.

FATHER: Jason, do you know the story of Adam and Eve?

MAM: Of course he does, Father, I tell it to him every night.

(*lies*)

ME: Yes.

FATHER: Well, Eve is a temptress in that story. The devil gives her an apple and she makes Adam take a bite of it. (*Mam leaning in*) He doesn't want to at first, but she seduces him into taking a bite. Her lady tempting ways, which the

Devil controls, are too much for Adam (*Mam leaning in even more*) and he gives in and has a huge ... juicy ... bite ... out of the apple.

MAM: Whore! ... Sorry.

Silence in the room for a few seconds.

MAM: I beg your pardon, Father, please continue.

FATHER: You see, son, women are temptresses. They're controlled by the devil himself, and when they push against your body they give off a scent, a scent that men find very hard to resist, but you must resist, you must for God's sake and your Confirmation. When this woman is rubbing and rubbing off yeh, push her back and say NO!

MAM: Harlot! ... Sorry, father.

Silence ...

FATHER: Now go in peace, my son, and don't be at that kind of thing again.

Turns to my mam and kisses her on the lips instead of cheek.

FATHER: See you next Sunday, Eithne.

Well, at least he wasn't a kiddie-fiddler.

MAM: Of course, Father. Now out the door you, yeh little pup yeh!

ME: Okay, okay.

My mam whacked me out of the church and down the steps. She had cleansed me, shown me the' way, no more mickey carry-on for me. I was to stop for good ... Was I, bollix! That very night and for a good few months after I was at it again, no more love-bites, but lots of this ...

THE ORDER OF SNOGGING ANTICS, AS IN, FIRST TO LAST BASE

FIRST: Tongues, snogging, getting off, wearing the face off someone.

SECOND: Grinding, or dry riding, this done with all clothes on.

THIRD: Outside boob (basically squeezing a poor girl's boob through several layers of jumper, sweater, coat).

FOURTH: Inside boob (here, you had your hand on the actual boob).

FIFTH: Outside outside fanny.

SIXTH: Inside fanny.

SEVENTH: Well, it's a bit graphic, but we all know what I'm talking about here.

Normally this ended with lads running around shouting, 'Smell me finger, yeah!'

But never the willy in, though, it was all innocent enough. I wasn't to lose my virginity till I was 18, when I told the girl I had lost it the year before in Spain. She said she'd never believed me as she watched the expression on my face as it happened for the first time.

Wide-eyed

DAD: Everyone up, I've a surprise!

My dad roared up the stairs at us all. It was around midnight, he woke us all up, my two sisters, brother and my mam. She went mental. We all gathered in the hallway.

MAM: What in the name of God are you doing?
DAD: I've a surprise in the garden.

We all went outside into the garden, PJs on us all, Dad full of drink.

DAD: Ta-dah, a new car.
MAM: *(complete U-turn)* Oh lovely, we'll look great heading up to the church for the Confirmation in that, Paddy, well done.

My dad had gone and bought a new car. He never consulted my mam on this, he just went off, traded in his old car and got a new Ford Cortina, pale blue. People used to call them a solid IRA car.

Dad made us all get into it then and there, at midnight, and drove us all around the housing estate. We were all half asleep, but my mam was delighted now, hoping the neighbours were looking out the window at her new family car.

My dad said he'd had to celebrate when he got the car, so, as usual, he'd gone from the garage straight to the pub, to celebrate with the lads.

Eventually we got back into our driveway. All headed to bed. The next morning, we were all downstairs having our breakfast in various parts of the house. My dad then arose with his head banging. He walked into the kitchen and actually said ...

> DAD: I've a surprise for yeh all.
> MAM: We know already, Paddy.
> DAD: Ah, you looked out the window.
> MAM: No, you came home jarred last night, woke us all up and drove us around the estate in the new car, kids and all, at midnight.
> DAD: Did I?
> MAM: Jesus.

My mam left my dad in the kitchen, staring into his coffee as he tried to remember driving us around in the night. Mam then picked up her address book and said she'd be busy on the phone for a while and no one was to annoy her.

She put her mug of tea at on the telephone table in the hall and started with A. She rang everyone in that address book, started by saying hello and how are you, then went on to say, 'Oh, I almost forgot Betty, Paddy went and got a new car for the Confirmation. It's in the driveway right now.'

By the time she was finished, she'd made sure the whole road, even aunties and uncles, all knew we had a new Ford Cortina.

Every evening when my dad came home from work, my mam would make him drive her up to the shops, she didn't even need anything, and she made him drive really slowly along the road.

If she saw anyone walking along, she'd make Dad stop, then she'd roll down her window.

MAM: Hello Mrs Farrell, just heading up to the supermarket in our new car, we got it for the Confirmation.

She'd then roll up her window and order my dad to drive on. This went on for a couple of weeks, until the Murphys down the end of the road won a car on a quiz show.

I actually remember the name of the show, it was 'Mike Murphy's Micro Quiz-m'. Our Murphys won an amazing, brand new, top-of-the-range Ford estate car; my dad's car was second-hand.

Just to tease my mother, if she was in the garden talking to a neighbour, the Murphys would slow their car down as they passed by, to rub it in her face. Fair is fair, my mam did it to them. Mrs Murphy would lean out of the window, look at my mam and say:

MRS MURPHY: See you at the Confirmation, Mrs Byrne.
MAM: Oh of course, Mrs Murphy. (*said under breath*) Showy-off bitch.

Confirmation

This was a different ball game altogether from the Communion. First, we were going to collect *a lot* of money over the next couple of days because I was now 12, and we were seen as men and women of the Church, not children anymore. We were full members of the Holy God crew.

We didn't have to wear silly suits either, we all wore whatever cool clothes we wanted. But still styled by our mothers, of course.

The morning of the Confirmation was madness, with my mam running up and down the stairs, trying to iron clothes and deliver them to each child. She was also trying to make sure we were all fed, as it would be a long day and we had booked our lunch at a Chinese restaurant. I'm not sure why, but as far as I remember that was where most people were headed and the Chinese was going to put on a special deal for Confirmation-makers who had basically never eaten Chinese food before.

I sat downstairs watching the telly with my little sister, Eithne, who was around three or four. We were very close and I loved looking after her, she was the smallest little cute package.

A wildlife programme was on the telly, but I wasn't really minding it as I was busy reading *The Beano*. These ducks came on the telly and my little sister said ...

EITHNE: Look, Jason, ducks ... wank, wank ...

I burst out laughing. I couldn't believe what I'd heard. My mam then came in to tell us to hurry up and my sister again pointed at the telly …

> EITHNE: Look, Mammy, ducks … wank, wank …
> MAM: What?
> EITHNE: The ducks, Mammy, they say wank, wank…

My mother looked at me. I was in tears with laughter, so she started to belt me, blaming me immediately.

> ME: I didn't teach her that! She doesn't know what she's saying, she thinks that's the noise that ducks make.
> MAM: I don't care who taught her, you un-teach her now, she cannot leave this house, on this day, saying … whatever she's saying … (*another belt for me*) and you shouldn't know what it means.
> ERIC: (*walks into room*) What what means?
> EITHNE: Eric, look, ducks, wank, wank.

Eric doubled over with laughter and my mam started to belt him too, then me again, and all through this Eithne wouldn't stop saying it because she thought what she was saying was causing all this excitement. In fact, she walked around the room in circles like a duck, while my mother tried to catch her … and while me and my brother howled with laughter.

> EITHNE: Wank, wank, wank … wank, wank, wank.
> MAM: Stop it, oh Jesus on the day of the Confirmation too.

My dad then walked into the room.

> MAM: Paddy, make her stop.
> DAD: I've enough of me own troubles, woman.

My mam stopped chasing Eithne around the living room.

> MAM: What is it?
> DAD: You put the toothpaste beside the arse cream and I'm after shoving half of the toothpaste up me arse and onto me piles. It feels like I'm on fire up there. I can't wipe it off cause that's only pushing it in further.
> MAM: What are you talking about, you fool? That's the travel toothpaste, oh Jesus, I can't believe you've done this on the Confirmation day.

Now me and Eric were uncontrollable, what with Eithne walking around saying *wank, wank* and my dad walking like a duck too because he had toothpaste up his arse, this had to be the funniest day ever in our house.

My dad stood there, squirming, his bum on fire.

> DAD: Jesus, I might have to go to the hospital.
> MAM: What, and miss the Confirmation? You'll suffer with your burny hole, now get in the car the lot of ye.
> ERIC: At least your farts will smell fresh, Dad.

Smack across the head from Mam ... then one from Dad.

We all gathered up our stuff and headed out to the car. Eithne had stopped saying *wank, wank* at this stage, and the four of us – me, Eric, Eithne and Rachel – all sat in the back, with no seatbelts by the way. They were never needed in Catholic Ireland because the backs of the cars were so stuffed with kids, if the car had rolled, all the kids would have been wedged together and could have used each other as airbags.

So we're ready to go to the Confirmation, my dad still squirming in the front with his minty hole, my mam disgusted with us all. My dad turned the key in the ignition and nothing happened … he tried it again …

> MAM: What's happening?
> DAD: The poxy car won't start.
> MAM: What? It has to Paddy, it simply has to … it's the fecking Confirmation car!

My dad paid the taxi driver as my mam and all of us got out of the taxi right in the view of *everybody*. My mam was so embarrassed. Her new Ford Cortina wasn't working, and the taxi had nowhere else to stop except right in front of the church door.

As my mam walked away from the taxi, she was pointing at my dad and saying to the congregation.

> MAM: Paddy is having a drink today, thought we'd leave the car at home.

Of course everyone, including Mrs Murphy, knew that all the men on the road drank and drove, it was like bread and jam, just something they all did, and they knew the local cops personally so it was never a problem.

I stood outside the church for a bit with all my friends, people walking up to us telling us we all looked MASSIVE! The mammies were in huge competition as we were on show for them, to see who was best dressed. If they were let, they would have put us on leads and walked us around the church grounds like show dogs.

Those women spoke to each other all day, every day, but I'm sure not one of them liked each other. The minute one of the mothers left the company of the women, they'd all bitch about that woman. It got to the point where they wouldn't dare leave the circle

The circle of women: rules and ways

I've seen them talking on the road for hours together because each one of them was too afraid to leave. They knew they were going to be bitched about if they left.

They would all agree at the same time to split and leave the conversation. I've heard them do it. But they were always very careful how they did it. If one said, 'Right, it's getting late, we better all head in', the rest might choose to hang on there for a little bit so they could have a good bitch about the mammy who just left. So somehow, they all had to agree to leave together.

This is how they did it. They would (and I've seen this) all back away from each other like gun-slingers from the Wild West, talking as they were walking, then back into their driveways, go in the door, have a quick look back out to see if any of the woman snuck out to start bitching again. Once they were convinced that they were all staying put in their houses, their doors would all close together at the same time. Genius.

They all watched each other like hawks, the window blinds were their best friend. My mother spent most of her days peeping out those blinds at other neighbours and if you looked carefully, you'd see another break in a blind across the road, mammies staring at mammies, the mad old cows.

Just to prove it, one day my mam got a phone call from Betty across the road, Karl's mam. She rang to tell my mother there was someone at our door. Amazing. The doorbell was broken and some salesman was trying to ring the doorbell and Betty was having a blind-peeping session at the time, saw that he couldn't get an answer at the door and thought to herself, Ah, I'd better ring Eithne, she doesn't know there's a man at the door to annoy her.

QUICK IMPRESSION OF SALESMEN AND RELIGIOUS PEOPLE AT THE DOOR VERSUS MY MAM AND DAD

Salesman vs Mam

SALESMAN: Good afternoon, madam, I have a lovely set of hand-painted pictures of the countryside.

MAM: Oh, I see.

SALESMAN: Now I'll do five for 20 pound if you can hand it over right now.

MAM: Oh I'd love to.

SALESMAN: Great.

MAM: But I'd have to ask my husband.

SALESMAN: Well, ask him.

MAM: He's not here, so maybe I could hang on to the paintings and you could come back for the money?

SALESMAN: No, I really must go, Madam.

MAM: Give us one, yeh scabby bollix.

SALESMAN: No. Good day, madam.

And the salesman would pull the door closed on himself.

Salesman vs my Dad

DOORBELL: Ding Dong.

DAD OPENS DOOR.

SALESMAN: Good afternoon, sir.

DAD CLOSES DOOR.

Short and sweet.

Religious people vs my Mam

RELIGIOUS PERSON: Good day, madam, could I interest you in the ways of Allah?

MAM: You people make me sick, and he's called Holy God!

DOOR SLAMMED SHUT.

Religious people vs my Dad

RELIGIOUS PERSON: Good day, sir, we're Mormons.

DAD: Ah come in and meet the wife. I was just heading out to the pub, but the wife would love to hear all about it.

My dad would lead them into the sitting room, leg it to the pub, then Mam would come in from the back garden with a pile of washing in her arms to find a bunch of strangers sitting on her couch, waiting to convert her. It was my dad's favourite trick.

So anyway, back to the Confirmation day. We all bale into the church, all of us feeling very important indeed and thinking of all the money we were going to collect.

We had an archbishop of some importance there, and all the mammies were excited as he was the Bruce Lee of bishops, so they felt like they were getting a professional mass said, the full works.

In the mass we all had to promise not to drink till we were 18, it was called *taking the pledge*. We all laughed because Pledge was what your mam used to clean the wooden table at home.

So we all promised, in front of everyone and Holy God Jesus, never to drink until we were 18. It was too late for many, though, as we had all been altar boys we'd already drunk a lot of wine.

Next we queued up to get the blessing from the Bruce Lee bishop. We each had a sponsor standing beside us, and my mam went with me as my sponsor. I had picked Peter as my confirmation name. So that's what the archbishop was going to use.

Just as we got a few people back from the archbishop, Eithne ran up to us, so my mam picked her up and held her in her arms. I thought this was lovely because now I had two sponsors, and Eithne would be my cute little one.

We got to the Bruce Lee bishop, and my mam was bowing and kneeling and standing and genuflecting the whole time she was in his presence. He then asked me my Confirmation name. I said 'Peter' and he said in a gentle voice, 'Jason James Peter Byrne' ...

EITHNE: Look mammy, ducks … wank, wank!

The whole church looked towards the archbishop and us. Eithne had just seen a small duck-like symbol on the bishop's outfit, God knows what a it was doing there, but Eithne made sure everyone knew.

My mam grabbed the Confirmation candle off the archbishop, grabbed me by the hand, left me with my dad and then ran with Eithne in her arms out of the church, Eithne shouting *wank, wank* and pointing at the archbishop as she was carted off into the distance.

After the mass, we all headed home in the taxi again. Then I was then sent around the neighbours, just like the Communion, and collected fivers this time at each door. I was minted by 2.00pm, the whole lot of us were. That done, we all got into the Ford Cortina, which turned out to have a flat battery, so my dad got Bert, our neighbour, to give it a jump with the leads and it started up alright.

We headed off to the Chinese restaurant, I think it was called Lau's or Luu's. The six of us sat around the table, none of us had ever eaten Chinese food before, so this was scary.

My dad just kept throwing the wine into him. He was loving this place, as soon as his glass emptied, they'd refill it with wine. My dad then began to tell Chinaman jokes to the staff. They had barely any English, and my mam was telling my dad to stop, but he'd grab a passing staff member and say, 'They don't mind, do you? Do you? Everyone loves a Chinaman joke, for god's sake.' My dad would then continue to hold the waiter by the collar of his jacket and tell him a Chinaman joke. My dad would burst out laughing at the punchline and the Chinaman would head off, having no idea what my dad had said, so I suppose, in a way, the language barriers were a blessing because it meant no one got offended.

Then, the memory of all memories happened. The waiter came to take our orders.

> DAD: You want a FORKING knife, eh? Eh?
> MAM: Paddy, stop.
> DAD: Sorry, son, what would you recommend? We haven't a bog about Chinese food.
> WAITER: The duck is very good.
> EITHNE: Wank, wank, ducks say wank, wank.

I nearly died laughing. My dad, locked, looked at Eithne and said:

> DAD: Good idea, Eithne, we'll all have a wank, wank.
> MAM: Paddy!
> EITHNE: Wank, wank.
> DAD: Wank, wank.
> ERIC: Wank, wank.
> RACHEL: Wank, wank.
> ME: Wank, wank.
> DAD: So that's decided then, six wank, wanks, please.

I thought my dad was going to need an ambulance he was laughing so much. But to our surprise, the waiter brought back food that we all liked.

Wank, wank must have meant something in Chinese after all because we were all eating it and I don't know what wank, wank was ... but it tasted great.

That evening I counted all the money I had collected and thought to myself, in a beautiful, reflective way ... what should I do with my money? Give it to charity? Give it to a beggar? Give it to my parents? ... no way! I was buying Stretch Armstrong ... because ...

... 2,000 years ago, Jesus said to the apostles, 'Make your Confirmation, collect money off everyone and buy a Stretch Armstrong, because it has feck-all to do with me or my dad.'

IT'S WHAT JESUS WOULD HAVE WANTED. AMEN.

CHAPTER 10
SCHOOL, SPORT, SPARTANS

Communion made, check; Confirmation made, check; love-bite, check; inside, outside boob, check; eye not turning in as much, check ... Time to move on out of primary school and into ...

SECONDARY SCHOOL

1. Bigger school.
2. Bigger boys (hairy boys).
3. Bigger girls (bigger boobs).
4. Bigger classrooms.
5. Bigger schoolbags (heavy, would need to be carried home with strap around forehead and bag hung down behind on back).

This was to be a very scary time in my life. We'd heard that on your first day at secondary school the sixth-year lads grabbed you and flushed your head down the toilet, but not to worry, this was a totally normal part of growing up and joining the big league.

I had an advantage over a lot of kids in there as I already knew a lot of the older lads. It was a bit like a gangster-type head or a *howayeh!* going into Mountjoy prison, 'Ah how are yeh, boys? Storeee?'

Karl was already two years ahead of me, Tally was a year ahead of me, and me and Ken Newman were the same age, so we joined together. The big thing was, I had Eric in there as a sixth year; the boss of the school corridors was my brother.

First morning and my mam was shouting at Eric to walk me up to the school. Eric said, 'He knows where the poxy school is, Mam,' and walked out the door. So I left on my own, huge schoolbag weighing me down, droves of kids walking up the road. It looked like a migration of kids, there were all the primary school kids walking up the road, then mixed in with them was us, the secondary school kids. Hundreds of kids.

I walked to Ken Newman's house, a few doors up, and he walked with me. Then Tally came out, belted me over the head and joined us, then Karl came out, and we all walked up the road together. Now I was excited instead of scared.

I entered the school with the lads. Karl and Tally split, knowing which way to go, me and Ken looked for Room 113, which was our registration room. We all sat in there with kids I knew but mainly not, but these kids were to become good friends of mine, and we'd be in each other's faces for the next five years, or six if you were thick.

In those days we did five years at second-level, but if you were a bit of a window-licker, you had to do fourth year, too; the rest of us did third, skipped fourth and went straight to fifth year. Nowadays, most kids are forced to do fourth year, or transition year as it's called, not because they're window-lickers but because leaving school at 17 was crazy.

Miss Allen came into the classroom and told us she'd be our tutor and we'd have to report to her every morning. She told us that as we were first years and her name was Ruth Allen, we would be called 1RA. Have a look at that again, 1RA, so at 12, 13 years of age we were in 1RA, or the IRA as we called ourselves. I mean, it was the funniest thing ever to be in that class. Kids would ask us what class we were in and we would stand up and say, 'the IRA'. My mother was furious.

Now we left Miss Allen and headed off to our different teachers, so exciting. In primary we stayed in the same classroom all day, but now we'd move from room to room after each class, for different subjects.

Subjects

ENGLISH, IRISH, MATHS, RELIGION (I know, best class too, it went on for two forty-minute periods), GEOGRAPHY, HISTORY, SCIENCE, FRENCH, METALWORK.

So exciting, these classes, and so different from primary school. Mad teachers teaching us, too.

English
Mr Burke

SKILLS ... calling people by their surname all the time. He taught like he was a proper English master in Cambridge, in fact I'm sure that would have been his dream, not teaching us fools. So we went into his class, we took out a book and read from the book aloud.

Even though I had my big glasses, a very tall frame and I looked shy, I loved it when Mr Burke asked me to read. In fact, I became his main reader in the class, although he didn't have much to choose from: there was either those mice-type children who read so quietly, it looked like they were just gently blowing on the book; then there were the really rough kids, who only a street merchant could understand; then there was, worst of all – and the teacher only picked this kid out once and never was he to read again – the stuttering child, God help him. It took him forever to get along the lines, but I would throw my hand up in the air and say, 'Please sir, can I have a go?', releasing everyone from high embarrassment.

Mr Burke had a harmonica and sometimes as I read, he would play it softly in the background. We couldn't resist throwing coins at him as he played, and he thought this was amusing, until Andrew Fitzgerald lamped a fifty-pence piece between his eyes and he had to go to the school nurse for stitches.

Irish/History
Mr Flanagan

SKILLS ... owned a moustache.

Loved this guy, he was cool, he had a moustache and would twirl it as he taught us. He was a damn good Irish teacher, and great at history. We never messed with this man, not sure why, we almost destroyed the rest of them.

Maths

Sister Brigid

Holy jaysus pants, what a five-year battle I had with this poor woman. A nun for a maths teacher, I couldn't resist messing so much in this class that me and Ken Newman had our own special table at the top of the room. It ran sideways to Sister B's table so she could keep an eye on us.

Well, keep an eye on me. Ken never did anything, I just got him into trouble all the time. I would cry with laughter because of the stuff that happened.

For example, I would pinch Ken under the table, he'd jump, causing the table to hop, and I'd say, 'Miss, it was Ken.' Ken would then get thrown out of class, poor Ken. We once changed the whole classroom around when Sister B went out to the loo or something, got all the tables and chairs and turned the whole room around, back to front.

When she came back in, she wasn't sure what had happened. She actually walked to the wrong end of the room, stood at her desk, then realised that the small window that normally faced her was now behind her.

Her face started to go red, she looked out at the class, and I pointed at Ken Newman and shouted, 'Ken did it!' Out he went, yet again.

Obviously she was a very religious woman, what with being a nun and all, so we would pray before the start of class and then again at the end. Now this is years before *Father Ted*, but I would call myself Father Byrne, call Ken Father Newman, and all the girls in the class were Sister so-and-so.

I even went as far as to get a wooden crucifix from my brother, who was in the church choir (never knew why, must have been a lady-chasing thing), and I would hang that around my neck. That wooden crucifix was about a foot long, and I would hold it as we prayed in the morning before maths.

Sister B couldn't tell me to take it off, I mean, how could she? It was a holy Catholic crucifix, so it would go against her beliefs to tell 'Father Byrne' to remove the cross. She knew full well what I was doing though, the little shiiiitt that I was!

Religion
Sr Theresa

SKILLS ... just trying to be young and cope with little bastard children.

This had to be my favourite class: it was easy, we spoke about God in a casual way, and Sr Theresa was lovely so we didn't really give her any hassle either. The only big memory I have of this poor woman was when she had to teach us sex education. Can you imagine? Us little shits, and the minute she said, in a very nervous voice, 'Right, children, today we'll be doing sex education', all the boys in the class yelled, 'Wey-hey-heeeeeeey'. All the girls, ever sensible, told us to shut up.

Why was it the job of a nun in a school to tell you about sex? Surely that was the parents' job.

In fact, I remember both of my sex talks with my parents. My dad walked into the kitchen, sat me down at the table and said:

> DAD: (*red face*) So, son, you know the ...
> ME: Ah jaysus, Dad!
> DAD: Fair play to yeh.

He then leaves the room, passing my mother in a hurry.

> DAD: (*to mother*) That's that all done then, he's fine. I'm off for a jar.

MOTHER FURIOUS.

> MAM: What?

Dad leaves, Mam takes his place, while holding her rosary beads.

> MAM: (*to me*) You know, son, when a lady and a man ...
> ME: Ah jaysus, Ma, not you as well, gross ...

MAM STANDS UP QUICKLY.

> MAM: Good man, glad we sorted that then.

I leave, not having a clue what it's all about. I only ever got road sex talk.

Once, Karl found a porn mag in a hedge. I don't know what it was about the '80s, but there were always porn mags in hedges. When I was a kid we didn't have dirty men hiding in the hedges, just dirty mags.

Karl took out his favourite pages first, then passed it around to us all in the field. My first girlfriend was a half-dressed lady in a field of sunflowers, I think I actually fell in love with her too. It was so innocent, as I wouldn't have had a clue how to take full advantage of said lady in the sunflowers – I probably didn't have the equipment either at the time.

She lived in my drawer in my bedroom, until one day I walked in and my mam had 'Helen' in her hands. Yes, I named her. My mother was furious, she actually said, 'I didn't think you were like that, Jason Byrne' ... Like what? Straight? Oh my god, what shame have I brought on the family, mother? She took the picture away, said she was going to the priest with it.

I was so scared, but of course in later life I thought it was hilarious to go to the priest with a picture of a naked lady. I'm sure he was disgusted at the door, in front of my mam, but I'm also sure that door was shut well quickly and he brought it into the study to check out in detail just how disgusting it was ('Ohhhhh, dirty lady in the field, thank you, Mrs Byrne').

So after loads of sniggering, red faces and a mortified nun, she got to nearly the end of the sex education talk. She had to ask this to round it all off: 'So, any questions, children?' More sniggering. She looked around at the class, no one had their hand up. 'Good, so …' 'Miss?' It came from the back of the room. Richard Howard had his hand up. Oh Jesus, not dopey Howard, the poor woman, what was he going to ask her?

This is word-for-word by the way.

> RICHARD: Miss, what if, when you're doing sex and you want to wee but also ejaculate at the same time, which will come out first?

The class exploded (excuse the pun). I thought Sr Theresa was going to die there and then. But the bell went, and we ran out of the class. As I passed her I heard her say, 'Thank you, Lord', as her eyes raised up to the ceiling, the source of her salvation.

Science
Mr Henning

SKILLS … Reading his newspaper as we copied text from our books into our copybooks.

We had to dissect stuff in his class, which was the best part. This teacher was on the way to a nervous breakdown, courtesy of us. In the science room, there were gas taps at each bench, which, when you turned them, made a small hissing noise.

Every time he turned to the blackboard, we would turn the gas taps at different times. As he spun around to us, we would stop really quickly. There is no competition between a 40-year-old man and a room full of quick teenagers. This drove him mad, as he could never catch us. I'm sure a twitch started to form around his facial area as the months went on.

I was called up in his class once, told to get the pheasant from the freezer for dissecting. So I brought back in a frozen pheasant and slammed it down on the table.

BANG!

One of the lads, Fitz, was sent to the metalwork room to get a hacksaw. When he came back, two kids held either end of this big bird and I was instructed to start hacksawing into the middle of the thing. As I was doing this, Mr Henning retched and spluttered as he tried to explain to the class where I was cutting into. For a science teacher, Mr Henning had an unusually queasy stomach, which we all knew and took advantage of as often as possible.

As I cut in, bits started to fall out all over the place. We started to pull out all its organs. Mr Henning was trying to stop us. At one stage I had its heart in my hand, just to torture Mr Henning. It was like *Lord of the Flies* in there, Mr Henning snapped and ran out of the classroom, never to return. The principal came in after about twenty minutes and we all got detention forever basically.

Mr Henning was replaced by a very stern man, Mr Barton. Even though he was in his seventies or eighties, we were afraid of this guy. He'd make us do horrible stuff to shut us up, which was karma for what we put Mr Henning through. He once brought in a load of lambs' lungs, put us into pairs and made us breathe down the windpipe and into the lungs to inflate them. Jesus, now that shut us up.

Metalwork

Mr Greasley

SKILLS ... being great at his job and taking no shit.

First day in his class, he made us all line up at our benches, then he walked around the metalwork room telling us how dangerous this room was, that we could lose an arm or a hand in the lathe, or drill through our hands with the drill, or burn our faces off at the forge.

As he was explaining this very dangerous environment, and to be fair it was very dangerous, Keith Higgins and Jason Keating were laughing together. He walked over, stood right in their faces and said, 'Something funny there, boys?'

Nobody said anything in that class ever again. *Ever*. Mr Greasley had respect from us.

Now, I was rubbish at metalwork. I'd say I was Mr Greasley's worst student. It was all down to my special eye, even with the op it would still have a little wander now and again. It loved to have a wander when I was trying to measure stuff or cut stuff. As a result, my stuff was always crooked and inches smaller than the other guys' stuff. Sometimes the right shape, but never the right size.

I would do everything opposite to what Mr Greasley told us. I didn't mean to, but I just did, probably because I was so nervous around all the equipment. He said to us, 'When you open the forge door, never look directly into the forge.' What did I do? Cut to: me at the school nurse's office, eyebrows gone and front of hair smouldering. I was that man's nightmare for five years.

Geography
Miss Turner

SKILLS ... had a chin you could rest a cup of tea on.

Main memory: using crayons to colour in maps. Stuck a fat crayon up each nose to pretend to be a monster, nose sucked crayons up too far. Cut to: nurse's office, her with pins stuck into the crayons, trying to pull them back down out of my nostrils.

French
Miss Holland

SKILLS ... repeating things loads, being terrified of kids, fear of public speaking, basically the skills of a person who shouldn't teach.

We studied French in the French lab, which had earphones with a mic attached at each table. What were they thinking? We would wear them to hear French tapes, and the mic was to repeat it back to the teacher.

We discovered fairly quickly that if you held the mic against the ear-piece and turned it up, it fed back. Well, it wasn't long before that French lab was beeping like a thousand metal-detectors on a beach all coming up with gold.

We drove poor Miss Holland out of the school. The French lab was stripped of its headphones, so then we had to listen to everything on a shitty tape-recorder. But it served us right, little shits!

Even though I honed my skills as a little bollix with the teachers, I became very popular in school with the students. It was a mixed school, so I mainly concentrated on the girls. I still looked weird: tall, thin, red hair, pudding-bowl haircut, huge glasses, you could see me blink from a mile away.

I had different names in school. Byrner, Redzer, Fanta Pants (due to my red pubes, which I didn't have yet) and Nessles: a little bully prick called me this because he said I looked like the Milky Bar kid. I'd tell him I didn't, and it was pronounced Nestlé anyway, yeh dick, whereupon he would simply beat the shite out of me.

I got to know the bullies, and the people being bullied. I ended up being like the UN in my school. Kofi Annan Byrne. Even though I looked like a nerd, I was always good with my mouth, so I was able to talk my way out of almost any situation, and I used humour to good effect.

Teachers never punished me, how could you? They were laughing as they gave out to me when I was bold.

Now that's a sentence that only Irish people will understand.

IRISH LINGO (SLANG)

1. **Give out** (trying to discipline someone, or scold if you're posh).
2. **Bold** (not brave, it means misbehaving).
3. **Amn't I?** (as in, 'I'm in the team, amn't I?').
4. **Gee** (with a hard 'g'; not a ju-jitsu suit, an Indian butter or an excited noise that Americans make, no ... it's a vagina).
5. **Pox bottle** (not a nice person).
6. **Gerrup ou'ha tha'** (I don't believe you, go away, you're having me on, etc.).
7. **Nil all** (0-0, in sports).
8. **Out of your box, out of your tree, out of your trolley** (if you're out of anything, it means you're probably drunk).
9. **Off your box, off your tree, off your trolley** (if you're off something, then you're also drunk. I think if you're Out, Off, or even On something, you're drunk, or high).
10. **Knock de bollix out of yeh** (not a vasectomy, but translates as 'I'm going to beat you up').

PE (Physical Education)

Pat McQuaid

SKILLS ... went on to be the president of the cycling federation while Lance Armstrong was there ('WHAT?!' I know).

Other main skills Pat had: too busy with cycling.

This was the subject where most of my mishaps happened, if you know what I mean. I tried every sport, here's a quick list.

SPORTS JASON ATTEMPTED

1. Running
2. Tennis
3. Badminton
4. Basketball
5. Soccer
6. Hurling
7. Gaelic football
8. Bowling
9. American football
10. Table tennis

I injured myself in nearly every sport I played. I was now a teenager, you only had to look at me and I'd fall down. I also had my funny 'fixed' eye to compete with, too. I was growing so fast, but only up, not out as well, so it was like trying to live in a tall, skinny tree on stilts.

I was driving my mam and dad mad at home, too, knocking over this and smashing that, all by accident. If you've ever seen the movie *Avatar*, when he gets into his new body and starts to run around, knocking over stuff and getting too excited, that's exactly what it's like to be a gangly teenager.

I was now in a more powerful body, well, in my case a longer body. Mad things were starting to happen downstairs, too. One day I had a willy that looked like a baby albino slug ... actually, a blind baby albino slug; the next day, and I'm not sure who put it there, but I had a proper mickey, a *man's mickey*.

While I was sleeping, Holy God or someone must have snuck into my room, unscrewed the tiny slug thing and replaced it with a mickey. Man, was I excited, but I wouldn't leave it alone, it was like a new toy. I couldn't wait to have a shower after PE in school.

When I did, one of the lads pointed and shouted, 'Look, Jason's got a new mickey.' Oh yeah! I towelled myself slower that day. Finally, I was able to change beside Con Ryan, the silverback of our class, he had hair everywhere and could use his mickey as a scarf. I'm sure he was 48 years of age, he even had stubble, for Christ's sake, something I wasn't to get until I was 25!

Of course, with my New Mickey came the *faster powers*. I joined everything in school, but as I say, I managed to injure myself in every one. I was just too excited when I played and I always wanted to win, but didn't always have the skill, therefore injured myself trying to get there.

If this book was a movie, we'd show a montage of injuries. But this book is a book, so I'll take you through them and you can use your lovely heads to work out what it might have looked like.

Basketball

One day while playing basketball – now remember, there were no sports glasses back then, the fancy ones that strap around your head. No, if you were a kid in the '80s playing sport, you had to wear your stupid big normal glasses, and keep pushing them up your nose while you tried to see through the steam-blind lenses.

So anyway, I was bouncing the basketball, doing pretty well as I was using my legs to keep bodies away from me, then in an instant my glasses fell to the floor. I missed the basketball as it headed towards my hand, it went past my hand and towards my nose.

BANG!

I was out cold for around a minute. I woke up and didn't know where I was. Got home and my mam freaked out, not because she was worried about her son being unconscious but because the ball had knocked my eye into the side again. I didn't even notice until my mam roared, 'Your wonky eye is back!'

It only lasted the day, but she banned me from playing basketball ever again. The lads called me 'The Eye of Jordan' for a while.

Table tennis

The next sport I got injured doing was table tennis. I know, I know, who in the name of God gets injured in table tennis? JASON BYRNE does, that's who!

This is a pretty quick one. Tony Mitten, no one would play with him, he was all a bit broken as we'd say, he threw the ping-pong ball up in the air to serve it, swung the bat as hard as he could, let go of bat, bat flies right across the table, over the net and smacks into my head. New black eye. Mam went mental again, eye didn't stay in this time, but girls were kinda digging my black eye. The lads called me 'Ping-pong Owww' for a while.

Hurling

Got knocked out by a *sliotar* to the head. We didn't wear helmets then, flat caps were still the thing. Of course, no flat cap is going to stop a ball the strength of a cricket ball when it bounces off your head. The lads called me 'Dent Head' for a while.

Tennis

Attempted to jump over net to celebrate win, basically ran straight into net, got caught in it, fell, busted my forehead, I think both my eyes went in that day. The lads called me 'Fish Boy' for a while (because of the *net*, yeh dope!).

Soccer

Went up to head a ball near the post, headed the post instead, knocked out again, busted ear. The lads called me 'Ear and In' for a while.

Gaelic football

Got attacked by two seagulls while waiting to go onto pitch. I was eating a sly sandwich, the seagulls attacked me for it, had several beak marks on face for a few weeks. The lads called me 'Bread Head' for a while.

American football

Couldn't afford padding, none of us could, need I say more? We didn't call each other anything after this, we only played it once, against a team from America who had all the gear.

Badminton

Slow and funny, this is another eye injury story. I pointed at the shuttlecock as it came towards me from the sky, didn't get timing right, it landed right in the middle of the lens of my glasses, cracked the glass, glass in eye, hospital. The lads called me 'Shuttle *Cock*-eye' for a while.

Bowling

As in ten-pin bowling, picked up the ball, put my fingers in the tight little holes, went up to lane, threw out arm, ball didn't leave fingers, broke two fingers. The lads called me 'Let Go' for a while.

The other club I couldn't wait to get into was THE SPARTANS. This was run by Father Olley. He was one of those very trendy priests, the type who would wear all the gear and the collar, but his shirt would be short-sleeved, oh yeah! We loved this guy.

The Spartans did cool shit, like camping, climbing, skiing holidays, cycle days, but you couldn't go if you weren't a Spartan.

You had to check your name each week on the noticeboard in school to see if you were in. Places were tight, so you could only get in if someone left and you took their slot. It was that tight, that elite, that desirable. So, I'm leaning against the noticeboard one day in school, sick of checking the list at this stage, then just as the bell goes to head to class, I turn, look at the list and see my name on it.

Holy Shit! I was in the Spartans!

I legged it home that evening, told my mam, and she tried to be excited for me but she didn't know what it was and was too busy with my sister, who had nearly died at the weekend.

OH YEAHHHHHHHH, I FORGOT …

Eithne had died at the weekend, but she didn't, but we thought she had, but she didn't. She was out the back garden, playing on the swing, when she fell off it backwards, banged her head, and fell unconscious. I saw all this happen from the kitchen window and shouted to my mam.

Now, First Aid was not a strength among people in the '80s. Today, it's part of 'one's skillset' no less, but back then, it was wing and a prayer stuff. So instead of walking out to my sister, picking her up, putting her into a recovery position and calmly talking her back around, my mother thought it best to do this:

MAM: Eithne! Eithne! Wake up! (*this screamed while shaking Eithne like a ragdoll*)

Then Joan Priestly, next-door neighbour, opened her back door to see what all the commotion was about.

JOAN: What is it, Eithne?
MAM: Little Eithne is out cold.

Joan ran into our garden and now my mam and Joan were both shaking Eithne. It was like a scene from the movie *Airplane!*

I went inside to dial 999 and call the ambulance, which arrived very quickly. The ambulance men prised Eithne away from my shaky mam and shaky Joan. Mam and Joan then got into the ambulance with a limp Eithne (no breadman this time), and off they went, screaming and trying their best to shake her awake.

The ambulance pulled away, and I was left alone. I remember looking out the window, thinking, My God, she's dead. My immediate next thought was: maybe Mam will let us have a dog again now. Yes, the insane logic of a child, people.

About half an hour later my dad pulled into the driveway, coming home from work. This was going to be good. Remember, no mobile phones for communication, so my dad had absolutely no idea. He came in the door, asked where everyone was, I told him what had happened to Eithne and that she had been taken away in an ambulance. My dad calmly said ...

DAD: What? What? What happened? Where is she? Jesus, is she alive?

He grabbed his car keys and ran out the door, got back into his car, and sped off to my little sister's rescue. Except I didn't know what hospital she'd gone to, and so neither did my dad. He just drove off as fast as he could towards no one and nowhere, in a total panic. You could hear him beeping people out of his way as he went to find his daughter in the many hospitals across Dublin.

Again, I was left alone looking out the window, wondering if maybe Dad would bring home burgers and chips to calm me down if my sister died.

Eric, Rachel and I sat in the sitting room, waiting. A taxi pulled up outside, it was around 9.00pm at this stage, and my mam got out, looking exhausted. Then Joan got out. Then my sister jumped out and ran towards the door. Damn, no puppy for defo now, she looked fine.

She was fine too, it was a simple knock on the head, and luckily for her she sustained no further damage from the First Aid administered by my mother and Joan. My mam flopped onto the couch. Eithne sat on my lap, not a thing wrong with her.

MAM: Where's your father?
ME: Not sure, he headed off to find you.
MAM: Gobshite.

Then the headlights lit up the driveway, and a few seconds later my dad burst in the front door, then burst in the sitting-room door.

DAD: Jaysus Christ, where were you? I looked in every hospital in Dublin.

MAM: And in a pub too, by the smell of yeh.

DAD: I didn't have any dinner. I had to stop into a pub on the way to get a basket of chips, woman.

MAM: Well there she is, not a bother on her.

DAD: Thank jaysus for that.

Dad sat heavily into a chair at the dining table, looking way worse than Eithne ever had. He looked up at us all.

DAD: Chips and burgers?

ME: Yes!

MAM: I thought you had that already in the pub?

DAD: You know I hate eating when I'm drinking ... (*stops talking as he hears himself*)

I ran out to get the chips and burgers. What a result, and Eithne wasn't even dead.

The Spartans

I got into my tracksuit and headed up to the school hall. Club started at 7.00pm, and I was *so excited* as I knew I'd be given a special outfit with SPARTAN written on the back of the sweatshirt.

I walked into the hall where my fellow Spartans were all warming up. I felt great, saying hello to guys I knew, also to some Spartans I didn't yet know. Father Olley walked towards me, obviously to welcome me into the elite club that was the Spartans. He put his hand on my shoulder and asked me what I was doing there.

My jaw dropped. People gathered to hear what was going on, my eye started to turn in, my face started to turn red.

> ME: I was on the list, sir.
> FATHER OLLEY: List? No you're not.

He then brought me out to the school hall noticeboard, where the lists were also posted. He pointed at my name in the reserves. I was *next* in, but he had no idea when that would happen.

I turned on my heel and left, to sniggers, and I cried all the way home. I was devastated. When I got in, my dad was in the living room, watching the telly while reading the paper. He never really noticed if we were upset as kids, but my eyes were all puffed and my face red from crying.

> DAD: What's wrong with yeh?

I tried to tell him without crying, but I did that crying and talking at the same time thing that's really hard to understand.

> ME: (*crying*) I went up ... (*breath, sniffle, cry*) ... went up, to join the Spartans (*sniffle, whimper*) ... and, and, and (*breath*) Father Olley said I wasn't in the club ... (*cry, cry, sniffle breath*) ... and I

was only on the reserves ... (*breath, breath, breath*).

DAD: Right, come on. Priest wanker.

My dad popped me into the car and we drove up to the school hall. Oh shit, what had I done? What was my dad going to do?

We marched into the hall, my dad walked through everyone, didn't give a shite. He went right up to Father Olley, who was standing watching kids climb ropes.

DAD: Here, you!

ME: (*to myself*) Oh no.

FATHER OLLEY: Yes, sir?

DAD: I'm this kid's dad, and he tells me you said he isn't in this club of yours.

FATHER OLLEY: Yes, there's a strict policy here, sir, there's not enough room, so he's on the reserves.

DAD: Listen, Father, unless you want that white collar shoved up your arse, he's in tonight, okay?

Father Olley was terrified, even though he was a trendy priest, he was no match for my auld fella. He conceded and let me in, then my dad rubbed me on the head, took out a ten pound note and shoved it in the priest's pocket.

FATHER OLLEY: Oh sorry, Mr Byrne, I don't take money.

DAD: Well give it to your boyfriend God instead. Later, son.

I was now a Spartan, and I was so proud of Dad, even if he was the maddest bollix ever. There should be a T-shirt with 'Give it to your boyfriend God instead' written on it. My dad paused at the door, lit a fag under the 'no smoking' sign and left like a hero from a Western, except he had no hat, just a good head of hair.

CHAPTER 11
YOU CAN'T KEEP A GOOD BYRNE DOWN

Parp!

> DAD: You can keep the change.
>
> MAM: Paddy, Jesus Christ those Guinness farts are too much, open the window, Jason.

I opened the window in the kitchen while my dad cried with laughter at his farting antics. He always laughed at this, but he also made the rest of us laugh with the way he would process his farts.

His favourite was to lean to the side – this was the warning move, your only chance to take evasive action – fart, then for some reason he'd say, *(parp)* 'You can keep the change' straight after. I loved that saying, or *(parp)* 'Take it outta that' or *(parp)* 'That's for yourself'.

Another favourite of his, at the dinner table, was to fart and then kick the dog under the table. 'Filthy dog, and in the middle of the dinner, too.' But there was never a dog under there, and if there had been, he would have dropped dead of gas poisoning.

Dad always made us laugh, he had a great dry wit and amazing comic timing. I was up in the house recently, visiting the two of them. My mam was pointing out my first wellingtons to me, they were tiny. She put these tiny boots with a blue ribbon around them onto the palm of my hand.

MAM: They're your first ever boots.

And in perfect timing, like it was rehearsed, my dad passed us in the background.

DAD: They're off a bleedin doll.

And he continued walking, leaving Mam furious.

Apparently, Mam had in fact got the boots off a doll, put a blue ribbon around them and then told me they were my first boots. It's what mothers did then, and now, because it's their job to make their kids feel special and she always did that. Unfortunately, it's the job of a dad to ruin everything.

DING DONG ...

DAD: Doorbell!

He always did this when a noise went off in the house. If the phone rang, he'd shout 'PHONE! PHONE!' and let it ring for ages, then he'd finally go and answer it. As he walked towards it he'd shout, 'Right, I'll get it meself, but I don't know why I'm bothering, it's never for me!'

He'd then pick up the phone and say, 'Hello, 980345, Paddy Byrne speaking', just like a secretary in WWII working for Winston Churchill. My dad would say, 'Yes?', then hang up after a few minutes.

I'd lean over the stairs, or one of my two sisters would, asking who it was. He'd tell us he didn't know, they never said.

My dad's pet hate was not introducing yourself when you were on the phone. He'd say, 'Hello, this is Paddy Byrne', but on the other end there'd be a young voice saying, 'Is Jason there?' because you didn't say your name on the other end. My dad would just hang up.

> DAD: The height of bad manners there again. Children, tell your friends to tell me who they are. I like to know who I'm talking to!

The phone in our house, and in many '80s households, was a very stressful thing to have to look at each evening. It was the biggest bill in the house, and that stressed my dad out no end.

He put a tiny padlock on the phone once, so only he and my

mother could open it to dial out. If we wanted to make a call, we had to ask permission for the key.

Thank God we never needed to use the phone in an emergency during the padlock days. If there had been a fire or a break-in, we would have all died or been battered to death. I once asked my dad what we should do if there was a fire and we needed to ring the fire brigade. 'Open the window and shout out of it,' my dad said, laughing to himself.

The big house phone was so different then, nothing like the sleek phones of today. It took half an hour to turn the dial and, young people reading this, we had to put our finger in the gap with the number we wanted, then turn the dial all the way clockwise, wait till it came back to the start, then choose our second number in the sequence. The house would have burnt down while you were trying to dial 999 anyway.

My mam entered a competition on some radio show, and the DJ was about to ring the winner and he said that if the winner wasn't in when he rang them, then they wouldn't win. And that's exactly what happened. The phone rang on the radio show, and at the same moment our house phone started ringing.

Mam went running around, desperately looking for the padlock key.

> DJ: It looks like a southside number, but they mustn't be in.
> MAM: They're ringing us, they're ringing us! Where's the bloody key to the phone?

DJ: Well they're not in, so they can't win.

MAM: We are fecking in, I can't find the fecking key!

The phone rang out, and my mam didn't win the cash prize. From then on, she hid the padlock key under the seat of the phone table, a hiding-place we all knew about, all but Dad. My God did he freak out when the bill came. We had all been using it on the sly.

DAD: We're going to need another bloody mortgage with this phone bill, yeh bloody bastards!

My dad then began to read out the numbers on the bill ...

DAD: Who's 980766?

ME: Karl.

DAD: He lives across the road! Use your legs to ask him a question.

Dad then rattled off a lot of numbers, they were all my mam's calls.

DAD: This is bloody women all on the street, woman. For Christ's sake, shout over the wall to them. Right, from now on we DON'T LET THE FINGERS DO THE WALK-ING, you let your *bleedin' legs do it*!

I came in the door one day and saw my Dad with his arms behind his back, walking up and down the hallway, shouting to himself. He waved me into the kitchen as he kept roaring into the air, like he was dictating a very important letter to his secretary, which he didn't have.

Mam was making the dinner. 'Who's Dad talking to?' Mam said he was using his new hands-free system. 'He's talking to his mate, Pat, and showing off at the same time.' I had another look out into the hall. The phone receiver was resting on some sort of speaker, the speaker was then amplifying Pat's voice so my dad could hear it. But the only way Pat could hear my dad was for my dad to shout as loudly as he could; to Pat, it sounded like my dad was in a different room.

> DAD: So are we going snooker later, Pat?
> PAT: What!?
> DAD: I said, SNOOKER! Are we going snooker later?
> PAT: I can't hear yeh, Paddy!
> DAD: SNOOKER!
> PAT: Snooker? Are you saying snooker?
> DAD: Ah bollix.

Whereupon Dad picked up the phone and continued the conversation without his hands-free system. When he'd finished talking to Pat, he put down the phone, leaned into the kitchen and said to my mam:

> DAD: That thing is a load of bollix, lucky we got it for free, I'll sell it to Tony later.
> MAM: Charming language.

Dad had gotten the hands-free speaker from an office in Guinness's that was getting cleared out. The amount of stuff he brought home each month from offices being cleared out would have meant everyone leaving the company. I think my dad and his mates probably had their own special way of clearing out offices.

LIST OF STUFF THAT WAS 'JUST LYING THERE' IN WORK

1. Hands-free phone system (Dad: 'lying there').
2. Phone table (Dad: 'just standing there, no one needed it').
3. Tea set (Dad: 'they don't even drink tea').
4. Mirror (Dad: 'there was four of them, who needs four mirrors?').
5. Inkwell and pen (Dad: 'he uses a typewriter').
6. Typewriter (Dad: 'he has a secretary').
7. Waterford Crystal whiskey glasses (Dad: 'they were in a box').
8. Statue of Red Rum, the racehorse (Dad: 'it was behind a couch').
9. A pair of wall-mounted gold lights (Dad: 'they've a new ceiling light').
10. Grandfather clock, no messin' (Dad: 'he got a new digital watch').

The answering-machine changed the average Irish household in the '80s. What a day we had, all of us in the hall, watching as Dad set it up and then got my mam to record the message. Eric,

Rachel, Eithne, me and Dad all sniggering as Mam tried to put a posh message on the machine. My dad thought he was a movie director for the day.

He knelt on the ground beside my mam, while she got ready to talk into the machine. We tried to stay quiet.

DAD: And ... action (*he actually said 'action' followed by a finger point*).

He pressed Record on the machine. For years the message on our answering-machine was ...

MAM: What? What? Now? Speak now?
DAD: Message, message.
MAM: Oh hello ... this is the Eithne, or sorry, Byrnes' house ...

Followed by a howl of laughter and a BEEP!

DAD: Ah for jaysus' sake, we're going to sound like mad yokes.
ME: Erase it.
DAD: Don't know how.

As far as Dad could see, there was no erase option on the answering-machine, so we were stuck with ... *What? What? Now?* etc. But then, that's exactly what I loved about my house, nothing ever went smoothly.

Back to DING DONG ...

DAD: Doorbell!

I went to the door, it was Karl.

KARL: Get money.

He was heading to the shop. I went back into the house and asked my dad for money. He said to get his trousers; my dad sat in his underpants a lot while watching the telly. My mam had asked him many times why he did this, he said it was because he didn't want to crease his trousers while sitting in the armchair.

He was like Superman, with a weird twist: if the phone rang and it was one of his mates in the pub, he'd quickly grab his trousers, which hung in the hallway, put them on like a flying cape and out the door to save the day ... in the pub ... talking shite.

So anyway, I got his trousers from the hallway, while Karl waited in the doorway. I stood next to my dad while he rummaged in his trouser pockets.

> DAD: How much do you want? Jaysus, I can't be doing this every day, we'll be on the streets if this keeps up.
> MAM: Just give him some money, Paddy.
> DAD: There you go.

A pound note.

> ME: Thanks, Dad!

Me and Karl left the house, I had a whole pound note to spend, Karl had 50p. We got to the shop, and Karl took my pound.

> KARL: We're buying fags.
> ME: What?
> KARL: Look.

Karl pointed at his upper lip, where a small bit of dark hair was sprouting out.

> KARL: I've got a moustache now, they'll serve me fags no
> bother. You wait here.
> ME: Okay.

Karl went into the shop. I was so scared, but remember, I was scared of my own shadow. I was looking around to see if anyone knew us, but this was the local shop, so loads of people knew us. I said hello to a steady stream of my neighbours as they walked into the shop.

They were just saying hello in their normal way, but I had *Guilty* written all over my face. What if my mam or dad arrived at the shop? Or even my sister Rachel, she hung around there a lot? Eric would love to catch me at something like this, he'd rat me up to Dad straightaway.

This was as bad as taking drugs. My parents had warned me not to smoke, even though my dad did and would smoke in the house beside us, and in the car with the windows rolled up, so technically we were smoking right along with him ... *buuut* ... we weren't allowed to put a fag in our mouths and light it up.

SHIT ... TING ... MY ... SELF.

Out comes Karl, he gives the thumbs-up and starts to walk fast out of the shop and over to me.

KARL: I've got them, go, go, go!

The two of us walked down that street like we'd just robbed a bank. I couldn't see where Karl had the smokes, but he had them. I was so nervous I was bursting for a poo. They say that's why robbers leave poo in your house when they break in, just too excited by the robbery.

Karl ducked into the Mini Tunnel. This was a smaller version of The Tunnel, near the shops. It was used for a quick snog with a girl or a quick piss or now … FAGS, OR CIGGIES, OR SMOKES.

SHIT … TING … MY … SELF.

In the bushes of the Mini Tunnel and out of the sight of neighbours, Karl took out 20 John Player Blue … This was scary, but also amazing, there we were, 13 and nearly 15, with our own fags. Karl unwrapped the plastic off the box, then he opened it to reveal the brown tips of the fags. My God, we were actually going to do this.

Karl nipped one at the end, pulled it out and put it in his mouth, then turned the box to me. I did the same, so that now we both had fags in our mouths. They felt like baseball bats between our teeth.

We had no idea what we were doing. Karl got out the matches, struck a match, it broke. Oh Jesus, I looked around to see if

anyone could see us, no one, still safe. Karl struck the second match, and that went out too. Oh God, maybe this was a sign? I was hoping we wouldn't have to do this, that we could just throw away the fags and forget about it.

But before I knew it, Karl had a lit flame hovering in front of me.

KARL: Suck.

I sucked. I felt the back of my throat burn. Karl sucked on his. We both coughed out smoke. It was horrible, we both hated it, but wouldn't admit it, not ever. So we smoked a whole fag each. As we were in the process of doing this, Karl's older sister, Orla, passed by us on the path, and then she stopped to talk to another girl.

KARL: Don't move, man. That's Orla, she'll rat us out no bother.

We held on to each other in the bushes until they left. Then out we came. We were giggling like mad, we had, as best mates, just smoked a fag each. We agreed to do it again tomorrow. Karl said I should take the fags into my house as he was older and they'd never suspect me.

Karl put the fags down the front of my jeans. 'Now, can't see them at all.' If we were smugglers, we'd have been sent down years ago. Karl handed me an evergreen leaf that he'd picked off the bush.

KARL: Here, chew on that, it gets rid of the smell.

We walked home, both chewing evergreen leaves and smelling of fags. Got to my house and Karl agreed to go in with me, the plan was to hide the fags in my room. I opened the front door, my mother was standing in the hall.

MAM: Alright, lads?
ME: Oh yeah.
KARL: Mrs B.
ME: Just heading upstairs.
MAM: (*beady eyes*) Right, well off you go then.

We both walked past her, and yes! She didn't notice my bulge. We went upstairs and into my bedroom. I closed the door behind me, then took out the fags, put them on the bed and ...

WHOOSH!

The door flung open.

MAM: I knew you two were up to something, it was written all over your faces!

Yes, the unknowable ways of the mammy ... they *always* know. She grabbed the fags from the bed.

MAM: Who the hell owns these? You're in a lot of trouble, the both of yeh ...
DAD: Ah, there they are.

Dad walked into the room behind us.

MAM: What?

DAD: Me fags.

MAM: But you smoke Carroll's.

DAD: I changed.

MAM: When?

DAD: Yesterday, must have left these on your bed, son, when I was looking out the window there, at … something or other.

My dad took the fags out of my mam's hand and headed out of the room.

DAD: Come on, lads, outside. On a day like this, you two should be out playing football.

Dad then semi-pushed me and Karl down the stairs, he got to the hall door with us, then gave us each a belt over the head.

DAD: (*whisper*) Don't be smoking, yeh pair of gobshites. Look at me, I can barely get up the stairs I'm so wrecked. Now, I won't tell your mothers, but if I catch you with these again, I'll bury the both of you.

MAM: (*from inside*) Paddy!

DAD: Coming, love … now go.

Dad put a John Player Blue in his mouth, lit it and walked towards Mam, coughing because he wasn't used to smoking them.

For the whole day my dad smoked John Player Blue in front of my mam, just so I wouldn't get into trouble, and they say he didn't make any sacrifices for his kids. Smoking John Player Blue instead of Carroll's was like drinking piss instead of water as far as my auld fella was concerned. But I loved him a long time for that one ...

FiVE THiNGS THAT MADE ME LOVE MY DAD EVEN MORE

1. **Never took shit off anyone.**
2. **Funniest dry-wit man on the planet.**
3. **Good for nothing, great for everything.**
4. **Loved his own farts, wife and family.**
5. **Would give you his last penny and do anything to defend the family.**

DAD: Jaysus, he's done it!

We all jumped around the living room. Then we ran out of the house and onto the road. I had Eithne on my back, Rachel and Eric were running alongside us. Mam was jumping about too.

Stephen Roche had won the 1987 Tour de France! Our road was going mental. In fairness, most of us didn't even follow cycling, but Stephen Roche was a local and he had just won the Tour de France. So now the whole of South Dublin was a cycling expert, and everyone was wearing yellow tops.

I had a yellow polo-neck that was my mam's from the '70s. It was amazing to see a local man, from such a tiny island like Ireland, win the Tour de France.

My dad walked out of the house behind us, pulling on his coat as he walked.

DAD: Let's celebrate, everyone!

We all cheered, as we watched our dad and loads of other dads with their coats on, heading off to celebrate in the pub on our behalf. Fair play to the dads, what would we do without them? How would celebrations ever get done in this world without the Irish dad?

Later that evening, we were all sitting in the living room when the phone rang and Mam went out to answer it. Phone down.

MAM: Your father's had a heart attack. I'll kill him!

Best sentence in the world.

So off we went in the car: Eric in the front, Rachel, Eithne and me in the back seat, my mother moaning as she drove.

MAM: I swear to God, when I get to this hospital your father better be dead, because if he's not, I'll kill him myself. He's drank himself into a heart attack. I don't know how many times I've warned him, but oh no, he just keeps going. Well, I can tell yeh, if he's in a wheelchair after having a stroke, he can wipe his own arse, because I'm too young to have a dribbling husband ... I can't believe we're all back in the hospital, first you, Rachel, and now your father, I can't take this anymore.

RACHEL: It wasn't my fault.

MAM: I know, I know, dear.

My sister Rachel had just come out of hospital after having heart surgery a couple of months earlier. It was a proper scary time. The school doctor had called my mam into the school to tell her that Rachel had a hole in her heart.

My mother didn't stop crying all day, she thought it was her fault, a hole in the heart, maybe it was something she didn't eat while pregnant and Rachel came out unfinished.

MAM: (*to the doctor*) I always knew her arrival was premature, she wasn't ready, I could see it in her, her skin just didn't look full enough, like a sponge cake coming out of the oven too early.

Turned out it was no one's fault, she was born with a hole in the back of her heart, she was operated on, and they did a great job. Rachel never complained, that was, and is now, just the type of person she is. Her chest was cracked open and stapled back together and you'd think, when talking to her afterwards, that she'd just had a run-of-the-mill appendix op or something. So brave, she was.

I remember the day we collected her from the hospital. She was so thin, and all the nurses were crying as she left. They all loved her because while she'd spent a long time on that ward, she had never complained. I'd say she was their favourite patient.

My mam went up to the hospital reception desk.

> MAM: Hi, do you have a Paddy Byrne here, please?
> NURSE: Oh right, do you know what he's in for?
> MAM: For being a gobshite, Nurse.
> NURSE: Oh we all have one of them. Drink, was it?
> MAM: I warned him to stop, but now he's gone and had a heart attack and I don't even have the big shop done.

The Big Shop
Normally done on a Saturday, trolley filled with stuff, in other words a big load of shopping to last five people all week.

The Small Shop
A few bits and pieces for the dinner, normally done on a Wednesday.

> NURSE: Oh I hear you Mrs Byrne, my fella wouldn't get off the fags, now he has goitre, and half his face missing with the cancer.
> MAM: Oh Jesus.
> NURSE: Tell me about it.
> MAM: I know.
> NURSE: What are they like?
> MAM: Like having another kid.
> NURSE: I hear yeh. St Monica's Ward, love, room 45, if

he's with the VHI we'll move him out of that ward into a semi-private room. Do you have VHI, love?

MAM: I think so, he probably drank it though.

NURSE: Yeah, I'd get him out of that ward before he catches God knows what from God knows who. The children aren't allowed up there.

MAM: Okay.

We all got into the lift and headed to the cardiac wards, or the heart wards as my mother called it. We got to St Monica's Ward, asked the young station nurse which one was room 45.

STATION NURSE: No children up here.

MAM: Listen here, missy, and before I ring your mother, who I know well (*she didn't, but always pulled this move*), their father is dying and they would like to see him now before he passes on.

The station nurse walked us all quickly to the room, not because she thought my dad was dying but because she was more worried about my mam telling her mother on her, who my mother didn't actually know. They had some power then, did the mammies.

There were a load of beds all lined up along either wall. The last time I had seen this many beds in a room was in *Carry On Doctor*. It smelled weird and a lot of these men looked like they were on their last legs. Horrible coughs and weird breathing accompanied us as we walked along between the beds. There were machines helping some of the men to breathe. I looked towards one bed and a curtain was drawn smartly in my face, followed by some heavy moaning.

This was WWII for the modern era. These men were in a bad way. I was frightened to see my Dad – would he have tubes down his neck, or a heart machine thing keeping him alive? We all feared the worst …

… until we got to my Dad's bed. There he was, sitting up, reading the paper, looking happy as Larry, and people all around him half-dead.

DAD: Ah there you are, did yeh bring me any chocolates or flowers?

I gave him a hug, Eithne and Rachel jumped up on the bed, Eric waved to him and sat down in his teenage way.

MAM: What have you done now, you gobshite yeh?
DAD: I was sitting in the pub, and Bang! Pains in the chest, next minute ambulance, suspected heart attack.
MAM: Suspected? It better be real or I'll kill yeh meself. I haven't been able to do the big shop or even get a dinner on.
DAD: It wasn't my fault, the lads were going mad for Stephen Roche, then the owner put on a happy hour, and Bang! Lads dropping like flies, there's Pat over there.

We looked over to see my dad's mate, Pat, in the bed across the room, he'd collapsed too. He gave us a little wave, he was weaker than my dad though.

DAD: And you see this bloke beside me? Bollixed. Doesn't even have a heart anymore, it's some sort of pump in there.

Of course as we all know, no heart, then you're dead, but Dr Byrne was filling us in nicely on his advanced medical knowledge.

DAD: And this guy on the other side? Liver packed in, and he's as yellow as a Chinaman.
MAM: Paddy!
DAD: Just saying.
DOCTOR: Ah Mr Byrne, and your children who aren't allowed in.
DAD: Doctor, hello there.
DOCTOR: Shall we move this lot on, so we can have a chat?
DAD: Not at all doctor, give me your worst, I'm ready for it. I want my family around me as you tell me.
DOCTOR: First off, you said to the nurse a while ago that you weren't feeling too good.
DAD: Yes. I do not feel right at all. Can't put my finger on it, Doctor, but yes, not right at all. If I'm a gonner then I'm ready for it.
DOCTOR: That's because you're sober, Paddy.
DAD: What?
DOCTOR: Sober, Paddy. You haven't been sober since you were 15, so this is the longest you've been off the booze.

MAM: Can you believe it? He doesn't feel well because he's sober.

DOCTOR: Now, you did have a minor heart attack.

MAM: Jesus.

DAD: Right.

DOCTOR: Now you'll be fine on meds, but the bad news is ...

We all held our breath as the doctor delivered the life-altering news.

DOCTOR: ... no more drinking.

Holy shit, the doctor would have been better off telling my dad he had cancer or a week to live, but *no more drinking*? This was going to be good.

DAD: What? What?

MAM: Well, thank you, Doctor, it needed a heart attack and someone like you to stop him from drinking, I can't wait for this.

We left the hospital, leaving behind my dad sitting up in his bed, in shock after the news. What was he going to do?

A couple of days later he arrived back in the house from the hospital.

DAD: I'm home.

ME: Dad, you're alright.

DAD: I feel great, let's celebrate.

He put down his hospital bag in the hallway, turned around and walked back out the door, headed up to the pub.

MAM: *Paddy!*

Dad in the distance, walking down the driveway.

DAD: Those doctors know nothing!

There was no way he was going to stop drinking. He cut down loads, but the pub was his everything, his mates, his info about people in the area, you just had to go to the pub if you wanted to know what was going on.

My dad was a Byrne, and they didn't die off easy anyway. My grandparents lived into their eighties, a minor miracle given that my grandad's diet was Guinness and huge hearty dinners, although he didn't smoke and he did cycle to the pub regularly.

We Byrnes were all pretty strong.

'Here he is,' some auld fella screamed at the top of his lungs. *Stephen Roche* got out of a car and waved to us all. We were in his mother's garden with thousands of neighbours, celebrating his homecoming.

His mam and family were making tea for everyone and handing out sandwiches. Me and Karl, Ken Newman, Brian Roche (no relation to Stephen, but he told everyone that he was his cousin so we could get nearer to Stephen and the free food) and Tally were milling into the sandwiches and cake.

We didn't even know these neighbours, they lived in a different housing estate from us, but everyone knew where Stephen Roche's mam lived and everyone knew what time he was arriving back to his mam's house.

We didn't have Twitter then, no, we had the MOUTHY MAMMIES, they sent messages to each other quicker than the web could now.

RTÉ news was there too, recording it all with their cameras. They interviewed Stephen Roche on his mam's garden wall.

Us lot stood behind him, we had manoeuvred into that pole position because we kept telling people that Brian Roche was Stephen Roche's cousin and to 'let us through, for God's sake'. So there we were, making faces and sticking our fingers up at the camera (little bollixes).

The interviewer could barely hear what Stephen Roche was saying with all the cheering and when he asked for a bit of quiet, we all started cheering even louder.

What a great day that was. I got home exhausted. I was met in the hallway by my mother.

MAM: Have a good time at Stephen Roche's house, did we?

ME: Oh yeah, Mam, it was great, there was free cake and crisps and the telly were there.

MAM: The telly?

ME: Yeah, the telly.

My mam took off her slipper and started to whack me around the hall in circles with it.

MAM: The world (*whack*) and its mother (*whack*) seen you (*whack*) and Karl (*whack*) Mc(*whack*)Dermot (*whack*), Brian Roche (*whack*), Kenneth Newman (*whack*) and Ciaran (*whack*) Tallon (*whack*) all sticking your (*whack, whack, whack, whack, whack*) fingers up on the telly behind (*whack*) Stephen Roche's (*whack*) head, little (*whack*) bastards (*whack, whack, whack, whack, whack, whack … drop slipper, pick it up … whack, whack, whack*) How will I be able to show my face at mass?'

I ran up the stairs, to avoid any more whacks, laughing as I ran.

MAM: (*shouting up the stairs*) I wouldn't laugh, son, I'll beat yeh unconscious if I get yeh again.

For some reason this was legal, well, in her head.

CHAPTER 12
PEBBLES iN MY POCKETS

'Woooooooooo!' The crowd cheered as some sort of rave music played. We were in Dundrum Shopping Centre (the modest old one, not the Celtic Tiger one) and four Mexicans from God knows where – yeah, I know, Mexico, but where did they come from? – were doing Yo-yo tricks.

I was 14, and the Yo-yo craze had started. Everyone watching clapped along as these guys did tricks with their Yo-yos. They had Coca-Cola ones, Fanta and 7UP ones. They were twisting the string and still making the Yo-yo spin, amazing.

We who were lucky enough to be there that day were witnessing the birth of 'THE STUNT YO-YO'. Not an ordinary up-and-down Yo-yo. Oh no! Stunt Yo-yos!

I had to get me one of those. So we all headed home to see if we could get money to buy a stunt Yo-yo. The only thing was, they were a tenner. We all headed into our gaffs (houses) for a coordinated assault on our fathers' wallets.

Dad was watching *Blockbusters* on telly. Eric was on the couch with Mam beside him, knitting.

DAD: I'll have a B please, Bob.

This was the only reason he watched it, just so he could shout various letters at Bob Holness.

MAM: Stop shouting at the telly, Paddy.

DAD: Well he can hardly hear me, now can he?

MAM: Then why are you doing it?

DAD: Fun, have you ever heard of fun?

MAM: Ha! You? Fun? Your idea of fun is sitting on the jacks for hours, reading a newspaper.

ME: Dad?

MAM: Oh hiya son, your father may not be able to talk to you, he'll be too busy getting into his red coat to head off to Butlin's for some 'Fun'.

DAD: What? A C please, Bob. Aaaahh, they picked O, stupid way to go across the board.

ME: Can I have money for a Yo-yo?

ERIC: Whaaaaaaaat? Don't, Dad.

ME: Shut up you.

DAD: A Yo-yo, what the hell do you want a Yo-yo for? There must be loads in the attic.

ME: No, this is a special stunt Yo-yo, Dad.

DAD: I knew a Yo-yo once, Chinese girl, worked in Bang-kok ... Ha, ha, ha ...

(So many things wrong with that sentence on so many levels.)

MAM: Paddy!

ME: It's just a tenner, Dad. They're really good, they have 7UP and Fanta written on the side of them.

ERIC: *A tenner?*

ME: Shut up!

DAD: I tell you what, son, here's a pen and paper, now go out on the road and write down everyone's name who wants a Yo-yo and I'll get the lot ... hahahahahaha ... or, or your mother could knit you one there ... hahahahahaha!

ME: (*I knew what he was doing*) Ah, Dad!

ERIC: Nice one, Dad.

DAD: A tenner for a Yo-yo? Will yeh feck off, for a tenner I'd want the thing to be made out of gold and making wishes. A tenner for a Yo-yo, go away outta that.

I left the room with Eric sticking his fingers up at me in triumph. My mam didn't even look up from her knitting, she just belted Eric.

DAD: (*from the living room*) H please, Bob.

CONTESTANT: H please, Bob.

DAD: Yes!

BOB: What H is a dwelling ...

DAD: House!

PING.

CONTESTANT: Home.
BOB: Correct.
DAD: Bollix!

Why did I go in and ask him? I should have known that was going to happen. The last time I asked for something I'd really wanted he'd caught me out big style, I should have learned my lesson from that.

Boot skates were a *big* thing. There were boys and girls all skating up and down the road with their boot skates and leggings. Yes, even the blokes wore leggings.

I asked my Dad for a pair. He said no bother, he'd get them on the way home from work the next day. So I ran home from school, did my homework and waited at the window for Dad to arrive. My mam was very suspicious that Dad had promised me a pair of boot skates, especially as it wasn't even my birthday or Christmas.

The car arrived in the driveway, Dad got out of the car, opened the boot, took out a box. Yes, this was it, he'd actually done it!

I ran to the door, grabbed the box off Dad, thanking him as he handed it over to me.

DAD: Open it on the kitchen table.

I put the box on the kitchen table, my mam looked on with squinty eyes. I opened the box, pulled out a pair of black welling-ton boots with old shitty skates taped to the bottom of them.

I have never seen my dad laugh so hard, he even started to cough and splutter into the sink. My mother thought he was going to have another heart attack.

Rachel and Eithne came in to see what was going on, and they started laughing too.

Then I started laughing, he was a bollix, but that was funny.

> DAD: The ... best ... boot skates ever ... I better patent them, hahahahaha ...
> MAM: Paddy! Don't mind him, son, he's a gobshite.
> DAD: ... you'll look great in them at the roller disco ... hahahahahaha.

In fairness to the lot of them, on my next birthday I got my boot skates. I loved them. Karl, Tally, Ken, Brian, we all had them. Never took them off. We'd skate to the shops in them, or to training, we used them to go everywhere.

Even when we were being chased by local bullies, they couldn't catch us as we could skate off at speed. But soon the bullies had skates too, and a massive Boot Skate Chase would start up as we skated around corners with skill. Could have been a PS4 game.

The main reason for these boot skates was the roller disco. This was possibly the best thing about the '80s: the roller disco. We'd climb onto our bikes with our boot skates around our necks and cycle from Ballinteer to Dún Laoghaire to a place called the Top

Hat. Bleedin' miles away, but we didn't care. We cycled out there loads, be it for the roller disco or for the Forty Foot.

The Forty Foot

This was in Sandycove, Dublin, right out on the tip of Dublin Bay. A lovely spot. Just down the road from Dún Loaghaire and up the road from Dalkey. It was full of posh people and visiting rough-heads like us. Sandycove was a small beach until the tide came in. Then behind Sandycove looking into the sea was THE FORTY FOOT.

Best laugh was to walk around to the bathing area. There you would find auld fellas in the nip with their mickeys out (i.e. naked men). They'd sit on the rocks starkers, like seals bathing in the sun, anyone could walk in there, but when we went in, you could see the dirty auld fellas getting edgy. If you walked by an auld fella in the nip, you had to say 'Mickey' under your breath. Oh Jesus, I was in tears with laughing. The line of us would walk past an auld fella and as each one went by him you'd hear, 'Mickey ... Mickey ... Mickey ... ' all said in different tones and different accents.

The auld fellas were disgusted because they could hear us and see us laughing. We didn't care. What were they doing, hanging around on rocks in the nip with kids everywhere?

You'd then go beyond the dirty auld fellas and the Forty Foot was there before you. You could dive off rocks into it, or just walk down the steps into it. Amazing place to swim and even better today because, as far as I know, the Mickeys are all gone now.

The other reason to bike out to Dún Laoghaire was for the Rainbow Rapids ... said in a very thick Dub-a-lin accent.

The Rainbow Rapids

We loved this the most. There was no water park in Ireland. This place had two water slides, no pool, just two water slides. You'd head in, buy a ticket, get a wristband, then you could go up and down the slides as much as you liked for as long as you liked.

We'd go there at the weekends, or in the mornings during the summer months, staying all day and leaving in time to be home for dinner. I felt sorry for the lads running the slides.

LADS: Don't go down the slide in pairs.

We'd go down in pairs, sometimes even threes, and nearly kill ourselves on the way down and then nearly drown one another in the plunge pool at the bottom. We'd stick our fingers up at the poor lad as we disappeared down the tube.

LADS: Don't slide down backwards.

We slid down backwards. In fact, anything he told us not to do, we did exactly that. On top of each other, with a life-ring, without a life-ring, jockey-back, slide down head first on your belly, head first on your back, all flicking the V's as we disappeared down the tube.

Once, three of us got stuck in a bend and blocked the pipe, they had to switch off the water and walk down the tube and get us out.

We were barred for life after that. But we came back the following week, flipping fingers at the same staff member.

ME: (*sliding away, fingers in the air*) Yeh bollixxxxxxxxxx!

Before we headed back home after a day's sliding, we would always go to Teddy's ice cream shop straight across the road. *Best. Ice cream. Ever.* It's still there, but I'm not sure if the ice creams are still the size of your head.

Once I'd had a Teddy's cone, I was full for the evening. I wouldn't be able to eat my dinner. My mam would flip out and say, 'There's no dessert if you don't finish your dinner.' Too late, Mam, already had dessert, that's why I'm not hungry.

Rainbow Rapids was closed down in 1997, no one was sure why. Rumour had it that rough kids, or bigger boys as we called them, had stuck razor blades in the joins of the slide, so when kids went down they were being slashed.

This was a load of me hoop. First, you went rushing down those slides at a million miles an hour, you definitely wouldn't have had time to plant razor blades in the joins.

In fact, the only way you could have got razor blades into the join of the tube would have been to close down the place for a week, while the delicate operation of carefully attaching razor blades to the joins in the water tube was being carried out. No, fact was that either someone sold it or it went bust.

My mates weren't too impressed with my logical answer, so it was deadners all round. They preferred the razor blade story.

DEADNERS: a heavy thump to the top of the arm/shoulder area.

Alternatively you could administer a …

DEAD LEG: a heavy thump to the leg.

Both areas were legal if you did or said something stupid.

TOP FiVE REASONS FOR GETTiNG A DEADNER

1. If you were too logical or smart (deadner).
2. If you farted, didn't say 'taxi', then someone else was allowed to say 'sixer', which meant six deadners in a row on the arm (six deadners).
3. If you said too loud in class that Miss forgot to give you all homework (deadner by many, while you said 'fair enough' in between each thump).
4. If you said something silly to a girl that she tutted at, and your mate fancied that girl (deadner).
5. If you took too big a bite from an offer of a chocolate bar (deadner).

If you ever did or said anything really bad, then you would receive many Deadners, they'd rain down on you relentlessly, followed by a huge Pile-On.

PILE-ON: many children piled on top of you, until removed by a teacher; many have not made it out of a pile-on alive.

A MINUTE'S SILENCE HERE FOR PILE-ON VICTIMS ....

How did we get this far from the stunt Yo-yo?

So ... a tenner for a Yo-yo? I called over to Karl to see how he was getting on in his quest for money for the stunt Yo-yo. As I walked up his drive, he opened the door, holding a bit of string and an apple in his hand, his dad, Paddy, laughing behind him as he sent him out the door. The door closed over to ...

PADDY: A tenner for a Yo-yo, I ask ye?
ME: No luck then, Karlo?
KARL: No, Dad gave me this apple and string to make a Yo-yo out of it.
ME: How will we get one?
AUSTIN: Hiya, lads.

Austin Murphy. What. A. Bollix. The rich kid on the road. He had a Coca-Cola Yo-yo in his hand and he was doing tricks with it.

AUSTIN: How do you like my Yo-yo, lads?

We pretended to be friends with him so we could have a go of all the stuff his dad bought him. I say he was rich, well, they were in housing estate terms, his dad was an accountant. They got everything first and it was never on HP (hire purchase, the way the working classes lived and got into debt). Oh no, Austin's stuff was paid for outright.

They even went to *America* on their holidays and came back with American accents ... wankers.

Austin was the first on our road with a BMX when it was the craze. Now those bikes were expensive, but this little bollix had the best one, top of the range, you could have bought a small car for the price.

They had the first video-recorder on the road, too, and what does Austin do? Charges us all 50p in to see *Rocky*, the scabby little shit. You'd know he was an accountant's son alright.

Bollix, like I said, but we pretended he was the best in the world, just to get a ride on his poxy bike. But you had to ask for a go.

> ME: Give us a go on your bike.
> AUSTIN: I have to ask me mam.
> ME: She's not even looking.

Then you'd get a go.

In the '80s in Dublin you had ask for a go of almost anything.

1. **Give us a go of your bike.**
2. **Give us a go of your sandwich.**
3. **Give us a go of your cigarette.**

4. **Give us a go of your girlfriend.**
5. **Give us a go of your ma. (This was highly insulting, but not as insulting as, 'I've pictures of your ma in the bath', to which I would reply, 'Well to have them you'd have to get my mam's permission to stand at the side of the bath while taking said photos because if you approached the bath from the outside, you couldn't see in, as the glass is frosted, and before you say *through the open window*, our window doesn't open in the bathroom.' Deadner, deadleg, followed by a succession of deadners.)**
6. **Give us a go of your dog.**
7. **Give us a go of your doorbell (if it had a special chime).**
8. **Give us a go of your swing.**
9. **Give us a go of your pencil, calculator, etc.**
10. **Give us a go of your glasses. (This happened quite a lot to me, and when they'd put my glasses on they'd say, 'How do you see through these bleedin' things?' I'd then say, 'They're not your prescription, they're my prescription, that's why you can't see through them.' Deadner.)**

So there was Austin with his poxy Yo-yo and myself and Karl with an apple on a string. We had a go of Austin's Yo-yo for a bit, but then his mam shouted out the window to him ...

AUSTIN'S MAM: Don't let people play with your Yo-yo, Austin, it's your Yo-yo, only for you to play with. Maybe you should come inside and play with your Yo-yo!

Austin went red, then we both gave him deadners for his mam saying something so sexual, and then we teased Austin about playing with his Yo-yo on his own in his bedroom.

Oh by the way, if there's any mams reading this, a little bit of advice: seeing your child out on the road from your window, thinking he needs your help, do not, *do not* shout out a window, this will bury him or her into way more trouble than necessary.

Austin left us. Karl had an idea how to make money. Remember, he was two years older than me so he was nearly sixteen at this stage. He said he knew a guy up in the supermarket who might give us a small job, then we could get the money for the Yo-yos. I agreed. We headed up to Superquinn, Ballinteer.

Superquinn, Ballinteer

The *posh* big shop. My mam would only ever do her big shop there, and in doing so, she classed herself as upper-class. She would never shop in Quinnsworth, would never, ever set foot in CRAZY PRIZES (to be honest, I never understood this, as their prizes were truly crazy), no, it had to be Superquinn for my mam.

We walked into Superquinn, it was busy. Me and Karl looked like we were there to rob stuff, we were nervous looking for this guy. A security guard came up to us, to ask if we were alright.

KARL: Yeah, cool, man. Do you know if Tony O'Neill is here?

He said yes, told us to wait by the door and he'd get him. After a short wait, Tony O'Neill arrived.

TONY O'NEILL
AGE: 25
POSITION: In charge of Fruit 'n' Veg.
SKILLS: Acting like he's 14; also talks to his fruit 'n' veg.
HOBBIES: Sticking his tongue in and out of his mouth like a snake, weeeiiirrrd.

> TONY: Well, lads (*tongue going in and out, trying not to look*). How can I help you, Karl? (*tongue going in and out, now mesmerised by it, can't stop looking, sly deadner from Karl*).
> KARL: How are yeh, Tony? Looking good, looking good.

He looked like a tall, wide dwarf from *Snow White*, with a snake tongue and more spots on his face than face.

> TONY: Alright Karl, what do yous want?
> KARL: Just a small job, nothing too serious.
> TONY: Right, wait there, I'll ask the manager.

He went off with a waddle, and we watched as he spoke to the manager and pointed to us at the door. The manager nodded and out came Tony.

> TONY: (*tongue in and out*) You're hired, you have to collect trolleys. Get all the loose ones around the place and stick them into each other against the wall.

KARL: So stick them into each other against the wall?
TONY: Yes, stick them into each other against the wall.

Karl made Tony say this many times before pretending to get it. We were to start the next day. A Saturday. Very Busy.

Me and Karl pushed hard on the huge line of trolleys we had made and put them against the wall. We were having a laugh. Old women kept asking us to help them out with their trollies to their cars, but we didn't get a tip off any of them, it wasn't America after all, this was scabby Ireland.

Instead of a tip, they'd hand you fruit or an old sweet from their purse. We collected trolleys all day, from 9.00am, a Saturday I remind you, so trolleys being used all over the camp and remember, no coins in the trolleys back then, so people just left them sailing loosely in the car park and bushes. Some even brought the trolley home; many a trolley was played with in our housing estate.

The day came to an end at 8 pm, me and Karl were knackered. We had collected hundreds of trolleys and done a great job, too. Tony walked by us with his coat on.

KARL: What's the story, Tony? How did we do? Where's our wages?

Tony pointed to his Boss, who called us over.

GLENN: *(knew this because it was written on his poxy badge)* Well done lads, you worked very hard.

Yes, this is it, money for Yo-yos and God knows what else! We had worked a 12-hour shift, and Karl reckoned we would get at least £2 an hour for our troubles and that was his low estimate. My God, I couldn't wait.

KARL: Yes it was hard, but we loved it, sir.
GLENN: Well let's reward your hard work.

He turned to a counter with cigarettes, drinks, sweets and, more importantly, a cash till at it. He reached down, picked up two packets of cheese and onion crisps and two super cans of Coke. He handed a packet and a can to Karl and a packet and a can to me. Our jaws fell open.

GLENN: That's for free, lads. Well done, nice crisps those, and that can is no ordinary can, that's a *super can* of Coke. See you next week, same time?

He walked back into the shop, me and Karl walked away slowly, still gob-smacked, holding our crisps and super can.

KARL: Tony is dead!
ME: Holy shit, crisps and a can of Coke, is that it? No cash?
KARL: Tell no one about this, not even your special eye bollix.
ME: I won't.

We never went back to work for Superquinn. We egged Glenn's car when we found out where he lived, and somehow a sign appeared on the wall of the lane that led up to the shops that said: TONY LOVES MICKEY.

But still, no Yo-yo …

> KARL: Time for a bit of light lifting.
> ME: What? We're not going back in there.
> KARL: No, you dope, robbin' stuff.

Karl had a great plan: we were going to kind of rob the money for the Yo-yos

I … WAS … SHIT … TING … MY … SELF.

Here was the plan.

Sundays, we'd all go to mass together, the boys and the girls that is, and we'd sit at the back, mess for a while, get the name of the priest because your mam always asked for the name of the priest who'd said mass. After mass, we'd take the money our dads had given us and go outside to the newspaper stall to get the paper and bring it home.

This Sunday would be different! We'd go outside to the stand with the Sunday newspapers, nick the papers, keep the money. This was foolproof because no one would dare rob outside a church on a Sunday … would they? … crazy idea …

SHIT ... TING ... MYSELF ...

Sunday. Mass over. Karl and myself edge up to the queue for the newspapers, it's packed with people coming out of mass, all stopping to talk to each other. The Paperman always stood away from his stand, with his money pouch tied around his waist. He thought he'd better protect his money, but for some reason he never protected his newspapers.

He'd have a huge bag of papers around his arm, surrounded by people handing him money and grabbing papers. Chaos.

Karl just picked up two papers from the stand, Sunday ones, so a bit more bulky than usual, handed me one, and we walked away. Free papers, and we had the money our parents had given us to buy the papers.

I ... WALKED ... DOWN ... THAT ... ROAD ... SHIT ... TING ... MYSELF.

Anyone, adult or child, who said hello to me and Karl was just ignored, we walked as fast as we could, but we were careful not to run in case someone thought that odd.

But we made it.

> KARL: (*out of breath with fright*) Holy shit, that's three quid each, seven more and we're in the Yo-yos.
> ME: I don't know if I can keep this up.

KARL: Let me check your eye ... yeah ... that op has saved us a lot of bother, I can see it trying to turn in, but it just won't. Okay, I'll meet you later for the next move. The shop.
ME: Oh God, do you think so?
KARL: Man! Come on, 7UP Yo-yos.

It's 5 pm or so, and up we walk to the shops. We have to get fags for my dad and Karl's mam. This was a big one, pull it off and we'd make another fiver between us, because they always let us keep the change.

In we went, shop pretty full, it was a small newsagents so if there were fifteen people in it, it was packed. The owner never liked this because it meant he couldn't keep an eye on all the light-fingered kids.

The fags were behind the counter, but they were located just where the counter ran out, so you could walk up to the fags and pop them in your pocket.

If anyone had been watching me and Karl, it would have been plainly obvious that we were up to something because we looked so guilty.

My eyes were shifting from the shopkeeper to Karl, who was now right beside the fags, waiting for the shopkeeper to serve someone down at the other end.

Then, Bingo! Someone asked for an ice cream, a 99 too.

Shopkeeper had to turn his back on everyone. Karl jumped in and grabbed the fags, I needed a nappy at this stage, he then passed the fags to me.

Just as he did this, he walked out, meaning for me to follow quickly after him.

'YOU!'

I looked up and the shopkeeper was pointing his finger, well 99, straight at me. I was caught, it was over. I searched for Karl, but he was already gone.

Just as I was about to open my mouth to say sorry ...

> GIRL: I didn't mean it, I'm sorry, don't tell my mam.
> SHOPKEEPER: I've been watching you for weeks, you've been stealing stuff out of here for ages, well it's the Gards [police] for you, missy.

I was frozen to the spot. He wasn't talking to me at all. It was the girl in front of me, and when I say in front of me, her head was under my chin. Around me, a few others had frozen to the spot, no doubt a few other shoplifters in there with me.

We all shuffled out of the shop slowly, like a Spike Milligan sketch. Karl ran over to me, half laughing.

> KARL: (*small laugh*) Holy shit, man, that was close.

ME: It's not funny.
KARL: It so is, come on.

I handed Karl his mam's fags and I kept my dad's.

We now had nearly all the money for the Yo-yos. We were just a little short.

We sat down on the edge of the road, we were so close, all we needed was a couple of quid each to get the Yo-yos.

KARL: Little black babies!
ME: What?
KARL: Little black babies, the poor little black baby box in the house.
ME: The *Trócaire box*? No way, no way, that's for the little black babies.
KARL: We only need a few quid from it. Where's yours?
ME: On top of the telly.
KARL: On a food scales?
ME: Yep, you?
KARL: Same thing, but it's in on the kitchen table. Use tiny pebbles to replace the money you take out, but be careful not to put too many in, just the right amount.
ME: Are you sure?
KARL: Come on, we've seen *Indiana Jones* loads. Just copy him.

Our mams had put the Trócaire box on a food scales so that our dads couldn't rob it for beer money.

The Trócaire box

This was such an Irish thing. Trócaire is an Irish Catholic charity that helps the poor in Third World countries. Every Easter, during Lent (Jesus died on the cross so we could all have chocolate), all the school kids in Ireland were given a little cardboard box – flatpacked, then you popped it up into box shape. You put in coins during the four weeks of Lent, then donated all the money to poor kids in Africa. There was a picture on the front of the box of a poor little black baby. That is why they called it 'Money for the poor little black babies'. We used to send all sorts of stuff to Africa, or 'The Missions' as it was called. At mass there was a basket at the altar and people put baked beans and jelly into the basket for the poor little black babies.

I'd have loved to have been in Africa when those packages arrived.

This one is from Ireland.

Oh no, is it beans and jelly again?

Yes, beans and jelly again.

Jesus, okay, start up the fire, we'll make jelly beans again.

Somehow I think that means something different somewhere else.

I sat in the living room, staring at the Trócaire box. It was on top of the telly, for God's sake, on a food scales. In full view! It may as well have had laser beams protecting it, like in *Mission Impossible*.

My dad was in the chair again, this time watching *Countdown*.

DAD: A vowel please, Carol, a consonant please, Carol, ooohhh I tell you, I'd give *her* a vowel, what? What? What? Ehhhhhhhh.

MAM: Paddy, I'm off to put the dinner on.

DAD: Okay, Carol, I mean Eithne (*Dad winks at me*).

Now there was only me and my dad in there. The ad break came on for *Countdown*.

DAD: Right, time for a tea. (*To the kitchen*) Eithne, tea ...

No answer.

DAD: Tea, it's the *Countdown* break!

No answer.

DAD: Right, I'll get it me feckin' self then, jaysus.

Dad left the room. This was my chance. I leapt up, took out the tiny stones from my pocket. I first checked the weight of the box, then I took the Trócaire box off the food scales. I felt like *Indiana Jones* in the Temple of Doom. I then took out £2 in change, put the box back on the food scales and filled it with tiny stones till it came back to the proper weight. I closed the lid, left the room. I banged against my dad as I went through the door.

DAD: Take it easy, son, mind the tea.

I said nothing, legged it out of the house and waited for Karl on the wall outside Newmans'. Karl came out.

KARL: Did you do it?
ME: Did it.
KARL: Right, let's get some Yo-yos.

Mine was a 7UP Yo-yo, Karl's was a Fanta one. We walked up the road, playing with the Yo-yos. Rest of the lads and girls came over to us. We were *the business* with our new Yo-yos.

After many hours of stunt Yo-yo training, it was time to go in, but I had to hide the Yo-yo. If my mam knew I had a 7 UP Yo-yo, she would kill me.

I sat at the dinner table with my Yo-yo in my pocket.

MAM: Nice day everyone?

Eric mumbled.

YOUNG EITHNE: I buried a frog.

Whatever that meant.

MAM: Rachel?
RACHEL: Oh, I had a great time watching Karl and Jason playing with their new 7UP Yo-yos.

The table went quiet. I stared into my mash, going very red.

MAM: New 7UP Yo-yo?
ME: I borrowed Austin Murphy's one.
RACHEL: No he didn't, it's in his pocket there.
MAM: Take it out.
DAD: Do as your mother says, son.

I took out the Yo-yo and placed it on the table.

DAD: Wow, a real 7UP Yo-yo.
MAM: Paddy!
DAD: I mean, where did you get the money for that?
MAM: The truth now.

I searched in my brain for lies, but the floodgates opened.

ME: (*said very fast*) All we wanted was a 7UP Yo-yo, we didn't have the money, so we stole the papers from mass, kept the money, then headed to the shops and me and Karl stole cigarettes, kept the money again, but we still didn't have enough, so I stole the rest from the Trócaire box and re-placed the money with tiny stones.

Silence in the room. If there was a camera panning around the room at that moment, you would have seen my sister Rachel grinning, my sister Eithne covered in beans, my brother Eric grinning, my mam with her jaw in her lap and my dad smiling, but quickly changing the expression to a badly acted face of horror.

Karl was grounded for life. He's 45 now and still grounded, as far as I know. We were made apologise to the newspaper man, give him back the money, then down to the shopkeeper, apologise, give him back the money, get barred. Then I had to earn back the Little Black Baby money with chores around the house. I, too, was grounded for life.

The Yo-yos were put in the basket on the altar for the Little Black Babies. Now they'd have a delivery of cans of beans, jelly … and two super Yo-yos. I wished I was a Little Black Baby then. Lucky bastards, getting our stunt Yo-yos.

But one thing did stick out at the end of all this. When I was made sit in front of my mam as she poured out the Trócaire box, it was nearly full of little stones. I had only put a tiny amount in, where did they come from?

I looked to my dad.

> DAD: I can't believe you filled that box with tiny stones, yeh bollix ye.
> ME: But …
> DAD: Don't *But* your father, son, terrible thing to do.

He then winked at me, showed me some little stones in his pockets, stood up and put a handful of change into my pocket without my mam seeing.

> DAD: (*whisper*) We have to look after each other in this house, son. That's to go towards your next Yo-yo. Right! I'm off to celebrate.
> MAM: Celebrate what?
> DAD: Victory among men.

Off he went to the pub. I was left with my mam's rubber gloves on me, polishing the TV screen. Oh to grow up soon.

CHAPTER 13
BONFIRES AND ONE-LINERS

DAD: I don't believe this for a minute! Eithne! Eithne!

MAM: What is it now?

DAD: I'm on the last half of the wall here and I've run out of wallpaper. I measured the wall and worked out exactly how much I'd need. How has this happened?

MAM: Maybe you measured it all wrong.

DAD: But it's a small room, it just needed eight rolls, and I've only six.

MAM: Look, I haven't time for this shite. I've no idea where your wallpaper is gone.

CUT TO: THE NIGHT BEFORE.

My mam up all night, covering our school books with *wallpaper*. In school, everyone's books were covered in the funniest designs. It didn't matter how tough you were, your Maths book could have a lovely wallpaper floral display or your Science book could be covered in some satin wallpaper that made a funny noise when you ran your finger over it. Or even little bits of woodchip inside the wallpaper ... *ooohhhh fancy*.

No matter who you were, you were never slagged off for having wallpaper on your books because everyone had it. And everyone's mam did the covering, at night, while the dad was in the pub, without a clue that his wallpaper was going onto school books, nor would he ever know, because those worlds never crossed.

It was your mam who sat with you every evening and went through your homework. Well, she didn't have to do mine any more because I was in bigger school, and if I didn't have my homework done, I'd get a belt off the teachers, so I made sure I had my homework done. But Mam still sat with Rachel and helped her; Eithne was still too small to have started school. Eric had left school at this stage. He was a proper man now and was to leave the house soon.

It would be great when he left – not great because I'd be losing a brother but because I might just get a room to myself.

Anyway, the thing was, it was the mothers who did everything to do with school. The dads hadn't a clue about any of that.

In fact, I'm sure dads didn't even know where kids came from. One day you come home from work and there's a little new person running about. All you see is another mouth to feed, but that's all you want to know: the school meetings, plays, general kids' stuff just didn't happen in a 1980's dad's head.

My mam also did the vast majority of the work in the house. She loved to sing and dance as she did this, very happy lady, and when she wasn't, you wouldn't know. These women had a special way of dealing with depression, which was to push it all to the way back in their heads and pretend everything was alright. They were warriors, those mammies.

Let's be honest, those were great days.

THiNGS YOU DiD AS A KiD WHEN AN ADULT SHOULD HAVE BEEN PRESENT

1. Light fires.
2. Go camping/hiking.
3. Chop down trees.
4. Trap animals.
5. Learn how to swim.

The swimming pool was an awful place, but it was where I learned how to swim. Today you'll find a hundred kids splashing around on a Saturday morning, being taught by qualified instructors, but back then there were no swimming lessons. We would queue up outside the pool, towels under our arms. It was 15p in, and you'd be given a ticket to hand in as you entered the swimming pool. Then it was into the changing room, togs on, run through the cold, disinfectant foot pool, then cannonball into the big pool.

The poor lifeguard was sick of telling us: no running, no jumping, no dive-bombs. Jesus, me and the lads did those three things for the whole hour. I stayed in the shallow end; I still couldn't swim, but I couldn't tell the lads that.

Once, I was walking along the edge of the pool, at the deep end. One of the lads pushed me in. I put my arms out over my head and did a perfect dive into the pool, surfaced like a pro and began to swim, it was amazing ...

    KARL: No you didn't!
    ME: Shut up you.
    KARL: Tell the truth.
    ME: Alright.

I stayed in the shallow end for weeks and a little girl, named Orla Hayden, aged 8, taught me how to doggy paddle. I did that for weeks until eventually I got the confidence to put my arms out. I did all this with my glasses on, never putting my head under the water. Then one of the lads got me goggles, and I finally took my glasses off. The next few weeks were spent gently placing the goggles on the surface of the water, so I could just see my feet at the bottom. Another few weeks after that, I had my head under. Then I lost the goggles and I had to use just my glasses again to see to the bottom.

The lads were bored waiting for me to go to the deep end, but after months of careful visits to the swimming pool, I did it.

SHIT ... TING ... MYSELF ...

But I had to learn to do it. If I wanted longer in the pool, then I had to deal with the deep end, for reasons which will become clear shortly. Eventually, I was doing it without even thinking. It was so much fun, the lot of us going mental and splashing about. Then the lifeguard would blow his whistle when the hour was up.

LIFEGUARD: Everyone out!

All the kids jumped out of the pool, except for us. We would sink to the bottom of the deep end, all holding our breath, me wearing my glasses underwater, waiting until the lifeguard let in the next batch of kids and the hour started again. Then we'd surface and swim away. Lifeguard never noticed, not surprising given that the pool was so full, you were barely able to swim. Anyway, we were just another bunch of annoying kids to him.

Off to the side of the swimming pool was a side room. (It was actually the room where my crèche was all those years back.) It was also used for functions, hence its name: THE FUNCTION ROOM.

That was where I learned how to ballroom dance. The lads didn't know about that particular hobby, I just did it to keep my mam happy. She needed some sort of Ballroom in her life, so she lived it through me, I suppose.

But if I'd known how cool it would become, as in *Strickly Come Dancing* on the BBC, I would have been up there every day, practising my heart out. My mam still says to me, 'You haven't made it until you're on *Strickly*.' So much for my career.

So I joined Pat Sharkey's School of Dance.

It was only once a week, thank God. I was paired with a very odd-looking partner. I was tall, so Pat Sharkey himself said I had to dance with a tall partner because her shape suited my shape. So I danced with this girl who looked like a really tall, skinny duck.

Pat Sharkey would bang his long stick as we danced around the room. I think he saw himself as the dance teacher from *Fame* (look it up, youngsters).

PAT: Dance, children, dance.

I moved around that floor like Bambi on ice, and my duckling partner wasn't much good either. I never really got any better. I went for a few weeks, then Pat Sharkey pulled my mother to the side and whispered those awful words into her professional dancer's ear: 'Your son can't dance.'

My mother wept in the arms of Pat Sharkey and I was never to return to Pat Sharkey's School of Dance.

DAD: Why do you have the boy dancing? You'll turn him into a fairy.
MAM: Dancing is not for fairies, all the men I danced with were amazing.
DAD: Did they marry?
MAM: No.
DAD: Fairies, the lot of them.
MAM: Well it doesn't matter now, he can't dance anyway.
DAD: That's because he's a man and not a fairy, for feck's sake.
MAM: Well I'm not giving up. He can audition for the Tops of the Town.
DAD: Ah jaysus, not that thing again.

Tops of the Town

This was one of the biggest competitions when I was a kid. Different areas would compete against each other in amateur dramatics. All these mad women, some kids and normally one man who was a widower or a divorcee would join the group. They would do songs, sketches, stand-up, big dance routines; to be honest, it was the funniest thing I've ever seen on stage, a collection of the worst acts you could ever find all under one roof.

My dad hated this time of year, when my mam would be practising in front of us all. We had to turn the telly off and she and her mates would be dancing in the front room, with tap shoes (on a carpet) and canes, and top hats. My mam was the only one with any timing.

So this year, myself and a few of the lads were roped into heading up to the Function Room, because my mam said they were desperate for boys. First night they had myself, Karl, Tally, Ken and Brian all dancing in the middle of auld ones with top hats and canes, trying to tap dance. As soon as the first song ended, the lads all ran out the door. I looked at my mam, shrugged my shoulders and followed.

The point to all this is ... my mam's group had entered a competition that was to be held in the school hall. Two communities going head to head: it was Ballinteer Am Dram versus Wickham Am Dram. Big rivals. Big battle.

The winner of this would go on to the Gaiety Theatre in Dublin for *the Final*. I sat in the audience in the school hall with my dad, sisters and Eric, my mates were scattered around with their families, and we would signal to each other by sticking our middle finger up behind our heads.

We were sitting patiently in our seats when my mam came running down to us, dressed as an army sergeant. My dad burst out laughing.

> DAD: You're looking great there, Eithne ... A-tten-tion (*salute*).
> MAM: We need your help, Paddy.

DAD: What?

MAM: The comedian is too upset to go on.

DAD: Why?

MAM: It's his anniversary, so it upsets him.

DAD: Wife dead?

MAM: No, left him.

DAD: He's probably a fairy.

MAM: No he's not, now we need you to fill in.

DAD: Ah here, Eithne, no way.

MAM: You're always telling jokes.

DAD: Yeah, to the lads in the pub.

MAM: Well just pretend it's a big pub, now come on.

We all encouraged him to do it, as we knew this would be *absolutely classic*!

Mam dragged Dad out of the seat and off to the backstage area.

The show began. It was peppered with mad women doing awful dance routines and, in between, songs sung out of tune, dodgy impressionists, and mental 'comedy' sketches. But at the same time, it was really entertaining because it was *so* bad.

Now. Here came the best part of my young life.

MC: Ladies and gentlemen, PADDY BYRNE.

Out came Dad, had to be shown where the mic was. When he spoke into it, he gave himself a fright; if you're not used to hearing your voice amplified, it's very weird. He settled in, had a bit of paper in his hand, coughed and began ...

PADDY: Do you ever notice ... ahem ... sorry ... did you ever notice ...

Tries to read off the paper, audience coughing too, all sitting quietly.

PADDY: Yeah, no forget that ... (*reads paper*) ... I was in a supermarket the other day ... (*reads paper*) why was I there? (*still trying to read script*) ... these aren't even my jokes ...

Audience now getting very shifty in their seats. Then ...

AUDIENCE MEMBER: Get off!

My Dad looks up, sees the neighbour who heckled.

DAD: That's what your wife said to me last night, John Brophy.

The audience laughed ... Dad takes this in ...

DAD: Yeah and I wouldn't mind, but I bumped into a fellow on the way into your wife's bedroom as I was leaving.

Howls of laughter. My dad was now loving this, he went through all the neighbours in the audience ... upsetting them all, spilling secrets, getting men into trouble with their wives.

DAD: I know, Betty, that Paddy said he was in work, but if smelling of beer is work, then he's the best in the business.

Betty angry ... Paddy laughs ... Betty belts him ... Paddy stops laughing ...

DAD: I said to Bernie, do you like your pussy? Bernie says, 'Oh I love to stroke my pussy, Paddy' (*doing Bernie's voice and all*). She thought I was talking about her cat.

He got dirtier, more offensive, but audience were loving it – all except my mam and her am dram mates.

DAD: See that priest, he has a filthy habit, a nun's habit, in bed every night.

Room full of laughter, rounds of applause, priest mortified. Mother mortified.

MC comes on behind my Dad.

MC: Paddy Byrne, ladies and gentlemen ... boys and girls ... yes, Paddy, there's boys and girls in here.
PADDY: Sure they've all heard it before.
MC: Paddy Byrne, everyone.
PADDY: I'm not even nearly finished ... and Mary there ...
MC: Thank you, Paddy, we've loads to get through ... Paddy Byrne, everyone.

My mam ran onto the stage and dragged my dad off, audience all clapping and laughing as he went. Suddenly, he broke free of my mam and ran back to the mic, grabbed it and said ...

DAD: Dancing is for fairies! (*waving his arms in the air, with a 'let's hear more applause' gesture*)

Laughter all round.

He was then dragged back offstage by the combined strength of my mam and her mates, who pulled him to the side.

My mam wouldn't speak to Dad again for days, but he was a star around the housing estate, even got asked to do a few pub gigs. He said no, it was a once-off. My mam's group didn't get through. The judges said that upsetting priests, dancers and most of the am dram community in one show had never been achieved before, so Ballinteer Am Dram could hang their heads in shame. And they would be banned from any future competitions.

They had to regroup, change their name, and my mam had to sign a contract stating that her husband would never, ever work with them again.

My mother felt terrible.

Dad loved it.

Shortly after the Tops of the Town we had ...

HALLOWE'EN! A pagan festival, celebrated by Irish Catholics. Reason? Plenty of drink involved, day off work, parties in houses, stuffing yourself silly with sweets, jumping around a fire praising false Gods.

Basically, all the fun stuff Jesus doesn't want you doing.

The most important thing to get organised first is *the Bonfire*. All the housing estates in the area would build their own bonfire, the bigger the better. These days the parents will build the bonfire and monitor it; in the '80s, the kids were solely in charge of collecting the wood and piling it up into a monster fire hazard.

We would start on 1 October; Hallowe'en is on 31 October. That's one whole month of collecting stuff to throw on the fire. We were like little ants, busy busy at our task. As soon as we were finished our homework or it was the weekend, all the kids on the road headed off in different directions to find wood.

At first, we'd call into people's houses and ask them for something for the bonfire, and they would give us mostly small bits of rubbish to burn. It was handy for them because it meant they didn't have to burn it themselves out the back garden.

We'd bring all these items to the centre of the field and leave them in a pile. That's when the mischief would start. At this stage, judging by the pile, it looked like the bonfire would burn for about an hour. Not long enough! Time to bring in some heavy-duty fuel.

PALLETS!

The only place we could get wooden pallets was in the local supermarket ... at night ... when it was closed ... in other words ... WE FECKIN' ROBBED THEM! Me and Karl had no problems when the lads decided we were going to rob the pallets from Superquinn, Ballinteer (sorry, Mr Quinn, but you should have paid us in cash, not crisps and Coke).

Of course ... SHITTING ... MY ... SELF ... AGAIN.

I think I actually spent most of my childhood SHITTING MYSELF.

The pallets were always piled up against a fence around the back of the supermarket. When it got dark, over the top we all went, Karl, Brian, Ken, Tally, me and loads of others.

When we landed on the other side of the fence among the pallets, we were confronted by a similar gang of kids from Wickham Park.

ME: What are yous doing here?
WICKHAM CREW: We're robbing pallets.
ME: No you're bloody not, *we're* robbing pallets.
WICKHAM CREW: Piss off, we were here first.

ME: No you bleedin' weren't.
WICKHAM CREW: Yes we bleedin' were.

This is totally true: I was to see the same sketch played out on *The Life Of Brian* a few years later, when the 'People's Front of Judea' meet another group in the sewers of Caesar's Palace (not the Las Vegas one, the ancient one), both groups plotting to kill Caesar.

Suddenly, a light came on, lighting up the whole gang versus gang scene, and we all began to jump back over the fence, guard dogs barking in the background as we laughed and screamed our escape. The Ludford Drive gang and the Wickham crew all ran away together on that night as one, with guard dogs chasing us.

'BARK, BARK, BARK!'

We found out months later that Superquinn had no guard dogs. Tony was on night duty that night and he always kept a traffic cone handy, then if the security light came on, he'd pick up the traffic cone and start to bark into it. If you ask me, GENIUS! In those days you had to build and create, so fair play to Tony, best security guard ever. In fact, if you're reading this now, please go and find a traffic cone, keep it at your house, then hide in a bush if you see unwanted guests coming to the house, BARK away into the cone, and *hey presto!*, they think you've a menacing guard dog and run away.

Now, we still had no pallets, and no one was keen on another assault on Superquinn. Time to think of another wood we could use. Out came Brian Roche into the field, his dad was a builder and this mad fella walked over and slammed a chainsaw down into the middle of us.

BRIAN: Let's chop down some bastard trees!

We all cheered. I'm telling you, *Lord of the Flies*.

Night fell. In the distance, from the direction of The Tunnel (trees behind all the houses), came unusual sounds.

VROOM ... SPUTTLE ... TURN ... BANG ... CUT OUT ...

'Bollix!'

NOISE OF CORD BEING PULLED ... ONCE, TWICE, THREE TIMES ... VROOM, VROOM, VROOMMMMMM!

BRIAN: We're in business, boys. Die, trees!

Brian started to cut into a mother of a tree. We all stood in the dark with torches as Brian cut away at the tree with a face like Jack Nicholson in *The Shining*, the biggest grin ever on his face, as the wood chips few into his face-guard. (Well at least he was wearing a face-guard, I know a bunch of kids were just about to get crushed by tonnes of tree, but at least Brian wasn't going to get wood chip in his eyes.)

ME: Holy shit, man, it's going!

The tree began to tilt, Brian, the brave bollix, just kept going at it with the chainsaw.

VROOM, VROOM, VROOM ... silence ... *CREAAA-KKKK-KKKK*

BRIAN: Run, lads, it's falling.

But it was pitch dark, we didn't know which way to go. Torches crashed to the ground as we ran, mad laughter as we looked for cover, the tree seemed to fall forever, all the lads scattering left and right in a blind panic. In a panic of any sort, I'm the man *not* to be near. If you're near me in a panic situation, something bad is about to happen. If I was a fireman, I'd bring all the rescued people back into the burning building.

It felt as if loads of people were tripping me up, I hit the ground and a massive BANG! of wood fell around my head in the total darkness ... more silence, very deep silence after the ear-shattering noise ... then ...

BRIAN: Is everyone alright?
KEN: Yeah.
KARL: Where's Jay? Jay!

I was pinned to the ground, I couldn't move. Torchlight came jerking towards me.

BRIAN: Holy shit, lads, Jay's dead.
ME: I'm not.
BRIAN: He's not.

More of the lads and their torches arrived. Then sniggering, then belly laughter.

The tree had nearly crushed me to death, but somehow all the heavy branches and trunk had completely missed me. It was the lighter branches that had tripped me up and pinned me down.

KARL: Holy shit, man, you lucky bollix.

The lads helped me up, brushed me down. We then spent the next hour with little saws, axes and the chainsaw, breaking up that huge tree. In the middle of all this, the cops then arrived – some nosy bollix had called them because of all the noise. The cops stopped at the kerb, got out of their car.

TALLY: Cops.

Chainsaw off, torches off, sawing stopped.

The poor coppers didn't know what the fuss was all about. They walked right up to where we were, but we stayed totally still, like the Viet Cong hiding in the Cu Chi Tunnels, and they couldn't see us among the trees, even with their silly weak torch. They got back into the squad car, drove away, and we got on with our lumberjack stuff again. The cops returned twice that night, but still couldn't find us. The Tunnel was our territory, no adults could find us in there!

The next day, we all basically slept in school at our desks. The other students kept a lookout for us, to give us a heads-up if it looked like the teacher was about to spot us.

After school, we inspected the bonfire, and it was looking good. On top of the household rubbish now rested hefty chunks of tree trunk and heavy branches, with smaller branches at the bottom to act as kindling and get the blaze going. While we admired it, the cops arrived again, looked at our firewood.

COP: Alright, lads? That's some fire you have there. You didn't cut a tree down last night by any chance to get that nice wood?
KARL: No.
COP: No? Where did you get the wood then?
KARL: Found it.
COP: Found it? Really?
KARL: Yeah, it's bits from a tree that was chopped … fell … down.

The cop winked.

COP: Okay lads, I just hope you didn't chop a tree down for it.

The cop then headed off, he well knew it was us, but he couldn't be arsed writing up the report.

The weeks passed and we'd add wood to the fire when needed. But as the big night got closer, now we had to get kids to sneak out and stand guard overnight to protect the wood stockpile. It was fast becoming the best bonfire in the area, and we all know who that attracts ...

BIGGER BOYS!

Bigger Boys were fellas older and stronger than us from a different estate, and if they wanted something, they simply came in and took it. But not this, not the fire, we'd worked way too hard for this to let it go. So three lads would guard the bonfire each night with, get this, traffic cones.

On two occasions the lads/nightwatchmen hid in the bushes beside the wood pile and when the **BIGGER BOYS** arrived, the lads started barking into the cones. The **BIGGER BOYS** legged it. The traffic cone is mightier than the sword, people. It had to be because we were wimps.

'GET YOUR FIREWORKS, FIVE FOR FIFTY!' the woman with the pram full of fireworks roared out across the street at us.

Henry Street, Dublin City. What a great, exciting place to be on

Hallowe'en Day. We'd all headed in on the bus to get our totally illegal fireworks, with money given to us by our parents.

I didn't know what to buy.

FIREWORKS FOR SALE FROM A PRAM

1. **Sparklers**
2. **Roman candles**
3. **Catherine wheels**
4. **French bombs**
5. **Ear aches**
6. **Whistlers**
7. **Screamers**
8. **Spiders**
9. **Wolf pack**
10. **Dragon's tears**

It was endless. I have no idea where these old women with their prams got these fireworks, but we bought loads of them. There we were, 14, 15 years of age, buying bombs basically.

(For anyone who couldn't get money off their parents, a Mickey Dribbler was free. You'd get an empty Mr Freeze packet, light one end, then the plastic would drip and make a *whoop whoop whoop* noise as it fell. We called it a Mickey Dribbler because it was long, like a mickey, and the drips were the wee. Charming.)

Got home, armload of fireworks at the ready. It was nearly Hallowe'en night! *So exciting!* First things first, get into costume. My whole house got dressed up, and when the kids came knocking for sweets, my dad and mam answered the door in their gear: my mam dressed as a witch, same hat and wig for years; my dad dressed as a dead butler.

Dad would answer the door to the kids just to scare the shite out of them.

DAD: Agrhh, I'll kill yeh all.

Then he'd throw sweets and popcorn at them.

I brought my two little sisters around the doors. Eithne, the baby, was in a black bag with the top cut off, my mam said she was a Rubbish Child. Rachel was in a blonde wig, long skinny coat and high heels, my mum said she was a hooker.

DAD: A hooker? Very funny, trick or treat, trick, get it, *trick*.

I was dressed in my mam's black fur coat, with rubber gloves on my feet over my plimsoles and another pair of rubber gloves on my hands. Give up? I was a Gorilla. I didn't even have a mask, my mam just blacked up my face with face paint and put a red clown's nose on me.

We went around the houses, with black bin sacks to collect our sweets, we knocked at hundreds of houses, got back home with

a mountain of goodies. I delivered my sisters home safely, ate a few sweets, and started to leave again.

DAD: Where the hell are you going?
ME: To the bonfire.
DAD: Not until we set off a few of your fireworks out the back garden, son.

Karl, Tally, Brian and Karl had all arrived at this stage. We stood out the back garden as my Dad lined up the fireworks. My mam had Eithne in her arms, still in a rubbish bag. Rachel leaned against mam, sucking on a chocolate bar of some sort, still dressed as a hooker. Eric watched from the house, dressed as a teenager. I was still a Gorilla.

Dad read the instructions on the box of fireworks.

> DAD: Do not light in a built-up area ... bollix to that ... bury this firework to the dotted line indicated at the side of this box ... bollix to that, too. Right, let's do it!
> MAM: Are you sure, Paddy?
> DAD: Eithne, I do this every year, I know what I'm doing.
> MAM: Yeah, but I've never seen fireworks like that before, all in one box, where did you get those, kids?
> ME: Off the aul ones with the prams in town, Mam.

The firework my dad had on the ground was called The Werewolf. It had eight fireworks in it, and it would shoot one at a time into the air after you lit the fuse.

> DAD: (*with a fag in his mouth*) Stand back, this could be a bit hairy.

Dad lit the fuse with his fag, then he ran back to us against the wall of the house, at a safe distance of about 10 feet. The box said to stand 50–60 feet away. The fuse ran to the box, then the first firework from the Werewolf shot up into the air.

'OOOHHHHHHHH!' we all shouted, the same noise every person in the world makes when a firework whizzes up into the air.

Then, OH ... MY ... GOD ...

Straight after the first firework shot into the air, the force of its expulsion tipped over the box, the box that Dad was supposed to bury in the ground. We were all about to find out *why* you're supposed to bury the box in the ground. The top of the box, where the firework comes out of, was staring us all in the face.

DAD: Bollix…….. *Run!*

As we all ran back into the house, the fireworks started to shoot at us, missing us by inches and hitting the walls. We all screamed as we ran. My dad had to grab me as naturally my instinct was to run straight into the path of the fireworks. Somehow we all got into the house, my dad slammed the back door behind him and fireworks ricocheted off the glass.

MAM: You stupid bloody man, you nearly killed us all.

Me, Tally, Brian, Ken and Karl were all wetting ourselves with laughter. Eithne and Rachel were crying. My dad was trying not to laugh.

Me and the lads left my family in the house and we headed off to light the bonfire. Brian had got petrol from a machine his dad owned, so he doused the whole thing. We needed two ladders to get to the top of the wood pile, it was that incredibly big. Then Brian climbed down, we lit rags and threw them at the pile. It went up in a second.

It was amazing, all the kids gathered around it, like moths to a lightbulb. The BIGGER BOYS arrived with their cider, but never started any fights, we just sat around together and watched as the fire burnt itself down flat. THE BIGGER BOYS left then and the younger kids went home too.

Weeks and weeks of gathering wood, and after a couple of hours it was all gone. So we entertained ourselves a bit more by jumping over the fire, until it had died down to embers.

It was getting late now, but Tally had an idea: if he threw a can of baked beans in, it would blow up the fire and put it out. In other words, for people reading this book who have sense, if you blew a fire apart, it would literally blow itself into tiny bits and those tiny bits would go out by themselves. That's teenage logic for you, more hormones than brains.

Tally ran to his house and came back with a tin of beans. He threw it into the middle of what was left of the fire.

We stood around the fire, waiting, but nothing happened. The beans were silent in the middle, no explosion, no noise, no steam.

ME: Bollix to this lads, I'll give the tin a belt.

Before any of the lads could shout *NO!*, I reached for the beans with my stick.

Cut to: my front door, my mam and dad rushing to help me, Tally, Karl, Brian and Ken all holding onto me, my face covered in baked beans. The lads were covered in baked beans, too.

> ME: I'm blind, I'm blind!
> MAM: Jesus, what's happened to him?
> DAD: Yeh feckin' dope.
> KARL: Tin of beans blew up in his face.
> DAD: How?

Even with a face full of burnt-on beans, I managed to rat on everyone.

> ME: Tally threw beans into the centre of the fire, they wouldn't blow up, so I hit them with a stick and they blew up in my face, now I can't see anymore.
> MAM: Jesus, he's blind, Paddy.

My dad had a good look at me.

> DAD: I think you're right, Eithne. Lads, go home, I'll have to deal with this.

The lads left me, probably blinded for life, on the couch in the living room, covered in beans, dressed as a Gorilla ...

DAD: I'd say he's blinded for life now, Eithne.

MAM: Do you think so?

DAD: Yep, better stay still there, son, for an hour or so.

My dad left me covered in beans and blinded for life on the couch for *two hours*. It wasn't until after the two hours passed, me terrified that I'd lost my sight forever, that my dad picked the baked beans off my eyelids. The beans had welded the eyelids together, which my dad had spotted, but which he hadn't told me. He made me sit there in terror for two hours as punishment, then pulled the beans off.

DAD: Now yeh dope, you won't do that again.

ME: I can see!

DAD: You weren't blind in the first place, yeh mad thing, the beans stuck your eyelids together.

MAM: No more messing with fires and fireworks and beans, that goes for the both of you.

Me and Dad agreed ... *no more*.

The next week Dad took the tip of his finger off with a Roman candle, and I ended up in hospital with first degree burns from a Mickey Dribbler.

CHAPTER 14
PURPLE WEETABIX

KARL: Stay still, man.

ME: I don't want to do this.

TALLY: But you're the tallest now, Jay.

ME: But you're two years older than me.

KARL: Stay still.

Karl, Tally, Brian, Ken and me were at the back of Dundrum Shopping Centre.

We all hated the Dundrum Shopping Centre because they'd knocked down our bowling alley to build it, and my video shop had disappeared, too, where I used to get movie posters off the lady owner. That was a great shop, she would let you pre-book movies and ring your house when the movie was in so you could come and collect it. I'd cycle down, get me movie and poster, back to the gaff to Blu-Tack up the poster and watch the movie.

The bowling alley was a great hang-out place, with loads of kids everywhere. It had snooker tables, video games and, of course, ten-pin bowling.

LiST OF BOWLiNG ALLEY ARCADE GAMES

1. **1942**
2. **Donkey Kong**
3. **Galaxian**
4. **Pac-Man**
5. **Centipede**
6. **Kung-Fu Master**
7. **Frogger**
8. **Space Invaders**
9. **Bubble Bobble**
10. **Defender**

When you lost a life, you had to go and get more money, no respawning as the kids call it now.

Karl was the best on 1942, which was a WWII game. You were basically a little fighter plane called 'Super Ace', which tried to shoot down the Japanese air fleet. Karl was on it for so long that I had to go and buy him burgers and chips, then feed him the burgers and chips while he continued to play the game. He had a crowd around him, watching as he played, because he was close to finishing the game. Or 'clocking it' as we called it. The score would be 00000 at the start of the game, but if you got to 99999, because the game wasn't made to take a higher number, it would go back to 00000 so you 'clocked it'. Only the chosen few got to witness this phenomenon.

The tension was high as he went into *stage 42*! Then in came the big plane, people were cheering Karl on by now, and then … he did it … HE FINISHED 1942! This was a near impossible task for a human, but he did it.

After all that drama, we went outside Dundrum Shopping Centre where the lads proceeded to apply mascara to my upper lip. Tally had got it from his mam's bedroom.

KARL: Stay still.

They were trying to draw a moustache on my upper lip so that I could go into the supermarket and buy two litres of cider for our camping trip. I was only 16, and not the oldest of the lads, but I was the tallest. So the lads reckoned that with my height and a mascara moustache, I'd get served, no problem.

KARL: Done. You look 23, man.
TALLY: Yeah, you're old, dude.
BRIAN: They'll never guess.
KEN: You'll be grand, Jay.
ME: I don't want to.
KARL: Here's the money, go for it, man, all they can say is no.

I walked away from the lads, trying to put a 23-year-old walk on me so no one would notice I was 16. My heart was pumping through my chest as I walked into the supermarket. I didn't even get a trolley, I just picked up a basket and headed to the alcohol section.

I looked around at the other men and women in this aisle, all nonchalantly and legally buying beer and wine, and I copied their actions. As they picked up something, they would make a face, then put it back on the shelf, so I would pick up a wine, make a face, then put it back on the shelf.

I then went over to the cider. They were huge bottles, but again I picked up different ones, put them back down, as if the cider connoisseur had arrived into town. Then I put six two-litre bottles of cider into my basket, headed for the tills.

I'm sure I stuck out like a sore thumb. These other people had trolleys with food in them, as well as the alcohol. I just looked mental with my basket full of cider, no other items and a drawn-on moustache on my upper lip.

I joined the queue. All I wanted to do was drop the cider and run. I was sweating as I got nearer to the girl on the cash till. I had deliberately picked a younger girl, hoping she wouldn't give a shit. If I'd picked an older woman, she would have known my mam or dad or something. The person in front of me seemed to take ages, packing and packing, and my hands were getting sweatier and sweatier. I was sure the moustache was running, too. Finally, the person in front of me paid and left.

My turn. It was like trying to leave Iran in the movie *Argo*, that tense. I felt like I was about to be pounced on and put in jail for life, or hung, or beaten. Stop it, Brain.

GIRL: Next.

I said nothing. I just stood the six two-litre flagons of cider on the conveyor belt. She pressed the belt, it moved forward, the bottles wobbled and all fell over.

ME: Sorry, sorry.

Oh Jaysus. Disaster. I picked them up, put them back upright, noticed the security guard glancing over. Oh Jesus, I was dead now. The girl looked at me.

GIRL: Are these all for you?

Hold it in, Jason, don't rat, don't fall apart. But I surprised myself.

ME: It's a finals party for university.

Good one, Jason.

GIRL: Oh, I love a party, where's it on?

Oh Bollix, security guard walking closer to me.

ME: Trinity College Dublin.

That's the only college I could think of and it was miles away from where I stood.

GIRL: Trinity? But where's the party?
ME: College ... Dublin ...

Starting to fall apart like a cheap robot.

GIRL: Is it in a flat in Dublin?

ME: Dublin, yes.

Security guard now listening to conversation at the end of the till.

GIRL: Yeah, but *where*?

Trying to think of street names ...

ME: U2 Street.
GIRL: (*she looked at me for a bit*) You're weird.

Security guard's eyes peeled on me now. Sweat pumping.

She beeped through all the cider. I put three in one bag and three in the other bag, gave her a bundle of dirty teenage money. She took it and counted it like she was counting dog turds. Then she gave me the receipt.

GIRL: Bye, enjoy your party, if you ever find where it is.

I picked up the bags.

ME: (*broken voice*) Bye.

Walked by the security guard.

GUARD: Have a nice day, sir.

Sir?

ME: Dublin.

GUARD: Excuse me?

ME: I mean, bye, bye, thank you.

I walked towards the exit. I thought the whole shop was looking at me as I left. If this was a movie, all I could imagine was crowds of people in the shop all frozen, staring at me as I walked out of the supermarket at 16 years of age with six two-litre bottles of cider. Sweat pouring off me and my moustache melting.

I could see the lads up ahead, all I had to do now was get to them. As they came into focus, their faces looked all white, as I got near to them, they all ignored me, looking out into the car park the other way. Why were they doing this?

Just as I got to Karl, he said under his breath, while looking the other way:

KARL: Keep walking, keep walking, security guard behind you.

OH ... MY ... GOD ...

This was it, I was dead. My parents would kill me for this. This is what a drug mule must feel like right before they're caught, stripped and banged up in a tiny prison cell that's 100 degrees because they were stupid enough to take on the customs officials in some foreign hot place.

I walked past the lads, walked on down the path, I glanced over my shoulder and sure enough, the security guard from the supermarket was following me.

He sped up as I sped up walking. I went down the steps, headed across the field for home. I didn't look back, I just kept walking.

Breathe, Jason. I'll never do this again. I kept walking fast, away from the supermarket ... then ...

BANG! Hand on my shoulder. Game Over. I turned around to face my fate ...

It was the lads. Thank God! They ran up to me, just as frightened as I was, all with pale faces, giggling with fear and confusion.

> KEN: Holy shit, man, well done.
> BRIAN: Close one.
> TALLY: Hero, man, you're a hero.
> ME: What happened with the security guard?
> KARL: I reckon he was just following you to make sure you weren't buying drink for anyone else ... BUT YOU WERE, for us! You did it, man.
> TALLY: Now let's go camping!

We all danced around in the field beside the supermarket, holding the cider above our heads. Then I ran behind the bushes for a poo.

★★★

DAD: All set, boys?
ME: Yeah.

Dad was driving me, Ken, Karl and Brian in his car, two other cars were behind us, filled with more lads. Only kids from the southside, from Ballinteer, would be driven to a campsite. Most other kids got buses, then hiked. Not us. Not the LUDS, we were to be driven, which meant we could bring whatever we wanted because we wouldn't be carrying it there or back.

But we still went as light as we could.

LiST OF 'LiGHT AS WE COULD' ESSENTiAL iTEMS

1. A big yellow gas cylinder (Brian Roche brought it, would have done us for months, never mind a weekend).
2. 10 large boxes of cereal.
3. 10 pints of milk.
4. A heap of bread.
5. A tonne of sausages.
6. White pudding.
7. Bacon.
8. Frying pan.
9. Four pots.
10. The top off a gas cooker (six rings, massive).
11. Tents, duvets, pillows, blow-up beds.

12. **A shovel.**

13. **Umbrellas.**

14. **Firelighters.**

15. **Six bags of coal.**

16. **Spoons.**

17. **Forks.**

18. **Knives (various types), with chopping board.**

19. **A mountain of crisps and sweets.**

20. **48 toilet rolls.**

We hid our cider in the bottom of our camping bags. As my dad drove, we could hear items banging off the bottles as Dad went over bumps. He was too busy talking about camping and giving us mad tips.

DAD: I was a scout for years, did a bit of survival meself, lads.

I think the only time he was ever in a forest was in the clump of trees outside the pub where he'd have a piss on the way home, if for some mad reason he didn't have the car with him.

DAD: So if you're eating food, make sure you eat upwind so as not to attract any wild animals to the campsite.

What wild animals? This was *Ireland*, the only thing to attack would be a deer or a fox.

DAD: If you're cooking on the fire, make sure you cook upwind and, I cannot stress this enough, if you're having a shit, make sure it's upwind or a rat will gnaw your bollix off, very sore, very sore, those feckers don't bite stuff, they gnaw stuff off, much slower, more painful process. I knew a fella ...

He always knows a fella ...

DAD: ... who was camping, had a shit, pulled up his trousers, rat in his jocks, gnawed his bollix off.

We all started laughing, the man was mad.

DAD: It's not funny, lads, also be sure to bury your shit, so no one can track you, best to leave no clues.

We arrived at Clara Lara, the parents unloaded the cars, put our tents up, lit the fire, made us a quick snack, well, not all the parents, my dad was walking around the boundary of the campsite.

DAD: Just making sure no animals have left their spray anywhere, they're not in your territory, you're in theirs.

Dad walked around, sniffing, and if he thought he could smell an animal scent, he'd have a quick piss in that area. All the other dads couldn't believe what they were seeing.

Dad then walked back to join us. The other dads had finished setting us up, we finished off our beans and sausages, my dad zipped up his fly, lit a smoke.

DAD: Right, lads, I'm off. Don't die or your mother will kill me.

All the cars pulled away and were gone. We were left with the sound of the fast-running river, which we camped right beside, and the fire crackling away.

TALLY: Yes! Let's get drunk.

There must have been at least 8–10 kids there that night. None of us had drunk before, but we all pretended we had. Well, we had sips of Communion wine, but nothing like this volume.

We got to our bags, took out our two litres of Linden Village, we called it Lethal Village, and with good reason. We all poured out the top of the cider and refilled it with blackcurrant. Karl said this was best, so as not to taste the cider.

We all sat in a ring around the fire. I was so nervous.

ME: We better be careful not to get too drunk, lads, we could fall in the fire and melt or drown in the river or, worse still, wander off into the forest, never to return because a rat has gnawed us to death while we were in a drunken sleep.

Huge uproar of laughter, followed by many deadners and a quick pile-on. Karl shouted from the top of the pile:

KARL: Shut up and relax, yeh mad yoke.

Cigarettes then came out, we all coughed and spluttered our way through them.

If you ask any of these guys now as adults, every one of them would tell you that they didn't want to smoke and didn't want to drink at that age. But we had to, this was life, we were dipping our teenage toes into it, even if every time I dipped my toe into anything, I got into trouble, normally through my own fault.

The rules of the drinking were set down. When you had drunk your cider down to the label, you were allowed to rip the label off, this was intended to get everyone at the same level of drunkenness. If someone got too drunk, the rest would mind him.

ME: Agreed.

You could hear the twist and fizz of the tops of the blackcurrant-filled cider bottles as we opened them to begin.

As usual, my heart was thumping. I watched as the others drank, I had a small taste, ooooooh jaysus, that was horrible, it was like fizzy blackcurrant dish-water. As the minutes passed, lads were lifting their cider bottles to the dark sky, guzzling, the light from the fire making their two litres glow.

KEN: I'm down to the label.
BRIAN: So am I.
KARL: Label.
TALLY: Label.

All I could hear around the fire was 'Label, Label, Label'. I was nowhere near the label, so I quietly poured mine out onto the ground. The others couldn't see me do it because the light of the fire was in their eyes. I poured until it was near the label, then drank the rest.

ME: Label!

We all cheered. We'd made it to the label. We continued on into the night, trying to drink our cider. As we got a bit more tipsy, we got braver with the cider and began to drink it for real. I later found out that all the lads had poured out their cider to the label, with only a few mouthfuls of cider taken.

Even so, we all then drank at least one litre of cider that night.

Drunk

I remember feeling great, like I could say anything, we were all laughing, giggling and saying stupid shit, then it all went dreamy, and the rest of the night felt like I was outside looking in. I don't know what happened.

The next morning I awoke in the tent, with Ken and Brian beside me still asleep. But where was everyone else? I fell out of the tent, my head was killing me. I looked around the campsite. It looked like a scene from *Doctor Who*. There were purple pools of sick everywhere, even on the sides of trees and bushes. Aliens had been here, left their mark splattered all over the place.

No, it was blackcurrant sick from the twisted stomachs of a bunch of teenagers who'd never drunk alcohol before and certainly not a whole litre of cheap cider. I found Karl in a bush asleep, woke him, got him to the fire to warm him back to life.

I found Tally underneath another tent. Apparently, he'd tried to get into his tent in the pitch dark, blind drunk, and had literally lifted the tent up off the ground, got under it and fallen asleep on the bare ground. Brian and Ken were up by this stage, and they helped me get Tally to the fire, then the rest of the sick-faced lads arrived to the fire, and we all sat around moaning. Thank God there was no more cider.

TALLY: Let's do it again next week!

'YEAH!' we all cheered, none of us meaning it.

Bowl of Rice Krispies and some sausages sorted us out. As we sat eating our food, little did we know that the camping trip was about to turn sour ...

BIGGER BOYS! BIGGER FECKIN' BOYS!

About five of these **BIGGER BOYS** arrived out of nowhere. They were rough, well, to us they were. They took our food, our cigs, they even had knives out, waving them about. They said they wanted to camp on our site. They were about 18–20 I'd say, and not nice.

BUT there were five of them and about ten of us. This was a no-brainer for the southside Ludford Drive posse ...

WE PACKED UP OUR STUFF, TENTS AND ALL, AND LET THEM HAVE THE CAMPSITE.

ME: You're a dozy bollix, Brian.

BRIAN: It's not my fault.

ME: Can we just throw the gas cylinder in a bush?

BRIAN: No way, it's my dad's, he'll kill me.

We were now all *walking* to the next campsite. GLENDALOUGH. It was feckin' miles away from Clara Lara, about 8 miles, and we had no cars to carry all the stuff, so me and Brian had to carry his stupid big yellow gas cylinder. My hands were raw, we looked like Sherpas there was so much stuff on our backs, which made the journey all the slower.

One of the lads, Rocco, was a bit younger than me, and he was getting scared, kept saying he wanted to go home.

ROCCO: I want to go home.

ME: Well we can't, there isn't a phone anywhere.

ROCCO: If we see a car, I'm stopping it and asking them for help.

KARL: No way, we're not heading home back to the road after one night, all moaning and crying. We march on, or we'll be slagged to death when we get home.

Rocco was not happy. To be honest, I would have gone home too. After what felt like 18 miles, a car went past us. Rocco went to jump out in front of it, Karl grabbed him and sat on him. The car stopped.

CAR: Alright, lads?
KARL: Yeah, just hiking, sir. (*With Rocco under him, struggling*)
CAR: Okay, enjoy yourselves then.

He went off, Rocco started to scream at Karl. We walked on. It was about 3 pm by the time we reached Glendalough, after about a three-hour walk, exhausted. We got to the car park, looked around at the nice patches of grass.

KARL: Look, lads, lovely camping spots and the lakes, too.
ME: We can't.
KARL: What? Why?

There were signs everywhere saying NO CAMPING! I thought Rocco was going to explode. We sat on our bags, devastated, no one around and now no camping, and no phone anywhere out here.

Most people reading this would have just pitched the tents anyway, but Oh No, not the LUDS! If a sign said something, then we had to obey it, otherwise someone might … might … might … tell us off.

We walked on deeper into the forest along the edge of the lake. It was getting a bit darker now and we were in a small panic. As we walked, I noticed a tree with a swing wrapped around a branch.

ME: Look, lads, a swing.

I unravelled the rope, held it above my head and jumped in the air. I soared off down this ridge, towards the edge of the lake, but as I got nearer to the lake, the rope kept going towards the ground … you weren't supposed to *hang* from it, you were supposed to *sit* on it.

I hit the water at speed, the rope dragged me onto rocks and then into the water face-first. I hit the rocks with a bang, jumped up, knee-deep in water, the lads watching from the top of the ridge, too tired to laugh at me.

KARL: You total dope!

I climbed back up the ridge, soaking wet, with cuts all over my body and face. Rocco totally lost it then, he took out an apple, ate the whole thing in a second while screaming and crying. Then he took out a box of Weetabix, started to eat them with no milk or water while howling to himself.

I started to weep with my pain, and slumped to the ground. The rest of the lads just started hugging each other.

ROCCO: I want to go hoooome!

It was getting dark; what were we to do? Then, as if it was a sign from heaven itself, two nuns walked by us on the path. Before them they saw a group of young boys, crying, with mouthfuls of

Weetabix, one with cuts and bruises, weeping, the rest looking tired and scared.

This is what these nuns had been waiting for, we were the strangers Jesus had told them to help, this was their big Good Samaritan moment. What did they do?

They walked right by us saying …

NUN 1: Oh aren't you great boys.

Rocco grabbed one of their legs, spitting Weetabix onto her skirts as he howled for mercy.

ROCCO: (*through mouthful of Weetabix*) Helfffff uhssshhh!
NUN 1: Ho, ho, will you look at him, sister, full of life.
NUN 2: Ho, ho, kids these days.

The nuns peeled him off their legs and sped off down the path! Now what?

ROCCO: (*to the nuns*) Biffichessss!
ME: Ahh bollix to this, let's go back and camp where we're not supposed to. We're too tired and it's getting dark.

So we did. We picked up Rocco, who was still mumbling to himself, and started to walk back to the car park.

We dragged ourselves to the NO CAMPING area, my body was

still aching from being lashed into the rocks by the swing you were supposed to sit on, not hang from, and more and more of the lads were getting tired and weepy.

Then a cop car turned up. It was on patrol around the park. The cops swung over to us.

What a sight, a group of teenagers who looked like they'd been on a tour of 'Nam when all that had happened was an 8-mile hike because of a **BIGGER BOY** invasion.

GARD: Evening, boys, all okay?
ROCCO: Noooooooooooo!

Rocco threw himself onto the bonnet of the cop car, with the weight of his rucksack crushing him as he lay there, still eating Weetabix.

ROCCO: We want to go home!
KARL: He's alright, Gard, don't mind him.

As Karl said this, Rocco jumped into the back of the cop car, then Tally followed him, then as many of them that could fit in there.

The car drove off, leaving me, Karl, Ken and Brian to the elements. The lads were being driven to a hostel so they could ring the dads to collect us.

KARL: We're never going to live this down, boys, we couldn't even survive one night of camping.

I sat freezing on a rock while we waited for the cavalry to arrive, the sun was just going down over the lake, and as the sun left ... the midges arrived.

Midges love lakes, and Glendalough is a monster lake; thousands of them swarmed around us.

ME: Arghhhh, they're biting me everywhere.
KARL: Get a towel out of your bag, wet it in the lake, and wrap it around your head.

We all got out a towel, soaked it in water, wrapped it around our faces and heads, with just a tiny hole to see out of.

BRIAN: Smoke, they hate smoke.

Ken got out some smokes, dished them around to us all, we lit them and began to walk around in circles.

If you stayed still, you could feel them going down your back and into your trousers. I have never been so itchy. I feel itchy even remembering it.

An hour in and you could have written your name in the air with the thickness of midges.

So there we were, being eaten alive, walking in circles, with white towels wrapped around our faces and heads, a ciggy sticking out of the tiny mouth-hole and us puffing furiously. If anyone had seen us, they would have sworn they'd seen a cult at its dastardly work that night.

HEADLIGHTS!

Cars began to pull into the car park. Two, to be exact: my dad's and Rocco's dad's. Rocco, Tally and a few lads were there in Rocco's dad's car. Rocco was sitting in the front, looking way happier now. But still shook.

DAD: Holy Jaysus, the flies. Get in, lads, before we get the bollix ate off us.

We threw our stuff into my dad's car, even the stupid yellow gas cylinder, climbed in, shut the door, unravelled the towels. It was a bit of a squeeze with all the boys and the gear.

> DAD: You look like a terrorist group out there lads, (*being bitten*) me bleedin' neck (*slap*), bastards. So boys, one night of camping and it's back to your mammies, if I was you lot, I would have stuck it out for a bit longer.
>
> ME: Dad.
>
> DAD: Just saying, son, it's Dublin you live in, so the slagging will be massive when you get home. What happened anyway?

I told my dad the story of the BIGGER BOYS, the hike, the yellow gas cylinder, the nuns ...

> DAD: Nuns? Sure all they need is a good ride, miserable witches, sorry, son, continue ...

... the swing and the nowhere to camp. NEVER AGAIN.

Next morning, I walked out my front door, looking for any signs of slagging. The road was quiet. Slowly, Karl came out, then Brian, Ken and the rest of the crew, we all looked like we had chicken pox, bitten to death, the midges hitched a ride and ate us all the way home and while we slept.

We walked towards the field, where we reckoned we could hide from the rest of the road for a bit before the slagging started. Oh shit! The field was full of lads, waiting for us, they had all heard already.

TOM BROLLY: Here they are. How was the one-day camping trip, yeh big babies? *I want to go home, I want to go home, there's bigger boys, they might hurt us … Boo hoo.*

This went on for hours, slagging, laughing, the only person not there to endure it was Rocco.

Rocco didn't come out of his house for nearly two weeks.

Whenever lads went by his house, he'd hear …

LADS: Alright Rocco, there's a couple of nuns out here with Weetabix for yeh!

CHAPTER 15
'DON'T YOU FORGET ABOUT ME'

Start school early, leave school early, skip fourth year and leave even younger. I was only 17 years old in sixth year. *Seventeen!* That's way too young to be thrown out into the big world.

The way secondary worked was: first year, second year, third year, skip fourth year, straight into fifth year and, finally, sixth year. When I was a kid, fourth year was for the slow learners, it was like being kept back a year. In my school, if you were a fourth year, then you were a bit of a thick, which was mainly a phrase used by the teachers, not by us.

UNLUCKY BASTARDS IN FOURTH YEAR

1. **Colour-blind**
2. **Dyslexic**
3. **Asperger's**
4. **OCD**
5. **Stutterers**
6. **Hearing impairment**
7. **Intellectual disability**
8. **Bad home life**
9. **Autism**
10. **Not liked by a teacher**

These were all 'thick' children, apparently. I don't know how these kids survived school in the '70s and '80s. Teachers had no idea what they were dealing with and there were no allowances made, for anyone.

MAM: Tell him, Paddy, now it's important.

DAD: I'm telling him, now, you'll have to study hard this year, it's the Leaving Cert.

MAM: Yes, the Leaving Cert, you have to study hard.

DAD: I thought I was telling him?

MAM: Well, tell him properly.

DAD: I am telling him properly, what do you think I'm doing? Speaking yik-yak to the fella? ... Anyway, son, you want to end up with a good job ...

MAM: College, he wants to end up in college.

DAD: College? How much is college?

MAM: Oh, it's dear.

DAD: Exactly, so he'll need a job, we can't afford college.

MAM: You'll just have to work harder then, Paddy.

DAD: Harder? I don't think I could work much harder, I'm never out of the place.

MAM: Then give up the pints.

DAD: How in the name of God am I supposed to do that? I'll never be able to unwind after work.

MAM: Just go to the pub and don't drink.

DAD: What? Who? What in the name of God are yeh sayin'?

MAM: Go to the pub and have a juice.

DAD: I may as well go in with lipstick rammed up me hole, woman. Juice?

MAM: Just promise us you'll try your best in the Leaving Cert, son.

ME: I will.

DAD: Good man yourself. Right (*clap of hands*), I'm off to celebrate.

MAM: So that's it, that's the talk?

DAD: I talked, you talked, he talked, we all talked, so I'm off to celebrate the art of talking. *One orange juice please, barman!*

MAM: Very funny.

DAD: *Certainly, Sir, and will I be serving that in a bra or a knicker?*

Dad left for the pub to celebrate yet again. I was left on me own with Mam.

MAM: Just stay in at the weekends and study then. It's only

for a year, son, not even, counting the holidays.

RACHEL: Me hair's on fire!

Rachel ran into the kitchen with her hair smouldering.

MAM: What in the name of jaysus?

Rachel had been ironing her hair straight on the ironing board and had gently set her own hair on fire.

MAM: Jesus, it never stops in this house. Quick, here.

Mam shoved Rachel's head under the tap, as Rachel screamed and cried because she was about to lose her lovely long hair.

RACHEL: Me hair, mam, me lovely hair.

MAM: Don't worry, love, a side-parting always looks good on a girl.

RACHEL: No, mam!

TOP TEN WAYS MY SISTER TRIED TO STRAIGHTEN HER HAIR

1. Iron hair.
2. Back to radiator and lay hair across top.
3. Closed bedroom door on hair and dragged it through the gap.
4. Sat in front seat of the car and brushed hair as vents blew.

5. Sunbathed out the back garden, but this made hair more frizzy.
6. Watched horror films, because her mate told her it would scare her hair straight.
7. Laid house bricks on her hair as she pulled her head and hair tight.
8. Heated two small pots and dragged them across hair like a tongs.
9. Used actual fireplace tongs.
10. Sat in front of fire with hair draped over front of head, but this caused it to go on fire once too often.

MAM: Remember, Jason, study hard.
ME: Got it, Mam!

I made my promise to study as I backed out of the room, leaving the screams of my sister behind me.

★★★

AULD WOMAN 1: A vodka with no ice, but bring us a pint glass of ice separate, luv.
AULD WOMAN 2: Pint glass of MiWadi orange undiluted, luv.
AULD WOMAN 3: Six empty glasses ... oh and a coke, filled to the top, no ice, luv.

It was my sixth and final year in school, and I was supposed to be getting ready for the biggest exam of my life, but where was I? In the Braemor Rooms in Churchtown, working as a lounge boy in the cabaret room at the weekends.

Exactly where I shouldn't have been, in other words, but I think my mam just plain forgot I was doing the Leaving Cert.

My mam and some mammies from the road worked in the Braemor Rooms for a few extra bob, mainly to try and save for a holiday for their families. I was the first male ever to work on the floor of the Braemor Rooms. I always got good tips because of my big glasses, which I had to wear to write down the orders. The women felt sorry for me, so they'd give me 50p or even a pound extra.

This particular weekend, Joe Dolan was playing, and when he played here the place went mental. It was only ever full of middle-aged, and aged, women, and these women looked like the grand meeting of witches from Roald Dahl's book.

The maddest hair-dos you have ever seen and insane make-up, like their own young children had made them up before they left the house. All of them looking constantly surprised with their pencilled-in eyebrows floating high above their eyes. You would never guess their age, they were anywhere from 30 to 83.

AULD WOMAN 4: Just a pint of white lemonade, luv. I'm driving!
ALL THE AULD WOMEN: Ha, hah, haahahh,hahaha-hahahaha!!'

The whole table of women howled with laughter, God only knows why, but like I said, they were mad. I walked along their table and took their orders for soft drinks, pints of ice, slices of lemon, not one of them ordered alcohol, which was unusual.

The pressure was on. We had to get all their orders out before Joe Dolan came onstage, as once he started singing, they all jumped up on the tables and danced on them, basically filling every space in the room. They roared the songs along with their hero, Joe. He was amazing, he'd be on a tiny stage, with a full band squashed on there with him, women throwing knickers at him non-stop. He always stayed on the stage, though, because if he went among them, they'd rip him to shreds.

When Joe Dolan's set was finished, he'd leave the stage in a ball of sweat. The women all left like they'd danced and sang with God himself. Slowly but surely, the place emptied out, and we started the big clean-up.

It was only then I realised why all the women had been ordering soft drinks. I had noticed that they seemed very excited all night to have just been on soft drinks and ice.

Now, I had to pull all the tablecloths off the tables, which I did at the end of every night.

Underneath the tables, it looked like a recycling centre, if there had been any such thing in those days.

Empty bottles of vodka, whiskey, gin, in all sizes, plastic containers with God only knows what in them.

I laughed so much. Those women would only order soft drinks off me once in the night, then they got busy all night, pouring their smuggled-in booze into the soft drinks. Irish genius. No wonder they were all laughing so much.

The bonus was that they always dropped money and change onto the floor from all their jumping and dancing about. I gathered this up as I cleaned. It was my college fund for the college I would never go to.

Monday morning in school, I was exhausted. Our form teacher was going through our exams for that June. The Leaving Cert. I could still hear Joe Dolan in my head, I smelled of smoke and late nights. I hadn't studied at all.

Miss Allen says not to forget that our Engineering project is due in by May, as it will be marked separately. It's now April. Oh shit! The project is that music timing clock thing that some of the kids who don't work part-time in a cabaret club have been making at the weekends.

This might have all worked out well for me if I was living in a movie like *Goodfellas*. I could have sent in the mobsters from the Braemor Rooms to rough up the engineering teacher, who would then give me full marks, and I would still be able to work in the cabaret room and earn money.

But sadly, no; no mobsters, no help. But then, hang on! Dad is really good at making things. I'll get him to help me.

DAD: A metro ... what?

Dad looked at the Engineering sheet, front on, sideways, he even looked at the back, where it was blank.

ME: A metronome, Dad. It's used for the timing of music

when you're playing a piano or something.

DAD: And you want me to make it? I brew Guinness, son, how in the name of God am I going to make a metername?

ME: Metronome, Dad, it's called a metronome.

DAD: I don't give a bollix what it's called, I haven't a banger, son.

I slumped into the chair in the kitchen. Mam walked in. 'What's wrong with him?' Dad gave her the paper with the metronome on it. 'What is this supposed to be?' she said, looking at it.

I told her it was my big project for the Leaving Cert and it was due in next month.

MAM: How long have you had to do this?

I didn't even get the word *year* out, she just went straight into overdrive.

MONOLOGUE OF A RAVING MOTHER (*for best effect, to be read at high speed without taking a breath*)

A year, *a year*? You've had *a year* to do this and you're only showing us now? You promised to me and your father that you'd study as hard as you could, well here we are now and a fine mess we're in, how in the name of God are you going to make a meterbone? ... I don't give a flying feck what it's called, as far as I can see, it's called nothing, because that's what you've done on this, nothing, zero, not there. All the days I've been saying *study study study*, but no, no, you've been up there playing with the corner of the wallpaper, well, when you fail your Leaving Cert, don't come running to me, I warned you, pleaded with you, to make sure you did your work, Jesus Christ you'll be living on the streets at this stage, and you'll have wished, *wished* you made that mottophone ... I said I don't care ... wished you'd made it, because if you knew how to make it, you'd be able to make one, sell it and get off the streets, well no more Braemor Rooms for you, that is *final* in that place, I don't give a shite shite shite shite!

PHONE RINGS.

MAM: I'll get it, sure I have to do everything around here. Let's hope that's someone telling us where to get a motto-phone from.

She headed off to the phone, to tell whoever it was how much of a brat I was for not having my project ready.

Dad stayed with me. 'I'll see what I can find in work, son. They're normally clearing out the old offices at this time of year, there might be something we can use.'

DAD: What happened to your hair? It's gone.

Rachel walked in, with her hair looking like a Lego man had put it on sideways.

RACHEL: Dad!
DAD: What?

Rachel ran out of the room crying.

MAM BACK IN.

MAM: She burnt it.
DAD: She needs to stay away from that fire.
MAM: No! Burnt it with an iron.
DAD: What in the name of God was she doing with a hot iron in her hair? Did it get caught when she bent down to stoke the fire?
MAM: Not a fire iron, yeh thick, a clothes iron.
DAD: A what?
MAM: Exactly, you would never have seen one of those.

Dad grabs his coat off the back of the chair.

MAM: Where are you going?
DAD: I'm off to the pub to concentrate, I can't think around here.

So my Dad had to leave to concentrate ... on what? I wasn't sure. My sister sobbed in the background ...

WALLOP!

MAM: And *you*, you get that project done or I'll metronome you, yeh little shit.

★★★

'How are yeh, son, are you looking for you know, you know?'

I was in town, in an electronics shop, and it was full of kids my age. We had all got wind that they were selling the inside of a metronome, the whole electronic piece, which meant all we'd have to do was build some sort of casing around it.

This unnamed shop, which rhymes with FEETS, had seen the metronome on the Leaving Cert paper and recognised a solid-gold opportunity when they saw one. And man, did they sell them! The place was packed with kids not really buying metronomes.

ME: Yes sir, I would like to purchase a metro—
MAN: Hang on, hang on, if the schools find out we're selling a complete made one of those, we'll be shut down, so I can only help you there with your request.
ME: Can I have the bits needed ... ?
MAN: Yessssssss?
ME: A speaker, a board ...
MAN: Yessssssssssss?
ME: And ...
MAN: Annnnd?
ME: Annnnd ... eh ... other stuff.
MAN: Jaysus, here. Ten quid.

He handed me a plastic bag with all the components inside it. Like I was buying drugs on the street. I gave him the tenner, he then gave me a receipt, or so I thought it was, but it was actually the instructions for how to build said metronome.

I turned to leave, and the next boy took my place.

> BOY: Hi. I'm here for the metronome stuff.
> MAN: No you're not.
> BOY: I am.
> MAN: No, no, you're not, you get me, yeahhhh?
> BOY: Oh yeah, I'm not here for that ... emmm .... I need ...

I was put into Engineering because I was a boy, but I was always useless at making things. I should have been in Art because I was a dizzy little dreamer. I mean, where would you put a cock-eyed boy who couldn't cut, saw, shave or even *see* a straight line?

Of course, in Engineering. Well done, everyone.

I walked along the line of everybody's metronomes. Only one kid had made a fully mechanised metronome, and it was amazing. The rest of us had various casings with the pre-made electronic piece housed inside.

Most of the lads had really good casings. They had ones that looked like mechanical metronomes, but were cleverly disguised, ones that looked like tellies, one fella had even made a metal bear, and you turned the bear's nose to speed up the beats or slow them down.

Well, I was unique, I'll give me that. After five years of bending and heating and sawing and twisting metal, what do I decide to do? Much to the bewilderment of my Engineering teacher, I made mine from *wood*.

Yes. I thought it would be cool to make an old-style radio from wood, then pop the insides into the *radio*. Hey presto! The coolest metronome ever made!

My teacher said he thought it was a birdhouse. It got the first 'F' a project had ever received in the school. My teacher kept it in his class for years, to show students what not to do when making a project. I only got it back from him three years ago, after returning to the school to do a gig. God help my little cock eyes.

'Last day in school!'

That was that, it was our last official day in school and, truth be told, one of the saddest days of my life. I had just spent five years in this school with these guys, 13 years, even, if you count the kids who were in primary school with me.

So there were lots of kids jumping about cheering, but deep down we knew we might not really see each other any more. You see these kids every single day in school, share secrets and first experiences with them, so it was hard to believe it would just end.

God only knew what would happen to us all over time. I recently did a gig in Paris and there was an old school friend of mine in the audience. I hadn't seen him in ages. He told me who of our year was alive, married, divorced, jailed or murdered – yes, murdered, a guy in my class was murdered by his Thai bride.

So I was right to feel sad as we all ran around the school like loonies. We still had the Leaving Cert to do, but today was the final and last day of real school.

We were all called in to Assembly. The principal gathered the sixth years for a deep and meaningful speech about our future lives. God help us all, any kid with the wits to scrape his or her way out of this pit of despair had to go on to be a genius.

PRINCIPAL: This is your last day and traditionally you return later today, in costume, to egg the teachers, or throw vegetation and what-not at the school windows, walls and caretakers. Well, hear this, children, any child caught throwing anything at anybody today will not be allowed to sit the Leaving Cert.

TOTAL HUBBUB AS THIS 'THREAT' IS ANNOUNCED.

PRINCIPAL: I mean it. Now, go and enjoy your new lives!

BIG CHEER AS WE ALL LEFT THE HALL.

We all returned later, in fancy dress. I was dressed as a surfer dude and Ken Newman was dressed in my karate suit, sleeves rolled up, finished off with my yellow belt, yes sir, an actual yellow belt for real, I was lethal.

So lethal at karate, in fact, that I once made Graham Newman, Ken's brother, stand dead straight as I swung my leg over his head and down. I threw my leg in the air with a mighty swing ... and smacked him straight in the side of the head with my ankle, nearly killed the boy.

The school looked like a war zone, or a heavy political protest somewhere in China. We were armed to the teeth.

I had emptied my mam's cupboards, and I had various small bags of flour, eggs, tomatoes, sugar. We pelted the teachers as they ran for cover to their cars and buildings. The principal was out with a loud-hailer, roaring at us to stop, the more he roared, the more he got pelted. I was crying with laughter.

The principal kept pointing at children, shouting their names and then trying to write their names down on a very damp pad as he got covered in eggs. Safety in numbers, we thought, he can't stop all of us sitting the Leaving Cert. And that, people, is the first bit of politics all us kids learned on that day: stick together as a group and you're stronger. We were stronger. We all walked away from the school arm-in-arm, boys and girls, boys dressed as girls, girls dressed as boys, witches, and a lot of kids in cardboard boxes with just their underpants on.

The school and teachers looked like the inside of a very busy kitchen that had been overrun by a pack of monkeys. I heard later in life that as we walked into the sunset, teachers headed for car washes and hairdressers, depending on their level of goo coverage.

The principal never stopped any of us from sitting our Leaving Cert, just as we'd thought. Sure, he never even got one name down and, fair play to the teachers, they never ratted us out to him either.

So that was that, just one more thing to do together as a group …

THE LEAVING! OHHHHHHHHH SHIIIIIIIIIIIT!

'I haven't done enough, I haven't done enough.'

I walked up to the school on the first day of the final exams with Ken Newman, both of us shitting ourselves. I just knew I hadn't studied enough.

STUDY TIMETABLE

MONDAY … …start study, look out window, stop study, I'll do it later, older lads playing football, come home, I'll study tomorrow.

TUESDAY ... wake up, start study, hear telly, watch telly, doorbell, mates, I'll study later, no study later, I'll do it tomorrow.
WEDNESDAY ... start study, stop study, start study, stop study, start study ... DOORBELL ... gone ... I'll do it tomorrow.
THURSDAY ... right, lots to catch up on ... I'll do it tomorrow.
FRIDAY ... now come on! Right, right, right ... sunbeams in window, tennis matches start up outside ... I'll do it tomorrow.
SATURDAY ... IT'S SATURDAY, FOR FECK'S SAKE!
SUNDAY ... day of rest, I'll start properly on Monday.

But I never did. I didn't open a single book for the Leaving and to say I wasn't ready was a bit of an understatement... I WASN'T READY AT ALL! IN FACT, I NEEDED TO GO BACK TO SCHOOL!

The Leaving was harder than I could ever have imagined, and I don't only mean the exam papers, they were just one part of the hardship, oh and the fact that I didn't study.

It was everything. We were put into the gym hall, hundreds of kids all in lines, sitting an exam in an environment that we'd never seen or experienced before, horrible echoey hall, scattered with coughs and rustles of papers, with a dose of exam supervisors' shoes clip-clopping by as we tried to write at the speed of light.

Summary of the Leaving Cert

ENGLISH

Wrote loads, finished too early, spoke to people after and none of my answers matched theirs. I just pretended I was delighted with the stuff I hadn't written down.

IRISH

Wrote loads, finished too early, thought I did better on this, met kids outside, again no answers matched, more pretend excitement.

MATHS

Went in, wrote down my name, then left straightaway. Teacher really let me down on maths, she never cared. I was amazing at it in primary, but as soon as you're taught maths by a nun, it's all over. Most of us in that class failed the exam. I went to the field straight after with a couple of girls and lads and we burned our maths books.

FRENCH

We all barely managed in this exam. They had one tape-record-er at the top of the room, nobody could hear it, we complained, they said *they* could hear it. Barry Hennessy said that it wasn't them sitting the exam, it was us, and went on to call them WANKERS. No more exam for Barry. But yes, WANKERS!

HISTORY/GEOGRAPHY

Again wrote loads of stories about Hitler and Stalin, mainly that they had different moustaches. Geography, drew loads of pictures of mountains, valleys and tectonic plates. Wrote, drew and said too much again, basically no info but oceans of hot air, oh and moustaches.

ACCOUNTANCY

Boom, at last, did well! Simply maths to this, you knew on the day if your books balanced, you were right, so did well here, loved our teacher.

ENGINEERING

Hahahahahahahahahahaha! My favourite waste of time in school. This exam was held in our engineering room. We were told to wear shorts and T-shirts as it was going to get hot and sweaty. Jesus Christ, we were filing and cutting and forging and lathing all over the camp. Our exam was to make a working lock.

At the end of the day, we all handed in our locks. Mine was at least 3 inches smaller then everyone else's and wouldn't lock anything. I handed it to my teacher and he frowned at me. I blinked at him through my steamy glasses, bid farewell, as I would never see him again – until he gave back my metronome 20 years later.

DAD: Well done, son.

ME: I'm only finished the exams, Dad, not the results.

DAD: Doesn't matter. Here's to my son, the man, and the rest of the Leaving Cert lads!

EVERYONE: To the lads!

ERIC: Spas!

MAM: (*smacks Eric*) Well done, son.

Hugs from Rachel and Eithne.

Karl, Tally, Ken, Brian, Damo, Robbie and all the Dolans, basically all the lads who had sat the Leaving, all the lads who had finished it long ago and all the lads who would do it next year, plus the whole road, were all in my house: another excuse for a booze-up.

On went the Perry Como. Then, a bit of hush, and my dad stood in the middle of the room with his fancy moustache and rug hair ...

MAM: Go on, Paddy, give it socks.

DAD: (*to be pom pommed to 'Magic Moments'*)... Pom, pom, pom pom pom pom pom pom pom pom pom pom pom pom pom pom ...

He 'Pom, Pommed' out the whole of 'Magic Moments' without using one single word.

What a party that was......

Morning of the results

... September 1989.

So this is it, the Leaving Cert results. I woke up, had my tea and three slices of toast. Dad had already gone to work, Eithne and Rachel were gone to school, my brother had headed off to work.

It was just me and my mam. She said it would be alright. She said the thing loads of Irish mammies say:

'Sure if you don't pass, it's not the end of the world.'

You nod and nod, but you know in your soul that if you don't pass ... it *is* the end of the world. Because she'll kill me.

I grabbed my coat, told my mam I'd be straight back down with my results. We had no mobile phones then, and ringing straight from the school was never going to happen.

I called into Ken Newman on the way, and we headed up to the school together. All our old friends were there, people already jumping around, cheering, showing each other their results. Me and Ken just looked at each other and laughed. 'Holy jaysus, if I'm even a tiny bit happy, I'll be delighted.'

We walked into the office, gave our names and the secretary gave us our brown envelopes. Then we stood outside, away from everyone. I opened my envelope, saw all the logos at the top of the page. It was like I was opening a Wonka bar, waiting for that Golden Ticket to appear.

I pushed the sheet out with the subjects on it, my heart thumping. There were four C's, two D's and an E. Jesus, I did it, I passed, just barely, but I passed. An E for maths, well you'll get an E if you only write your name. Ken came over to me, and he had done even better than me. We jumped around in a circle, then joined the rest of the kids celebrating.

'I passed, I bleedin' passed!'

I turned to go back down the road to show my mam the results. I was held back at the elbow.

BARRY HENNESSY: Where are you going?
ME: Home.

BARRY HENNESSY: You are in your shite, we're all heading to Simple Minds in the RDS.

ME: But I've no ticket.

BARRY: I know a bloke, come on.

Cut to: my mam in the kitchen, looking at the clock, which tells her it's 8.00pm. I've been gone all day. I never returned to tell her the results, so she still has no idea if I passed or not, nor did any mammy whose kid went to Simple Minds that day.

Cut to: the RDS, kids jumping up and down, Leaving Cert results hanging out of their back pockets ... *two fingers to the world!*

NOW AS LOUD AS YOU CAN EVERYONE, EVEN YOU READING THIS BOOK:

'HEY! HEY! HEY! Oooooh, ooooooh, ooooooh aaaaaaaa ...

... Don't you forget about me, don't, don't, don't, don't ...'

JUMP IN THE AIR ... AND ... FREEZE.

ACKNOWLEDGEMENTS

A big thank you to:

My wife, Brenda, and my kids, Devin and Daniel.

My mam and dad, Eithne and Paddy, and my brother and sisters, Eric, Rachel and Eithne.

Nicky Phelan for the illustrations, Graham Thew for the design, and the team at Gill Books: Deirdre Nolan, Sarah Liddy, Catherine Gough and Teresa Daly.

Karl McDermott, Betty, Paddy, Orla and Roy.

Ciaran Tallon, Brian Roche and Ken Newman.

All my mates from BCS – there are too many to mention.

All my real uncles, aunties and cousins, and all my pretend uncles, aunties and cousins, including all my mates and neighbours from Ludford.

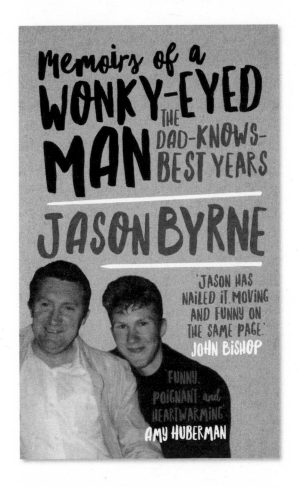